A Fork in the Trail

mouthwatering meals
and tempting treats
for the backcountry

Laurie Ann March

WILDERNESS PRESS · BERKELEY, CA

A Fork in the Trail: Mouthwatering Meals and Tempting Treats for the Backcountry

1st EDITION January 2008

Front cover photos copyright © 2008 by Laurie Ann March
Back cover photo copyright © 2008 by Photos.com (Jupiterimages Corporation)
Interior photos, except where noted, by author
Cover design: Lisa Pletka
Book design and layout: Lisa Pletka
Book editor: Laura Shauger

ISBN 978-0-89997-431-6
UPC 7-19609-97431-4

Manufactured in Canada

Published by: **Wilderness Press**
1200 5th Street
Berkeley, CA 94710
(800) 443-7227; FAX (510) 558-1696
info@wildernesspress.com
www.wildernesspress.com

Visit our website for a complete listing of our books and for ordering information.

Front cover photos: (clockwise from top left) Citrus lentil salad, sunset in Algonquin Provincial Park, water bottle sprout garden, chicken and apple slaw, cinnamon walnut buns, and blueberries in Bruce Peninsula National Park

Library of Congress Cataloging-in-Publication Data

March, Laurie Ann.
  A fork in the trail : mouthwatering meals and tempting treats for the backcountry / Laurie Ann March.—1st ed.
      p. cm.
  Includes index.
  ISBN 978-0-89997-431-6
  1. Outdoor cookery. 2. Backpacking. I. Title.
  TX823.M2742155 2008
  641.5'78—dc22
                                                                    2007039333

In memory of my brothers: Robert Bruce Langman, an avid hiker and friend who still walks with me, if only in spirit, and William John Langman, who nurtured my love of the written word.

To my darling son, Tobias, you help me see nature from a whole different perspective.

To my husband, Bryan, I couldn't ask for a better partner in life or on the trail.

Acknowledgments

I'd like to express my appreciation to Wilderness Press for their faith in my abilities, for listening to my ideas with open minds, and for helping me bring this book to fruition.

Special thanks to my mom, Janet Langman, for inspiring me with her creativity and for helping me adapt the family recipes for this book. Thanks to Nigel and Victoria March, my parents-in-law; your unconditional encouragement has kept me going through the tougher parts of this project. Thanks to Shelley and Claude Lauzon; after all, who else would listen to my half-baked ideas over and over again? You are the epitome of true friends. Appreciation goes to my sister Margaret Wellhauser for rescuing me when I misplaced the biscotti instructions and for teaching me about Italian food, and to my brother Dan Langman for always being there as my strong, silent supporter. Christine and Tim Conners have my gratitude for persuading me to create this book and for being mentors in the kitchen and in life. Your expertise, encouragement, and friendship are valued. Thanks to Brad Wipperman for being a great taste tester and a good friend and also to Krysia Lear for her guidance and wisdom.

My husband, Bryan, is a brave man who deserves an abundance of love and appreciation for being the guinea pig, especially with those recipes that were unpalatable and far from book worthy. Thank you for rescuing dinner with a last minute meal when I had a disaster, for eating breakfast meals at suppertime, and for doing the dishes over and over again. Last but not least, I must thank my son, Tobias, for being a great little outdoorsman and the toughest of my food critics. There is no better gauge than the honesty of a child when it comes to food.

I have connected with so many people on the trail, on canoe routes, and online who provided inspiration that it would take a full chapter to thank them all. Instead I thank all of you who took the time to speak with me about your wilderness cooking and eating experiences. Thank you all!

Contents

List of Recipes

Dinners

Desserts and Baked Goods

Preface

Who knew that the 16-year-old girl who boiled eggs until the pot went dry, causing the contents to explode on the ceiling of her parents' kitchen, would become a wilderness gourmet? This progression from cooking disaster to success was not without a few lessons that I learned the hard way.

After I'd been backpacking for many years, my usual fare consisted of trail mix, dried fruit, and a variety of tiresome, freeze-dried offerings purchased from a local outdoors store. It wasn't until my husband, Bryan, and I went on a trip with another couple that I discovered there was another way. It started on the first day of the trip when we stopped on a trail for lunch. There we were, firing up our stove to heat up a boring store-bought backpacker meal. I looked over to see the woman breaking a baguette while her partner retrieved other items from a cooler bag. Further inspection revealed that they'd brought a selection of cheese, pâté, and smoked oysters. Their lunch was more of an event, while our fare seemed even less appealing than it had on previous trips. I glanced back at our lunch and pouted. We enjoyed the rest of the day and made camp. When dinnertime came, Bryan and I set to work preparing another, store-bought meal. Along came the scent of fresh vegetables and a steak being grilled to perfection. Instead of pouting this time, I decided that we had to do something about the way we were eating! Our meals for the next few days were equally unappetizing as we watched our companions devour seafood pasta, bean salad, fresh baked pizza, and spaghetti with grilled zucchini.

Once we arrived back at home, we realized that fresh food wasn't going to work on longer trips. I had dehydrated foods decades ago as a teenager when I took a 4-H outdoor living course, and so I decided to try dehydrating some meals. I did some research and bought a dehydrator and a backpacker's cookbook. The first things I made were jerky and fruit leather. I was delighted to discover that the dehydrator I had purchased worked far better than the oven method I had used when I was younger. That being said, I was still intimidated when it came to dehydrating other foods.

After a few months I summoned up enough courage to dehydrate some spaghetti sauce. I thought it was great but felt I needed an expert opinion. Bryan came home from work to find two bowls of sauce and two pieces of crusty bread on the table. One bowl contained the sauce right from the pot, and the other contained sauce that I had reconstituted from dried spaghetti leather. Now my man is picky about his spaghetti sauce. The taste test was under way and he couldn't tell the difference! I was elated and all of my dehydration fears went out the window. It was time to test the recipe in the backcountry, but on our next trip I mistakenly added too much water and ended up with tomato soup. It still tasted good but was disappointing when we were expecting a thick and luxurious pasta sauce. Lesson learned.

I went on to purchase a selection of backpacking cookbooks to review for an online magazine. A chain of events led me to a friendship with a couple who had authored one of the backpackers' cookbooks, Tim and Christine Conners. They were working on a second book, and Christine asked me to contribute some of my creations to the book. I did so and found it very enjoyable. Then Bryan and I invited them to come to Canada where we spent a week in the wilderness together. I learned a great deal from that trip. One night Christine suggested that I write my own cookbook; I was very honored but didn't take it too seriously.

We returned home and a few weeks later she emailed me asking if I had started the book yet. Then another few weeks passed, and along came another reminder. I wasn't ready to write an entire book, but since I did want to teach I decided to create an online wilderness cooking course. Before I could do that, however, I needed to learn as much as I could about cooking in the wilderness. I spent a few years learning and putting my knowledge to use in the field. During this period I adapted family recipes and created many new ones, adding to my collection all the time. I explored different cooking methods, became adept at backcountry baking, and learned about appropriate storage and many types of outdoor cooking equipment. Along the way, I discovered that good-tasting food added to the wilderness experience and did not have to be labor-intensive at camp. When I finally started teaching my course, which was a great success, I found that I continued to have the urge to create even more recipes. It was then that I realized I had mastered the art of wilderness cooking and was ready to write this cookbook.

Lightweight, yet tasty recipes for backpackers and paddlers are the heart of this book. The wide selection of recipes ranges from quick and easy cooking to gourmet, including recipes to please children, canines, and car campers. Delicious food brings people together at the end of a hard day of hiking; hopefully these recipes will facilitate that type of eating experience.

Dehydration and pre-trip preparation at home are important components in many of the recipes within this volume. Even though you can use an oven to dehydrate food, purchasing a countertop dehydrator with multiple trays is a much better option. Dehydrating foods allows you to make meals several months before your trip. Proper storage and menu planning information has been included so that you can be sure that you will have the proper amount of food for your trip whether it's a weekender or a multiweek excursion.

As a wilderness cooking instructor I've taught hundreds of students how to cook great meals on their trips. It is my hope that this book will do the same for you that it has done for my students and my family—turn backcountry meals from mere sustenance into events that enhance the whole wilderness experience.

Laurie Ann March
October 2007

Chapter 1

An Introduction to Wilderness Cooking

A History of Wilderness Cooking

When European explorers and voyageurs traveled through North America beginning in the 16th and 17th centuries, their diet was quite different than that of modern-day wilderness travelers. Meals were based on animal foods and what could be gathered, which meant there wasn't much variety. Salt pork, cornmeal, flour, and beans were often the primary components of an explorer's larder. Pemmican, a mixture of animal fat and berries, was used by the fur traders. On their 1803–1806 expedition Meriwether Lewis and William Clark ate what meat was available and a variety of found plants and tubers. The fare of the old-time wilderness traveler included staples such as hard tack and Hudson's Bay bread. Cooking equipment was heavy and often woodstoves were packed in. People had to cure or dry their meats to prevent spoilage and to survive the winter months. Food was heavy, making travel arduous work—eating was more about survival than enjoyment.

When backpacking and paddling became recreational activities, the food choices changed dramatically. On long journeys some people arrange food drops and mailings. Freeze drying makes food more lightweight and allows for more variety. I remember my brother, who was an avid hiker, taking an assortment of trail mix, oranges, chocolate, peanut butter, cheese, granola, jerky, Mennonite sausage (cured farmer's sausage), and dried fruit on his trips in the 1970s. For main meals he'd take items from the grocery store such as boil-in-bag chili and a selection of canned items—it must have been extremely heavy. He didn't have high-tech cookware and did most of his cooking over a small fire. Oh my, how times have changed. Today's wilderness cuisine is far more interesting and palatable than the fare I remember as a child.

Innovations such as the Outback Oven and the BakePacker have made it easy for us to create baked goods in the backcountry. Modern, lightweight stoves with simmer controls make cooking a breeze. Marry these technological advances with the wide availability of international ingredients and you have the makings of a gourmet wilderness experience.

Food for Wilderness Trips

As I first started to embrace backpacking and canoeing, I decided to venture into the realm of prepackaged, freeze-dried fare purchased from a local outdoor store. After a while, I found that many of the foods had the same taste and that some were not to my liking, especially those where I could not control the spice. I was also concerned with nutrition and did not like some of the additives such as preservatives contained in the store-bought meals. When canoeing, I was able to take fresh foods for a few days with the aid of a small cooler, but that approach wasn't practical for backpacking or weeklong paddling excursions. My solution was to take homemade, dehydrated foods on our adventures.

Before starting you should consider the type of activity you are participating in. Backpackers will want to watch the weight of food closely; whereas, kayakers will be more concerned with bulk. Canoeists are afforded the greatest luxury and can sometimes take heavier foods depending on their planned route of travel. You'll also want to consider the area in which you are camping. Some parks and trails have strict bans on cans and bottles—bottles aren't a wise choice for obvious reasons, and cans are just too weighty.

Time of year and climate are important considerations as well. In cooler weather you'll have more flexibility with your menu as you can take items that might be prone to spoilage in hotter weather. Keep in mind, however, that you'll probably use more fuel in cold weather. I've found that the same is true for wet and rainy conditions.

Outdoor Cooking Equipment

There is no right or wrong choice when it comes to cooking equipment—it all depends on your individual needs and wants. If you are an ultralight hiker, you will want to keep your equipment simple and light. Groups and families can consider a more comprehensive kitchen if they plan to share gear. The following list includes some of the types of equipment you could consider for your backcountry kitchen; your choices will depend on your chosen menu and your style:

- Single-burner stove with windscreen (I recommend one with a refillable fuel bottle that can accommodate various fuel types if you are planning to travel internationally.)
- Fuel (The amount depends on the cooking times of your chosen menu—I always take an extra half bottle or canister depending on the stove type.)
- Heat exchanger (recommended for cold weather trips)
- Matches in waterproof containers
- Cooking grid (if weight isn't a consideration and you are in an area where you can have a cooking fire)
- Backpacker's oven (Outback Oven, reflector oven, or BakePacker)
- Lightweight pot set designed for backpacking
- Pot lifter
- Pot cozy or Nalgene insulator
- Insulated work gloves (for handling hot pots, cooking grid, etc.)
- Folding spoon that can double as a ladle (one with measurements is quite useful)
- Folding spatula

- Salt/pepper shaker (I prefer an all-in-one unit.)
- Backpacker's pepper grinder (an "essential" luxury item)
- Rehydration container (a pot or large Nalgene would work)
- Cup, plate, bowl, and cutlery for each person
- Water treatment solution (filtration pump, tablets, or liquid)
- Personal drinking water bottle
- Water containers (Nalgene bottles, Platypus bladder, or other container)
- A few extra ziplock bags in case of leftovers
- Thermos
- Parchment paper
- A sharp knife (I like a Swiss Army or locking blade knife.)
- Collapsible sink, camp soap, dish cloth, and scrubber or pot scraper
- Pack towel to dry dishes or a mesh bag to air-dry them
- Tarp, tent wing, or other shelter to cook under during inclement weather

You also need to consider the equipment you will use at home for your pretrip food preparations. Most things you will already have in your kitchen, but I strongly suggest you purchase a food dehydrator if you do not have one already as this book relies heavily on drying foods.

Cooking Methods

Choosing the most appropriate of the variety of cooking methods, much like the equipment, depends on the activity, location, and individual needs. While most methods—boiling, frying, heating, cooking in a foil packet, cooking on a stick, and grilling—are self-explanatory, baking methods for wilderness cooking require a little explanation. The easiest way to bake in the wild is to use an Outback Oven, BakePacker, or reflector oven.

Made by Backpacker's Pantry, the Outback Oven comes in two styles: the Ultralight and the Plus 10, the latter of which is great for larger groups. The latter comes with a riser, heat shield, lidded fry pan with a built-in thermometer, and a convection tent. You can bake almost anything you can think of in either style of Outback Oven, plus they both make wonderful pizza. I prefer the Outback Oven Ultralight, which consists of a riser, convection tent, thermometer, and heat shield. With the Ultralight you use your own pot set, thereby reducing pack weight compared to the larger model; I use mine with the largest pot and lid from my pot set. Both types of Outback Ovens work best over a stove that has a simmer control. It's possible to use the oven with a stove that has practically no simmer function; you just have to turn the convection tent frequently to avoid scorching the specially designed fabric. *Never forget the riser or you will instantly create a burnt offering!* I do not recommend using an Outback Oven with stoves where the canister is directly below the flame.

The BakePacker consists of a pot and grate system. You place the grid in the pot with enough water so that it will not dry out during baking and then you place your ingredients in a plastic bag that sits above the grate—my least preferred method because you are steam baking rather than traditional baking so you do not get that golden crust with breads and such.

Reflector ovens are generally homemade, are simple to construct, and work reasonably well. They work best with a small hot campfire. The oven is somewhat open, and you have to turn the dish often so that it cooks evenly. There are several websites with plans for building a reflector oven; I recommend viewing the list of oven plans at www.AForkintheTrail.com. The construction process isn't difficult and the final product should fold flat for storage.

You can also bake in other ways. Methods popular with outdoor groups for young people, such as the Boy and Girl Scouts, include baking in a paper bag, Dutch oven, foil packet, freezer bag, orange skin, tin can, or cardboard box oven. I have even cooked a turkey in a cardboard box oven; it was very accurate as far as temperature goes. For recipes and more information about some of these other techniques, see Chapter 12.

Spices, Condiments, and Fats

Spices and condiments can enhance a meal but a good wilderness cook should allow each person to adjust the spices to his or her taste. I always take the basics such as salt and pepper, but I also like to tailor my spice rack and condiments to my menu. Look for items such as mayonnaise in little packets that do not require refrigeration. Butter, oils, peanut butter, jam, and other such items can be stored in little Nalgene containers.

Butter has a very low smoke point, which means that it will burn very quickly. It is best to purchase regular salted butter for wilderness cooking; it will stay fresh longer than sweet or unsalted butter. If you will be traveling in hot weather, you might consider using ghee, or clarified butter, which will keep longer. You can find it at Indian grocery stores. Some people prefer margarine, but I really do not like the taste of it—plus it can separate in hotter weather. Also, some kinds have a very high water content that can adversely affect a recipe's outcome, especially if you are baking with it. My advice is to avoid margarine altogether and use butter unless you have a medical condition that prevents you from having the latter. Although olive oil has a higher smoke point than butter, it can add an unwanted flavor to some dishes so you might want to use a light vegetable oil or canola oil in some cases.

Using This Book

Dehydration times listed in recipes are approximate; you should check food periodically as it's drying. The cooking and rehydration times are also an approximation. Outside factors such as weather, altitude, and heat source can affect the cooking or baking time. You should read a recipe, including the instructions, through twice before you make it. Familiarizing yourself with the recipe in this manner will give you better results.

Serving sizes are what I would describe as average to hearty. All recipes, except for the baking ones, can easily be cut in half. Those of you who are solo hiking or solo paddling might consider making the recipe and eating it for dinner at home and then drying the leftovers or drying the entire recipe and dividing it into single servings. Because dehydrated food will keep for an extended period, doing the latter will give you food for additional trips. If a recipe involves dehydration, then the approximate time is listed at the beginning.

Where applicable each recipe includes icons to help make it easier for you to choose an appropriate dish. An 🍎 indicates that a recipe is vegetarian. Beverages and desserts are assumed to be vegetarian and so are not labeled as such. A 🪶 indicates that a recipe is especially lightweight and, therefore, more appropriate for an activity like backpacking.

Special Ingredients

A few ingredients used in this book need some further explanation and instruction.

Roasted Garlic Powder

To make roasted garlic powder, gather 1 bulb of garlic, some olive oil, and a pinch of kosher salt. Cut the top off a bulb of garlic. Drizzle the cut with olive oil and sprinkle with a little salt if desired. Wrap in aluminum foil. Bake the garlic at 350°F for 30 to 45 minutes. Remove from the oven and let cool. Squish the garlic out of the skin and spread it on a lined dehydrator tray to dry for 5 to 7 hours. When the garlic is dry, process it in a spice grinder or blender until you have a powder.

Roasted Red Peppers

To roast peppers place the whole pepper on a baking sheet in a 350°F oven for 45 minutes to 1 hour. Remove from oven when the skin starts to blacken. The skin will separate easily from the flesh. Allow to cool before peeling off the skin. You can also grill them until the skin starts to blacken and peel. If you prefer, you can buy roasted peppers at the supermarket.

Celery Leaves

Many people do not realize that the leaves found on celery stalks are good in salads and other dishes. They impart a mild celery flavor. Most often, the leaves are at the top of the celery; however, if you look closely you can sometimes find them hidden between the stalks.

Lemon, Lime, or Orange Zest

Citrus zest adds another layer of flavor to a dish because of the aromatic oils in the fruit rind. The easiest way to zest citrus fruit is by using a tool specifically designed for the task or a fine grater, but in a pinch you can use a knife. Remove the outer layer of skin being careful not to get any of the white pith. If you use a knife, you will need to cut the pieces into tiny slivers. Citrus zest dehydrates well.

Vanilla Sugar

To make vanilla sugar, place a vanilla bean in a ziplock freezer bag of fine white sugar and let it sit for a few days. Vanilla sugar adds flavor to hot beverages, baked goods, cereals, and stewed fruit. You can also substitute it for white sugar in any recipe.

Ginger

When buying ginger, look for pieces with a firm and smooth texture. Older ginger will be more fibrous, and young ginger will have a sweeter flavor. Freezing gingerroot is a great way to store it and helps it grate finer. An easy way to peel ginger is by scraping it with the edge of a metal spoon.

Physical Needs and Nutrition

When you are on a backpacking or paddling trip, you burn more calories than you normally burn at home. For backpackers much of this depends on the ruggedness of the terrain, distance, and pack weight. With canoeists and kayakers it is determined by the amount of paddling and portaging. Canoeists are notorious for doubling and tripling portages on longer journeys thus increasing their energy needs. Many backpackers I know are concerned about fats, but the truth is we need some fat in our wilderness diet and this need increases in colder weather.

Nutrition is also a factor—you want to eat enough food to meet your caloric needs but also want a good balance of foods to meet your nutritional needs. Both proteins and carbohydrates are important. Because of the amount of physical exertion involved in wilderness adventure activities, you can eat more simple and complex carbohydrates than you would at home. It is necessary to consume a variety of foods including fruits, vegetables, and legumes. You also need to make sure that you have enough fiber in your diet for obvious reasons. If you are a picky eater and tend to limit your diet, you might want to consider supplementing with a multivitamin.

You'll find that some days it is better to graze, or munch, while on the trail. Munching keeps your body fueled and is especially important for those who tend to skip breakfast. Grazing is helpful if you have a big day of travel ahead and don't have time to stop and prepare a lunch; an assortment of gorp (good old raisins and peanuts), dried fruits, jerky, homemade energy bars, and the like will keep you going.

Backpackers and paddlers also need to ensure that they consume enough safe drinking water. All too often I have traveled with people who ignored their thirst and ended up suffering the effects of dehydration, such as weakness, loss of coordination, thirst, nausea, and headache. In higher altitudes you'll need to remember to drink more water than you do at sea level.

Food Storage: Safe Practices at Home and Camp

Food storage is a question I have addressed many times with my wilderness cooking students. It's very important that you compress as much air as possible out of the bags you store your food in. If you don't plan to use the meals you dehydrate within a month or two, freeze them for up to six to eight months without compromising taste or quality. Recipes with sweet potatoes should only be stored for two to three months because their flavor can be compromised.

After the food has thawed completely, open the bag a little to let out any condensation that might occur, squeeze out the air, and close it again. If you aren't freezing the meals, keep them in a cool, dark, and dry place or in your refrigerator. Check your meals a few weeks before you go—if there is the slightest sign of mold, throw the meal out. It means that the meal didn't dry properly or became contaminated. This has only happened to me once, and it was because the bag wasn't properly sealed.

Storing Fresh Ingredients

While I usually try to avoid taking a lot of fresh foods because of weight considerations, you have a few options. Some require the use of a small cooler with ice and others require some creative packing. On weekend hiking and paddling trips, fresh food can be a nice alternative if you don't mind the extra bulk and weight.

Vegetables

Organic produce seems to last longer for some reason. Fresh potatoes (especially the little new potatoes) will travel well and are nice wrapped in aluminum foil and baked in hot coals. Fresh yellow onions last a week or more in a pack. If the skins start to show signs of wrinkling, use them right away. On a short trip where weight is not so much of a consideration, you can bring zucchini and grill it over a fire or pan-fry it with butter and Parmesan cheese. I have had fresh organic green peppers last a week in my pack. They are generally smaller than nonorganic peppers and fit nicely into a plastic container, which prevents them from being crushed. When I take one, I open the container every day at camp for a few minutes to let the contents breathe and reduce the humidity. I use some on a pizza, and then my family and I munch on the rest over the dinner hour. You can even grow sprouts on the trail to add a fresh crunch to wraps and trail salads.

Always store fresh mushrooms in a paper bag, or they will spoil quickly. If I take fresh fruit or vegetables in my pack, I wrap them in a paper towel to reduce bruising and then in a plastic bag that isn't airtight. Every day at camp I unwrap and check them and allow the air to dry any condensation. If something is ripening faster than I expected, I will juggle the menu to use the item before it spoils.

Fruits

Fruits like oranges carry very well and last a week or more. If you wrap an apple in some paper towels and place it in the center of your pack, it will last more than a week. More delicate stone fruits such as peaches, nectarines, and cherries bruise easily; they travel better in a hard-sided container.

Meats

If you plan to take fresh meat, double wrap it in freezer paper or newspaper and freeze it solid before your trip. Take a small cooler to keep it cold unless you will be consuming it the first day. Usually you can have fresh meat for two days, sometimes even three in colder weather. I don't recommend taking fresh chicken unless you plan to use it your first night. Since a cooler can be cumbersome and heavy, you really have to judge whether having fresh meats on a trip is worth the extra effort.

Cheeses

Hard cheeses such as Parmesan, Dry Monterey Jack, and cheddar will keep longer. If you want to store cheese for longer than a few days, wrap it in vinegar-soaked cheesecloth and put it in a ziplock freezer bag. If you want to use it for more than a week, go one step further and dip the cloth-wrapped cheese several times in paraffin wax. Cheese also keeps well wrapped in plain brown paper or butcher paper. Grated cheese does not keep long and should be used on the first night or two.

Storage Ideas

There are many ways to deal with food storage on trips. I really like reusable Nalgene containers even if they add a little weight. Freezer bags can be reused at home as long as they aren't damaged—just be sure to wash them and allow them to air-dry well.

I use a selection of the following containers and bags:

- Nalgene bottles in sizes from 30 to 500 milliliters,
- ziplock freezer bags, ranging in size from small to large,
- a hard-sided container for items such as crackers or tortilla chips,
- mini-ziplock bags or contact lens containers for salt and spices, and
- extra ziplock bags for leftovers or emergencies.

It is advisable to store foods by meal in larger ziplock bags rather than to store many meals in one ziplock bag. The bags often fail if they are opened and closed repeatedly, and being stuffed in a pack each day can be hard on them. Remember to take a few spares just in case. Wrap homemade granola bars and other similar items in waxed paper and then place several in a ziplock freezer bag. The waxed paper makes an excellent fire starter.

Protect gorp from being crushed by storing it in a wide-mouth Nalgene bottle. I actually store some of my gorp items separately from one another and mix it each morning. That way I will not have to dig through the mixture if I want to use an ingredient like the raisins in another recipe.

It is important that you also store your food safely. I double bag much of my food to prevent moisture from getting inside because it causes food to spoil quickly. At camp I try to keep the food pack out of the sun to reduce its temperature.

It is also important that you hang your food or use an approved bear canister in areas where there are bears; some parks and trails have hanging cables or bearproof boxes. But bears aren't the only problem—raccoons and other critters can be bothersome as well. If you are in bear country or above the tree line, be sure to use an approved bear canister. It is best to find out ahead of time what type of container is approved for the area you plan to hike in.

Because I don't like to hang all of my gear and my entire pack, I carry a nylon bag designed specifically for hanging food. The bag packs up small but will hold a considerable amount of food. Bearproof canisters are also available, but I find hanging the food just as effective. If you are on a paddling trip, you may have the luxury of a separate food pack or barrel, which should be hoisted up between two trees. You should hang your food before dark if possible—not only does this reduce the risk of attracting little nocturnal pests, but it's easier to find a suitable tree when you can see what you are doing. Be sure to use a good quality rope for food hanging. The inexpensive, yellow nylon rope that you can buy at the hardware store breaks much more easily than you would think. Use a marine-grade or climbing rope that won't stretch if saturated with water. If your clothes smell of food or you spilled food on them, you should hang them as well. Toothpaste, camp soap, and other scented items need to be hung with the food pack for safety.

As much as you try to avoid having leftovers, sometimes it happens. Depending on the item, you can store it for use the next day. Intentionally creating leftovers, such as bannock or muffins, makes the next day a little easier. Before storing baked goods, let them cool completely; then place them in a clean ziplock freezer bag or other suitable container. Be careful storing things such as rice unless the weather is very cool as it can develop bacteria that will make you ill. Anything you have rehydrated that contains meat should be packed out as it will not be suitable for consumption. If you have any doubts about the safety of leftover food, it is best to err on the side of caution. Depending where you travel, you might be able to burn your leftovers. I prefer to pack garbage out as it has less impact on the environment. At night hang the garbage bag in a tree just as you do your food pack.

Packing food for backpacking and paddling trips can have a steep learning curve. Here are some tips that I've found helpful:

- Plan your menu.
- Take a copy of your menu with you so that you can refer to it.
- Pack each meal separately in a larger ziplock bag.
- Bring extra ziplock bags in case one tears or you have useable leftovers.
- Repackage grocery store finds into ziplock freezer bags.
- Pack the name of the meal, water needed, and other trailside instructions with each meal. (Don't write it on the outside of the bag in case it wears off.)
- When baking, line your pots with parchment paper to make cleanup easier.
- Store liquids in leakproof containers, and put these in a ziplock bag just in case.

Hygiene and Cleanup

Hygiene is crucial, especially when it comes to food. Most times when a person becomes ill on a trip, it is from issues with improper treatment of drinking water, contaminated hands, or food-borne illness. Hygiene starts at home. When you are preparing your food for a trip, sanitation is essential. Wash everything thoroughly, and use only clean utensils, bags, and containers. Make sure you compress the air out of ziplock bags, and be sure that you dehydrate foods properly and thoroughly. Wash your hands frequently to avoid cross contaminating foods.

At camp and on the trail clean hands are important, too. If you don't have water to spare, use a hand sanitizer. Clean your body as well because bacteria can travel. Always wash your hands thoroughly before handling food. Each individual should have a personal water bottle for drinking. Don't share foods like gorp—each person should have their own personal snack bags. That way you won't pay the price if someone's hygiene is lacking. It is also a good idea to have your own personal eating utensils, plate, cup, and bowl.

Always be careful that you don't contaminate water containers with untreated water. It can cause illnesses from bacteria such as giardia and cryptosporidium found in water.

Dishwashing is important, too. Be sure to use a soap product designed for wilderness camping. Use camp soap with care, and be aware of the impact it could have on the region you are exploring. For example, camp soaps should never be used near or in alpine water systems. Never use a sponge to clean your dishes—they're notorious for harboring bacteria. Dispose of dishwater far from water sources and away from camp. Don't just dump it; throw it so that it spreads out over a larger area.

If you spill food, pick up the solid pieces, put them in your garbage bag, and then rinse the area well. Always keep a clean camp kitchen so you don't attract critters.

Preventing and Rescuing Meal Disasters

Meal disasters were my forte in the beginning. Fortunately I learned from my mistakes; hopefully you can, too.

It only takes a millisecond to turn spaghetti sauce into tomato water.

When reconstituting dried foods, less water is better until you get the hang of rehydration. You can always add more water. If you have to remove it, you will lose some of your ingredients and flavor. Don't rely on the measurements preprinted on water bottles as they aren't accurate. Use a folding spoon with measurements on it, or mark proper measurements on a cup or bottle before you go on a trip. Never rely on your memory for measurement amounts either. It only takes a moment to put a note in the bag with your meal so that you will know how much water you need.

Don't fret if you do end up with something soupy—just cook your pasta or rice right in the sauce. It'll increase the starch content but will also save your dinner. I always recommend carrying a little ziplock bag of cornstarch in your food pack for thickening in these situations. Cornstarch is the quickest and easiest solution, but you can also simmer the sauce to reduce the water if fuel consumption isn't an issue.

Burnt cinnamon swirl coffee cake is hard to get off the bottom of a pot.

When you are baking with an Outback Oven, remember that if you forget the riser your baking will smell really good when you put it on the flame, but within seconds you will face a burnt mess.

If it can tip, it will tip.

Place your stove on level ground. A stove that isn't level will teeter, and your dinner may end up as an offering to the forest floor. If your food falls on a solid rock, you can usually scoop it back into the pot using the "five-second rule." Food that lands on ground laden with pine needles is another story.

Keep your kitchen and eating area clean.

Our friend Brad dropped some noodles on the ground while serving his fettuccine alfredo. A few minutes later he commented on how cute the deer mouse munching on the spillage was, but then the mouse climbed the rock beside our friend. Brad was savoring his dinner when suddenly the tiny mouse jumped toward his plate, missed, and landed on Brad's shoulder. Noodles went flying! Brad's meal abruptly came to a halt, and cleanup was crucial. Those killer mice will get you every time! All kidding aside, critters can be an issue, and the last thing you want to attract is a large animal like a bear. Keeping a clean camp kitchen is imperative.

No amount of water can extinguish the burn from too much cayenne pepper on your tongue.

Never, ever pour spices directly over the pot. The lid once came off my bottle of cayenne pepper and about two tablespoons of spice fell into the pot. It was so hot that no one could eat it.

Bring an extra meal or two in case of an emergency.

An emergency could be weather related or result from an injury or from forgetting to use your noodle. While on a trip with a friend, my family and I stayed at a wilderness campsite that had a wooden privy. He was making pasta and had the bright idea that he would drain his pasta water into the privy—an act I have many issues with, sanitation being one of them. As he was draining his pasta, the noodles started to slide out of the pot and into the privy. The man tried to catch the noodles but dropped the towel, burned his hand, lost the pasta to the hole, and spilled some of the hot water on his leg. Luckily he wasn't seriously burned. He didn't have any extra food and would have gone hungry, but luckily we had an extra meal that we gave him.

Chapter 2

Dehydration Basics, Commercially Dried Foods, and Grocery Store Finds

Dehydration

Some of the ways to preserve foods so that they do not need refrigeration include salting, curing, smoking, sun drying, and dehydration. Dehydration is my preferred method. Salted, cured, and smoked foods have an added flavor that some people do not always want, and sun drying means that you have to wait for the right day. The first thing you need is a dehydrator. There are different ways to dehydrate food, most of which work decently; however, some are more accurate and cost-effective than others. What you are doing is slowly removing all of the moisture from the foods, which requires a heat source and time. The time necessary to dehydrate foods depends on your dehydration method, the humidity, and the size and type of food. In general, it takes between 5 and 20 hours to dehydrate most foods.

Types of Dehydrators

A homemade dehydrator consists of a wooden box with trays and a light bulb as the heat source. They tend to be bulky, but they work and allow you to do several trays at a time. You have to rotate the trays frequently, and you shouldn't leave it unattended.

Putting the food on cookie sheets in an oven set between 140°F and 165°F with the door slightly ajar works, too. You have to check on it often, turn the pans frequently, and can only prepare two pans at a time; it is not the most energy-efficient solution. It can also heat up the house so midsummer is not the time to use this method. Every oven is a little different so suggested drying times may need to be adjusted accordingly. In this case you'll have to keep a closer eye on what you are drying, checking as often as once every hour.

A retail dehydrator is the best choice. My preferred model is the countertop type that can accommodate numerous trays and has a thermostat. These units are cost effective and are not hard on the utility bill. They have a powerful fan, and you usually do not need to rotate the trays. Often you can turn it on late in the evening and turn it off when you get up in the morning.

Advanced Dehydration

Although at first it can seem quite intimidating, dehydration is pretty simple. Once you overcome your initial fear, you will find that you are dehydrating all sorts of wonderful meals. The tips below will help you succeed. Either line your dehydrator with the fruit leather trays that you can buy to match the unit or use baker's parchment paper. You'll want to line the trays when drying meals, sauces, and fruit leathers. Small pieces of fruit and veggies fall through the tray grid if you do not use a liner. Plastic wrap also works well. Using a liner makes cleanup much easier. Most fruit for leathers does not need to be cooked. Dehydrate pie fillings and condensed soups straight from the can. Cook sauces such as homemade spaghetti sauce prior to dehydrating them. When you're ready to dehydrate the sauce, filling, soup, or fruit purée, put a liner on the tray and pour the food on top. Leave about an inch of space on the inner and outer edges and spread the ingredients out until they are about a ¼ inch thick. It is a good idea to make the food on the center of the tray a little thinner than the edges to ensure that the ingredients do not pool thicker in the middle and that drying is even. Set the temperature on your dehydrator according to the manufacturer's instructions.

Most meat, including poultry and fish, can be dehydrated. Trim all visible fats off meats, and cook the meats well. Rinse any excess fat off ground meat. Make sure that the pieces are ground or small, approximately ⅓ inch wide. Place the cooked meat on a lined dehydrator tray. Ground meat is completely dehydrated when it has the consistency and texture of gravel. By chopping pieces small or shredding it, you will have an easier time drying and reconstituting them. When you dry chicken or pork, keep in mind that you will have to rehydrate these items with boiling water and that rehydration may take an hour. It is a good idea to plan chicken and pork meals for days where you will arrive in camp early enough to allow adequate rehydration time.

If you don't plan to cook them before dehydrating them, fresh potatoes and some vegetables such as corn, asparagus, broccoli, and cauliflower need to be blanched. To blanch them just drop the sliced or chopped items into boiling water for a few moments. You can also use a microwave to blanch your vegetables. Add a little water to the vegetables in a microwaveable bowl, and cook on high for about two minutes in a 750-watt microwave (adjust cooking time as necessary). Frozen and canned varieties can be put directly on lined trays.

When dehydrating items such as stews, chili, and goulash, separate the vegetables from the meat and the meat from the sauce because each item dries differently. For a stew, for example, I dry the gravy on one tray; the potatoes, turnips, and carrots on another; and the meat on yet another. Be sure to measure everything before separating and dehydrating so you will know how much water to add back later. Then place all the ingredients in a ziplock freezer bag along with a sticky note stating the contents, amount of water needed to rehydrate, number of servings, and the date you prepared it.

If well packaged, these foods will keep in your freezer for about eight months. Unfrozen the food can last several months as long as the package remains unopened and is stored in a cool dry place.

Rehydration Basics

You can use a large, wide-mouth Nalgene bottle or a ziplock freezer bag or simply rehydrate the food in a pot. Water of any temperature will work, but of course cold water will take longer. As I mentioned earlier, it is a good idea to take a copy of your menu with you on your trips. If you do so, you can look at your menu in the morning to see what you have planned for lunch and dinner. Then you can decide how and what needs to be rehydrated. For example, if you are having *Chili con Queso* (see page 90) for lunch, you will need to prepare the salsa that you dehydrated. Let's say you started with 1 cup of salsa and now have ½ cup of dried salsa. Because it is morning and you do not need this until lunchtime, you can use cold water and let the salsa rehydrate as you travel. Crumble the salsa up into a Nalgene bottle and add a little less than ½ cup of water to end up with close to a full cup. It is always best to put in a little less water than too much. You can always add a little more water later. Place the Nalgene in the top of your backpack or clip it to the outside of your pack. By lunchtime, you'll have perfect salsa that looks and tastes just like it did when you first made it and spread the contents on the dehydrator.

For the stew I mentioned earlier, you can arrange to start rehydration at lunchtime. Put the meat and all the other ingredients in a Nalgene bottle, add the necessary amount of water, and then pack it. If the meal is not hydrated enough upon reaching camp and mealtime is approaching, pour the contents into a pot and heat it almost to the boiling point. Take the pot off the heat, and place it in a safe spot with a rock holding the lid down—the heat will speed up the rehydration. If you forget to rehydrate a meal before you reach camp, add boiling water at camp to speed up the rehydration process. If you use boiling water in a Nalgene bottle, it is advisable to open it once in awhile to release the pressure from the steam.

I keep one Nalgene water bottle just for rehydrating meals. At cleanup time, I always wash it thoroughly and rinse it with boiling water. I also bring a few ziplock freezer bags for multi-ingredient meals. Be careful that you don't burn yourself when using very hot water in a ziplock bag.

Multi-ingredient Rehydration

Some items will produce flavored water that may overpower the dish. For example dried porcini and portabella mushrooms or green peppers can take over a dish pretty quickly. I have indicated in the recipe if ingredients need to be rehydrated separately. The best way to do this is to use freezer bags for the smaller ingredients and a wide-mouth Nalgene for the ingredient that require the largest volume. Be sure to let the steam out of the Nalgene as the food expands. As I mentioned before, you need to be extremely careful when pouring very hot water into ziplock bags. Sometimes I take a few small plastic containers for this purpose if weight and bulk aren't an issue.

Commercially Dried Foods

Sometimes a spontaneous trip means that there is no time to prepare food for a trip. In that case I recommend that you use a commercially dried meal. They tend to be expensive, but there are several brands that will do in a pinch:

- Alpine Aire
- Backpacker's Pantry, which also offers fare specifically designed for an Outback Oven and a more affordable line called Campfood
- Mary Jane's Farm
- Mountain House

Here are some specialty dried ingredients that will help with your backcountry cooking. Availability of these items may vary by region.

- Powdered whole eggs
- Powdered egg whites
- Powdered scrambled egg mix
- Powdered milk (nonfat and whole)
- Soy milk powder
- Powdered sour cream
- Powdered butter
- Powdered buttermilk
- Freeze-dried meatballs
- Freeze-dried meats such as chicken and beef
- Freeze-dried fruits and vegetables
- Tomato powder
- Dried soup base
- Powdered vegetable shortening
- Dried mushrooms (You can get great varieties at Asian grocery stores.)
- Powdered peanut butter
- Honey powder
- Instant wild rice
- Yogurt culture

Grocery Store Finds

If you want to mix your home-dried foods with other foods for variety, you will be quite surprised at what you can find in your local grocery store. Many times, you can find some really good fare if you check the vegetarian or international foods sections. Here are some of the things that I have found in my travels in both the U.S. and Canada.

- Muffin mixes
- Cake mixes (look for single-layer varieties)
- Jell-O No-Bake Cheesecake mix
- Instant pudding
- Complete pancake batter (you only add water to this type of mix)
- Bisquick
- Dried sausage and pepperoni (look for ones that aren't refrigerated in the store)
- Smoked salmon in a foil pouch
- Clams, shrimp, chicken, crab, and tuna steaks in foil pouches
- Spam in a foil pouch
- Instant mashed potatoes
- Scalloped potatoes
- Uncle Ben's Bistro Rice (heats in a frying pan in two minutes)
- Flavored rice
- Minute Rice or other five-minute rice
- Mayonnaise or Miracle Whip (in restaurant pouches)
- Soups (Knorr, Cup-a-Soup, and Lipton)
- Sauces mixes (McCormack, Knorr, and Lipton)
- Hamburger Helper and Tuna Helper
- Noodles and sauce or rice and sauce packets from Lipton
- Wraps
- Flatbreads
- Bagel chips
- Curry sauces
- Precooked bacon and bacon bits
- Pizza kits
- Powdered nacho cheese sauce
- Shelf-stable milk and juice boxes
- Coffeemate
- Stuffing mixes
- Dried mushrooms
- Bulk soup mixes
- Dried hummus mix
- Granola bars
- Cereal bars
- Energy bars
- Instant oatmeal
- Carnation Instant Breakfast
- Instant Cream of Wheat
- Ramen noodles
- Instant cappuccino
- Instant international coffees
- Instant coffee
- Kava

- Vegetable chips
- Wasabi peas
- Dried tortellini
- Gnocchi (some varieties don't require refrigeration)

- Cornbread mix
- Pizza dough mix
- Pringles
- Cheeses (look for unrefrigerated types such as Laughing Cow, Velveeta, Babybel, etc.)

Online Resources

There are many great online resources for prepared foods and ingredients as well. Some are listed here and an up-to-date list can be found at www.AForkin theTrail.com.

- **Gourmet House Wild Rice:** www.gourmethouserice.com—instant wild rice
- **Gibbs Wild Rice:** www.gibbswildrice.com—instant wild rice and wild rice cereal
- **Snyder's of Hanover:** www.snydersofhanover.com—a wide range of pretzels
- **Walton Feed:** www.waltonfeed.com—dehydrated ingredients, egg mix, sour cream powder, and butter powder
- **Mumm's Organic Sprouting Seeds:** www.sprouting.com—organic sprouting seeds
- **Minimus.biz:** www.minimus.biz—single-serving condiments, salad dressings, and other travel-sized items
- **The Spice House:** www.thespicehouse.com—specialty extracts and spices
- **King Arthur Flour:** www.kingarthurflour.com—dried egg products, organic ghee, flour, mixes, and spices
- **Bauly Specialty Foods:** www.bauly.com—freeze-dried fruits, vegetables, meat, whole meals, and meatballs
- **Emergency Essentials:** http://beprepared.com—dehydrated and freeze-dried ingredients and meals
- **Nesco/American Harvest:** www.nesco.com—food dehydrators

A chain named Trader Joe's (www.traderjoes.com), with stores throughout the U.S., has a great variety of spices, nuts, and dried fruits and vegetables along with foods such as couscous and soup mixes. Some of the items are in bulk so you only have to buy what you need. Unfortunately, online ordering is not available at the time of this writing.

Chapter 3
MENU PLANNING

One of the questions I am most frequently asked as a wilderness cooking instructor is about meal planning. I believe it is one of the biggest challenges facing anybody learning to cook in the wilderness. When my husband and I were first learning, we brought too much food, especially gorp (good old raisins and peanuts). We would look over the initial menus and feel concerned that we didn't have enough food, so we would pack extra food and end up bringing half of it home. After doing this a few times we realized we needed to make a meal plan and stick to it. Our simple menu plan consists of three meals and two snacks per day (I add an extra snack for cold weather trips) and the occasional dessert. Fresh foods can complement your backcountry menu if you don't mind the extra weight. Paddlers who are not embarking on large portages can afford more luxury when it comes to meal planning than backpackers can.

Keep in mind that most people eat more on trips than they do at home; after all you are expending more energy and your body needs to refuel. All too often, I see menus that include a great deal of foods such as candy bars and the like—not always a good choice. Sure, you will have energy for a little while, but after a spurt of sugar energy you experience a "sugar crash," which makes you feel zapped and lethargic—not a good combination when you still have half a day of hiking or paddling ahead of you. You also tend to live off your body's food stores in this state, instead of fueling your body. Foods that are nutrient rich will serve you better on the trail.

Planning for Solo Trips

Menu planning for a solo trip is fairly straightforward because you are on your own. Since you have no one to split the weight of cooking gear with, stick to a simple menu and avoiding the heavier baked goods if pack weight is an issue. Package your food in single servings and take along a copy of your menu.

Planning for Larger Groups

For larger groups meal planning is a little more difficult because you must take group dynamics into account. Some larger groups like to plan food so that the menu is shared; one person brings breakfast for the entire group, and someone else is responsible for dinner. Others plan so that certain people bring particular ingredients to contribute to the meal. From experience I know that this can be difficult to plan and organize, especially if you have fussy eaters. It can also be an issue for those who have larger appetites or for the whole group if someone forgets a key ingredient for a meal. I recommend handling things a little differently.

If there are more than five people, create subgroups, limited to about three or four people. Often subgroups form when a group naturally splits by family unit. Each subgroup becomes responsible for its own food, with all subgroups cooking meals in the same spot at about the same time. Before the trip, the organizer creates a menu plan and then sends it to everyone. Each subgroup can adapt the menu to suit its members' tastes and needs. Everyone ends up eating in the same area at about the same time in a much more relaxed manner. This method is also beneficial in case one group has to cancel the trip last minute. If food is done as one large group, it's more difficult to be flexible. Plus, organizing by subgroup cuts down on the amount of kitchen gear needed because each group can share items like a stove and water filter.

One thing that makes cooking easier in the morning is to assign chores. While one person dismantles the tent and packs the gear, the other can cook breakfast. This approach saves time and means you can get on the move early but still enjoy a hearty meal.

Mailing Foods

On thru-hikes and longer hiking or paddling expeditions, you may need to mail food packages or plan to shop along the way to restock your supplies. When mailing food, it is important that all your ingredients are dried properly, well sealed, and packed properly in a sturdy carton. You might want to include a food-safe oxygen absorber or two in the box to help keep the food from becoming stale. Oxygen absorbers can be purchased from Walton Feed at www.waltonfeed.com or Sorbent Systems at www.sorbentsystems.com.

Special Diets and Picky Eaters

Those individuals with dietary restrictions and others who are picky eaters should be responsible for their own food. It is easier for one person to pack a special diet than to expect the large group to conform to the restrictions. For picky eaters, especially children, it is best to test foods at home before the trip to ensure that there won't be any issues with the menu.

It is easy to convert most recipes to suit low-sodium diets or for vegetarians. However, people with illnesses such as diabetes will need to be especially careful when menu planning because of the fluctuations in blood levels caused by increased physical activity and any dietary differences. If you are diabetic, you should talk to your physician before going on a backpacking or paddling expedition.

People with food allergies have to be especially careful—it is best that those people plan their own menus and discuss any life-threatening allergies with the rest of the group. If someone has a deadly allergy to something such as nuts, it might be best that the entire group avoid bringing foods that contain those ingredients. There are many good substitutions for those with wheat, dairy, or egg allergies; more information on ingredient substitutions can be found in the next chapter.

Recipe Resizing

Increasing and decreasing a recipe's size is easier than most people realize. That being said I always test a recipe at home first to ensure that everything turns out okay. Most of the recipes in this book are easy to double or reduce by half. Recipes with sauces such as spaghetti, soups, stews, and goulash are easy to resize. Here are a few tips:

- When doubling a recipe that contains onions, only increase the onion amount by half.

- Be careful with hot spices such as chilies when you double a recipe—you can always add more when it reaches your plate.

- Mark the number of portions and predehydrated volume on a piece of paper and place it inside your storage bag/container.

- Never measure ingredients directly over the pot or bowl. If too much of something falls into your pot, you could have a dinner disaster.

- When you double some baked recipes, such as chicken pot pie, for a larger group, it is often better to prepare two of the recipe as opposed to trying to do one dish. You can cook one, and while everyone has a small serving cook the second for all to share; if you want to serve both at the same time, use two stoves.

Menu Plans

Print a small copy of your menu and take it with you so you can refer to it each morning and plan accordingly for the day. Make notes about what ingredients you may need to rehydrate at breakfast time for consumption at lunch. This preparation saves you from digging through the packs, which is especially helpful in inclement weather. The following sample three- and six-day menus were taken from actual wilderness hiking trips.

Three-Day Menu Plan

Day 1—Lengthy Travel Day

Breakfast	Maple Pecan Quinoa
Snack	Raisins
Lunch	Apple Peanut Salad Wrap
Snack	Beef jerky
Dinner	Salmon Cakes
Dessert	Dark chocolate

Day 2—Moderate Travel Day

Breakfast	Orange Cranberry Pancakes
Snack	Blueberry Banana Energy Bars
Lunch	Cream of Potato and Roasted Garlic Soup
Snack	Spicy Gorp
Dinner	Linguini with Red Clam Sauce
Dessert	Mocha Moosey Mousse

Day 3—Hike Out

Breakfast	Franola
Snack	Mixed nuts
Lunch	Curried Tuna and Couscous Salad
Snack	Dried mixed fruit
Dinner	Stop at a restaurant on the drive home.

Six-Day Menu Plan

Day 1—Moderate Travel Day

Breakfast   Breakfast Frittata
Snack   Fresh orange or dried fruit
Lunch   Lemon Wasabi Hummus with pita bread
Snack   Spiced Dried Pears and Apples with Walnuts
Dinner   Moroccan Chicken with Sweet Potatoes and French bread

Day 2—Lengthy Travel Day

Breakfast   Banana Breakfast Bar (Start rehydrating lunch
               ingredients with cold water.)
Snack   Pumpkin Pie Leather
Lunch   Broccoli Carrot Slaw
Snack   Ginger Cashew Bark
Dinner   Hungarian Goulash
Dessert   Mayan Hot Chocolate

Day 3—Lengthy Travel Day

Breakfast   Cherry Almond Granola with milk (Start rehydrating
               lunch ingredients with cold water.)
Snack   Fresh apple or dried fruit
Lunch   Citrus Lentil Salad
Snack   Teriyaki Jerky
Dinner   Harvest Pork and Apple Stew with jasmine rice
Dessert   Dark chocolate

Day 4—Moderate Travel Day

Breakfast   Harvest Oatmeal Bars (Let rice for lunch cook
               while you pack up your gear.)
Snack   Dried veggie chips
Lunch   Jasmine Rice and Shrimp Salad
Snack   Honey Mustard Gorp
Dinner   Chipotle Pork with Toasted Tortillas

Day 5—Short Travel Day

Breakfast   Chai Tea Breakfast Cake
Snack   Crunchy Berry Yogurt Leather
Lunch   Chicken and Apple Slaw
Snack   Spicy Gorp
Dinner   Quinoa and Spinach Soup
Dessert   Cocoa Mocha Fry Cookies

Day 6—Hike Out

Breakfast   Strawberry Peach Muesli with milk (Start rehydrating
              lunch ingredients with cold water.)
Snack   Smoked Salmon Jerky
Lunch   Carrot Raisin Salad with Peanuts
Snack   Hazelnut Currant Energy Bar
Dinner   Stop at a restaurant on the drive home.

Additional Items

Bring beverages, sugar, seasonings, creamer, milk powder, oil, butter, an extra
meal, and a few snacks for emergencies (in case you become stormbound, ill,
etc.).

Chapter 4
RECIPE CREATION

Creating recipes is only as limited as your imagination. You can use a variety of sources for inspiration such as your favorite cookbook, an old family recipe, online recipe collections, or even your favorite backpacking cookbooks. Experimenting can be fun and you will be pleasantly surprised at what you can create to enhance your wilderness trips.

Adapting Recipes from Home

Adapting your favorite recipes for wilderness cooking is easier than you might think. It can be as simple as dehydrating leftovers from today's supper. Leftovers such as stew, chili, and spaghetti sauce dry incredibly well. In fact, any recipe with a sauce that is not cream based should give you good results. Cook the recipe first and then cut the pieces small enough so that they will dehydrate well.

Meats that are not ground will dry and rehydrate better if you shred them after cooking. You have to be careful with fatty ingredients such as sausage or ground beef. I use extra lean ground meat and remove the casings from sausages. Cook the meat separately from the dish, and rinse it a few times under hot water. Then return the meat to the frying pan, reseason it, and follow the rest of the recipe.

You can easily replace eggs, milk, buttermilk, and sour cream in recipes with their powdered equivalents. Sour cream dries well in a dish such as beef stroganoff, but it does not dry well at all for use as a sour cream topping. Yogurt makes a wonderful leather and dries well when used as a minor ingredient, but you cannot dry yogurt to be reconstituted on its own. Feta and grated Parmesan cheese dry very well.

All vegetables dry very well except lettuce and most salad greens. Swiss chard and spinach dry nicely for use in soups and pastas. You can thinly slice vegetables such as zucchini, carrots, and parsnips, and dry them to make your own vegetable chips. Frozen vegetables are already blanched and you can dry them right from the freezer.

Recipes for baking are also easy to modify. The *Pear Berry Crumble* recipe (page 189), for instance, is a modification of a very old family recipe for apple crumble. First, I cut the recipe in half. Since there are no eggs or milk in the recipe, it was an easy one to change. I did not want to carry fresh apples and was becoming a little bored with apples anyway, so I decided to try dried pears and a mixture of dried berries at home using my camping pot and my regular oven. I rehydrated the fruit for 15 to 20 minutes in boiling water and then made the crumble mixture. It turned out very well. My family and I decided it was worth keeping, so I made the recipe again in our backyard using our backpacking stove and Outback Oven, which resulted in another successful crumble dessert. Finally we tried it and enjoyed it on a wilderness trip.

Creating Your Own Recipes

Creating your own recipes can be an adventure in itself. Be sure to test them at home first though—there is nothing worse than having to choke down a meal that did not turn out especially when you have no alternatives. When creating recipes be careful to use ingredients that complement each other. You can also base your creation on another meal that you enjoy. For example, rosemary, lemon, and garlic on roasted chicken is a classic combination that you could turn into an interesting lunch for a wilderness trip. At home you could sauté small chicken pieces with a scant bit of olive oil, the juice of a lemon, some rosemary, and a few cloves of chopped garlic and then dehydrate the mixture. Some possible uses include making chicken salad or enhancing a recipe that calls for cooked chicken. The only limit is your imagination.

Ingredient Substitutions

There are many products on the market that make ingredient substitution very easy, and there are some more creative ingredient substitutions.

Egg Powder or Replacer

You can purchase egg powder that is suitable for baking but not for use as scrambled eggs. If you have an allergy to eggs or you are vegan, you can purchase egg-free egg replacer at your local health food store.

If you prefer, you can make your own egg replacer. It is similar to egg whites and works well in white cakes, muffins, and cookies. The addition of oil mimics a whole egg in baking. To make the equivalent of one egg, mix 1½ teaspoons tapioca starch, 1½ teaspoons potato starch (sometimes found with the kosher foods), and ⅛ teaspoon baking powder together and store it in a ziplock freezer bag. Then when you're ready to use it at camp, add ¼ cup of water and 1 teaspoon of vegetable oil, and beat the mixture with a fork until it becomes a little foamy.

Ground flax seed can be used in muffins, breads, or other baked goods, but it imparts a flavor that might be unpleasant in a cake or cookies. Keep the ground flax seed cool and away from air and light to prevent it from becoming rancid; this recipe is not suitable for use in hot weather or more than two days into a trip. Store the seeds in the refrigerator until you leave for your trip. To make the equivalent of one egg, use 2 tablespoons ground flax seed. If you cannot find ground flax seed, then grind whole flax seed. Pack the powder in a ziplock freezer bag, removing as much air as possible and storing it away from sources of heat and light. When you're ready to use it, add 3 tablespoons of water to the ground flax seed and let it sit for 3 to 5 minutes. Add to your recipe like you would regular eggs.

Flour

You can increase the fiber in a recipe by replacing up to one-third of the white flour called for with whole wheat flour. This substitution, however, will change the texture, giving you a coarser and denser product. Pastry flour contains less gluten than all-purpose flour and is great for baked goods that require a finer texture. Buckwheat flour can replace up to half of the white flour in your pancakes. Quinoa flour adds more fat to your baking and can replace half of the white or all-purpose flour in a recipe. Quinoa flour also contains a good amount of protein. Spelt flour can be used cup for cup, but you need to increase the baking powder in the recipe slightly as spelt is heavier. Spelt flour is a good substitute for people with wheat allergies.

Meat

Many recipes in this book call for meats such as chicken, pork, beef, or seafood. You can replace the meat in recipes with textured vegetable protein, which you add at camp. You can also use tofu when you make the recipe at home as it dehydrates very well. Another alternative is to replace the seafood with a favorite vegetable. For the *Jasmine Rice and Shrimp Salad* (page 73), for example, omit the shrimp and add 3 ounces of rehydrated broccoli instead. You could substitute rehydrated asparagus for the clams in the *Orecchiette with Clams* (page 142).

Sweeteners

Both white and brown sugar can be replaced with Splenda or white or brown sugar. Read the instructions on the package for equivalents. Stevia is another good sugar substitute that is available at most health food stores. Raw sugar can be substituted for white sugar as well. Honey and maple syrup can also be substituted for one another in most recipes. Because honey is more acidic, you may have to add a pinch of baking soda if you are using it to replace maple syrup. You can also substitute real maple syrup for sugar, using ¾ cup syrup for every cup of sugar you are replacing. Since it is liquid and may change the texture of the recipes, reduce the recipe liquid by 3 tablespoons for every cup of maple syrup used.

Chapter 5
BREAKFASTS

I could not agree with the old adage "breakfast is the most important meal of the day" more, especially on a day when you are going to be doing a lot of physical activity. I come, however, from a long line of breakfast skippers. On my first backpacking trip, I did not plan for breakfast and was nauseous from a pounding headache each day by lunchtime. I felt so awful that I would not eat properly at lunch, and by the end of the day I was sluggish and downright miserable, which was not good for my body or my campmates.

When planning your breakfast options for a given trip, you should consider the type of travel (backpacking, hiking, paddling, or portaging); time of year; weather forecast; time needed for cooking and cleanup; and your group's general energy needs. Type of travel, in particular, makes a difference in your energy needs. You burn more calories backpacking and portaging than you do flatwater paddling. Time of year is important as well. I prefer a hot breakfast such as oatmeal in colder weather. Your body will also need more fuel when it is colder.

I always bring a few homemade energy bars in case I have to break camp quickly to stay ahead of the weather. Speaking of breaking camp quickly, make sure you take into consideration how long it will take to cook and clean up from your meal. If you have a long day planned, you may want a breakfast that is a little faster to prepare. You can prepare something a little more elaborate on a rest or short day. The breakfast menu usually correlates to the camping style of your companions. For instance, if you are traveling with people who like to break camp early, you should save the eggs Benedict for a rest day. Be sure to discuss meal times and styles with everyone before your trip to prevent unnecessary tension.

Eggs are a good source of protein and are fairly quick and easy to prepare. If you are backpacking, powdered or freeze-dried eggs are better than fresh eggs. You can use powdered scrambled egg mix for omelets and French toast. Powdered and freeze-dried eggs are also excellent for baking. If you are vegan, you can use a powdered egg-free replacement in baking. If you aren't worried about weight or bulk, you can take fresh eggs as long as you pack them carefully. Fresh eggs keep for about a week if you coat the shells well with petroleum jelly and place them in an egg container designed for camping and then in a ziplock freezer bag. Make sure you pack it safely in the center of your pack. I generally take a few extras because you cannot use an egg if it cracks. Of course, you have to wash the petroleum jelly off before you use the eggs.

Powdered milk is a good alternative to regular milk and is important, especially if you are traveling with children. Even though I am not a vegetarian, I use powdered soy milk because I find it a little richer and creamier than powdered skim milk. Powdered milk comes in both instant and noninstant varieties, but the instant kind is preferable because it mixes more easily.

Instant oatmeal is great for breakfasts, too; you can even make it in a mug. The nice thing about Quaker Instant Oatmeal, in particular, is that the individual-sized paper packets are actually waterproof. In our test kitchen, we immersed packets in cold water for 24 hours and the oatmeal was still dry.

Protein drinks and bars are common among backpackers, but I prefer not to use them. The taste is not always appealing, and one can tire of them quickly—they're best left to the adventure racers.

Baking for Breakfast

A few years ago, my family and I started baking for breakfast, and it has become a big hit. You can fry-bake or use an Outback Oven or BakePacker. Leave this sort of elaborate meal for days when you are not in a hurry or are staying put. You can use recipes from this book, modify your own, or look for commercial mixes that require few additions. Mixes often require only eggs, oil, and water. You can replace the eggs with powdered or freeze-dried eggs easily. You can also use commercial pizza dough mixes and items such as Bisquick as a base for both sweet and savory breakfasts. If you have ingredients that need rehydration, it is best to start that process the night before or use boiling water if you wait until morning. It's easy enough to put cold water and your dried ingredients in a Nalgene bottle and hang it with the other food overnight. Do not do this with beans or meats, however, because beans reconstitute very quickly and become mushy if left overnight and rehydrating meat right before you use it reduces the risk of bacteria.

Use of Leftovers

You might consider baking banana bread or muffins from a mix for dessert or reserving some herb bread from dinner. You can save these leftovers in a ziplock bag and have it the next morning with a hot beverage. If you are taking a small cooler for the first night, you can easily save other leftovers for the next morning.

Breakfast on the Go

Often you want to get going earlier; you might have a long journey planned for that day, be facing bad weather, or just want to enjoy a beautiful morning. On such days it's convenient to use foods you've made at home or leftovers from the previous night's baking. Several breakfast options are portable and are therefore perfect for eating on the go.

Homemade granola and breakfast bars are very convenient. You can increase the protein by using high-energy cereals and adding a variety of nuts or nut butters. Bagels travel well and can be prepared with peanut butter or other spreads and wrapped the night before and then eaten on the move the next morning. There is likely a wide variety of bars available at your local grocery store, but I prefer homemade bars. Fresh fruit is also great when you are on the go—although it can be heavy, sometimes it is worth the extra weight.

1 tablespoon orange juice

1 tablespoon lime juice

¼ cup macadamia nuts or
    hazelnuts

¼ cup medjool or honey dates

1 large ripe banana

1 tablespoon nonfat powdered
    milk or vanilla protein powder

2 tablespoons peanut butter

⅛ teaspoon cinnamon

Peanut Butter and Banana Dip

Dehydration Time: 10–15 hours
Makes 2–3 servings

Both the big and little kids on your trip will love this recipe reminiscent of a peanut butter and banana sandwich.

AT HOME

Combine all ingredients in a food processor and process until smooth. Spread on lined dehydrator trays and dry for 10 to 15 hours until thoroughly dried. Place the mixture in a food processor or spice grinder and pulse it until you have a fine powder. While it's not necessary to grind it into a powder, this step greatly speeds up the rehydration process. Package the powder in a ziplock storage bag.

AT CAMP

Rehydrate dip, using equal parts of boiling water and dried mix. Stir and let sit for a minute or two. Serve with fresh or dried apple slices and toasted whole wheat pita wedges.

Tropical Couscous

Makes 2 servings

Couscous makes a wonderful breakfast food since it cooks very quickly.

At Home

Place the couscous and brown sugar in a medium-sized freezer ziplock bag. Place the fruit, ginger, powdered milk, and coconut in separate bags, and put the bags in with the couscous. Add the butter to what you are taking on your trip.

At Camp

Bring 1¼ cups water to a boil. While you wait mix the couscous and brown sugar mixture with the fruit, ginger, and butter in a freezer ziplock bag. Place the coconut cream in a bag or container large enough to accommodate at least ½ cup of liquid. Add 1 teaspoon of hot water to the creamed coconut and mix. If you're using coconut powder, then you will need to add 1 to 2 tablespoons of water. To the same container add enough powdered milk and water to make a ½ cup of milk.

Carefully pour the boiling water into the bag with the couscous mixture. Let stand 5 minutes. Stir the couscous, scoop it in bowls, and top it with the milk mixture.

1 cup instant couscous

1½ teaspoons dark brown sugar

½ cup chopped dried pears, peaches, and mangoes

1 teaspoon crystallized stem ginger

½ teaspoon creamed coconut or 3 tablespoons coconut powder

1½ teaspoons butter (optional)

Enough soy or powdered whole milk to make ½ cup

1¼ cups, plus 1 teaspoon hot water, plus enough water to reconstitute milk

1¼ cups granola

½ cup freeze-dried mixed fruit

2 tablespoons butter

Enough nonfat powdered milk and
water to make ½ cup milk

Franola

Makes 2–3 servings

*I accidentally discovered franola, or fried granola, one
morning in late fall when my family was camped on a cold
bay. I couldn't face another cold breakfast so I ended up
putting a little butter in my frying pan and digging through
my pack to see what I could create. This brought some
warmth to the bitter morning.*

At Home

Put the granola in a ziplock freezer bag. Put the freeze-
dried fruit in another bag and place that in with the
granola. Pack the butter with the other butter that you will
take on your trip. Do the same for the powdered milk.

At Camp

Add a little cold water to the freeze-dried fruit and set it
aside. Use the milk powder and water to make ½ cup of
milk. Heat 2 tablespoons of butter in a pot or frying pan.
When the butter is melted, add the granola and stir until
it is hot. Add the freeze-dried fruit and mix until heated.
Divide the franola into two servings and top with milk.

Maple Pecan Quinoa

Makes 2 servings

A seed the ancient Inca used, quinoa, pronounced keen-wa, *is a good source of amino acids and complex carbohydrates. Because it has a bitter coating, you must rinse it very well. This cereal is as warm and comforting as a bowl of oatmeal but packs a lot more nutrition.*

AT HOME

Rinse the quinoa under cold water for at least 3 minutes. Drain well and then toast in a dry nonstick frying pan until the quinoa starts to pop. Allow it to cool and then place it in a ziplock freezer bag with the salt and vanilla sugar. Pour the maple syrup in a small leakproof container, wrap the pecans in plastic wrap, and place both in the bag with the quinoa. Pack the milk powder with the other milk powder you will take on your trip.

AT CAMP

Mix the contents of the quinoa bag with ¾ cup of water in a pot. Bring to a boil. Reduce the heat to a simmer and let the quinoa cook for 10 minutes, stirring occasionally. If it becomes too dry, add a little more water. Meanwhile use the powdered milk and water to make ½ cup of milk. When the quinoa has finished cooking, divide it into 2 servings. Top each with milk and a little maple syrup and sprinkle with pecans.

TIPS

If you are camping in cold weather and need to increase your fat intake, add a tablespoon of butter to the quinoa when it has finished cooking.

For warmer quinoa, add the milk to the pot when the quinoa has finished cooking and heat through.

Do not use fructose or corn syrup in place of the maple syrup.

½ cup quinoa

⅛ teaspoon salt

1 tablespoon vanilla sugar

⅛ cup maple syrup or 1 tablespoon turbinado or brown sugar

⅛ cup pecans

Enough nonfat powdered milk to make ½ cup, plus water as necessary

¾ cup water

Strawberry Peach Muesli

Makes 2–4 servings

2 tablespoons slivered almonds

2 dried figs

3 dried peach slices

¼ cup freeze-dried strawberries

¼ cup wheat bran

1 cup rolled oats

¼ cup oat bran

¼ cup wheat germ

⅓ cup shredded or flaked coconut

¼ cup sunflower seeds

A dollop of yogurt or enough nonfat powdered milk to make 1 cup milk

Muesli was one of my childhood favorites. This one has a summery flavor and travels well. You can serve it hot or cold.

AT HOME

Toast the almonds in a dry nonstick frying pan until they start to turn golden. Set them aside and let them cool. Chop the dried fruit. Toss the fruit and the wheat bran in a large bowl to coat. Add the toasted almonds, rolled oats, oat bran, wheat germ, coconut, and sunflower seeds and mix. Pour the mixture into a ziplock freezer bag.

Pack the powdered milk with the other powdered milk you will take on your trip. If you prefer yogurt, see the recipe on page 65 for *Trail Yogurt*.

AT CAMP

Pour the muesli into a bowl. If you brought powdered milk, mix it with water and then pour the milk over the muesli. If you prefer yogurt and brought it, top with a dollop of yogurt.

Cherry Almond Granola

Makes 6–8 servings

Sometimes I add chocolate chips to this recipe and eat it as trail mix instead of for breakfast.

At Home
Preheat the oven to 350°F. Mix the dry ingredients together in a medium-sized bowl. Combine the liquid ingredients in a small bowl and then add to the dry ingredients. Stir well. Spread the granola on a baking sheet lined with parchment paper. Bake for 25 to 30 minutes, stirring occasionally.

Remove from heat and let cool. After the granola has cooled, package it into ziplocks.

¼ cup wheat germ

2 cups rolled oats

1 cup slivered almonds

¾ cup dried cherries, chopped

¼ cup canola or vegetable oil

¼ cup honey

¼ teaspoon almond extract

Ginger Peach Granola

Makes 6–8 servings

Ginger and peaches go well together, and the ginger adds a little bite to this granola.

At Home
Preheat the oven to 350°F. Mix the dry ingredients together in a medium-sized bowl. Combine the liquid ingredients in a small bowl and then add them to the dry ingredients. Stir well. Spread the mixture on a baking sheet lined with parchment paper. Bake for 25 to 30 minutes, stirring occasionally.

Remove from heat and let cool. Once the granola has cooled, package it into ziplocks.

¼ cup wheat germ

2 cups rolled oats

1 cup walnuts, chopped

½ cup dried peaches, chopped

¼ cup candied ginger, chopped

¼ cup canola or vegetable oil

¼ cup honey

¼ cup oat bran

2 cups rolled oats

1 cup pecans, coarsely chopped

½ cup dried blueberries

¼ cup banana chips, broken into pieces

¼ cup canola or vegetable oil

¼ cup pure maple syrup

¼ teaspoon maple extract

Canadian Maple Blueberry Granola

Makes 6–8 servings

When my family and I are hiking in the Canadian wilderness, we often come across patches of wild blueberries, and there is nothing more Canadian than maple syrup. This flavor combination was the inspiration for this recipe.

AT HOME

Preheat the oven to 350°F. Mix the dry ingredients together in a medium-sized bowl. Combine the liquid ingredients in a small bowl and then add to the dry ingredients. Stir well. Spread the mixture on a baking sheet lined with parchment paper. Bake for 25 to 30 minutes, stirring occasionally.

Remove from heat and let cool. Once the granola has cooled, package it into ziplocks.

Date Raisin Hazelnut Granola

Makes 6–8 servings

This recipe tastes a little like a date square.

AT HOME

Preheat the oven to 350°F. Mix the dry ingredients together in a medium-sized bowl. Combine the liquid ingredients in a small bowl and then add them to the dry ingredients. Stir well. Spread the granola on a baking sheet lined with parchment paper. Bake for 25 to 30 minutes, stirring occasionally.

Remove from heat and let cool. Once the granola has cooled, package it into ziplocks.

TIP

To peel hazelnuts, which are also known as filberts, place them in a strainer and roll them with your hands, pressing lightly. The friction will remove the peel easily.

¼ cup natural bran

2 cups rolled oats

1 cup whole hazelnuts, peeled

½ cup dates, chopped

¼ cup raisins

¼ cup canola or vegetable oil

¼ cup honey

Mango Pineapple Macadamia Granola

Makes 6–8 servings

This granola has a tropical twist. It can be used as a trail mix if you leave the fruit pieces a little chunkier.

AT HOME

Preheat the oven to 350°F. Mix the dry ingredients together in a medium-sized bowl. Combine the liquid ingredients in a small bowl and then add them to the dry ingredients. Stir well. Spread the granola on a baking sheet lined with parchment paper. Bake for 25 to 30 minutes, stirring occasionally.

Remove from heat and let cool. Once the granola has cooled, package it into ziplocks.

¼ cup oat bran

3 tablespoons shredded coconut

2 cups rolled oats

1 cup chopped macadamia nuts

¼ cup dried mango, chopped

¼ cup dried pineapple, chopped

¼ cup canola or vegetable oil

¼ cup honey

⅛ teaspoon orange extract

Maple Peach Crepes with Custard

Dehydration Time: 8–10 hours
Makes 6–8 servings

You'll turn heads with this completely decadent breakfast that is surprisingly easy to make. It makes a great dessert, too.

AT HOME

Put the pecans into a nonstick frying pan and gently toast them. Allow pecans to cool and then wrap them in plastic wrap. Dehydrate peaches for 8 to 10 hours and then place them in a large ziplock. Package the maple sugar and instant custard powder in separate small ziplocks. Place the crepe batter in another ziplock. Put all the bags into the large ziplock bag with the peaches. Add the butter to any other butter that you will take on your trip.

AT CAMP

Pour boiling water over the peaches and let them rehydrate for approximately 15 minutes. Meanwhile make crepes according to the instructions in the *Basic Crepes* recipe and set aside. Make custard and set aside, preferably in a pot cozy.

In the pot or pan where you made the crepes, add a little butter, the rehydrated peaches, and the maple sugar. Cook until the peaches are heated through and the sugar is syrupy. Place each crepe on a plate and put ⅙ of the peach mixture in the center. Roll up each crepe and top with one-sixth of the custard. Sprinkle a few of the toasted pecans on each.

¼ cup pecans

6 canned peach halves, diced

¼ cup maple or turbinado sugar

Enough instant custard powder to make 1 cup of custard

1 recipe *Basic Crepes* (6 crepes, page 211)

1 tablespoon butter

1 egg

1 cup light brown sugar

1 cup buttermilk

2 cups all-purpose flour

½ teaspoon baking soda

½ teaspoon baking powder

¼ teaspoon salt

⅛ cup butter

½ cup walnuts, chopped

Nut Bread

Makes 6–8 servings

I remember my mom making this old family favorite with sour milk when she didn't have buttermilk. This bread is slightly sweet and has a sturdy consistency. It will last for several days in a pack.

AT HOME

Preheat oven to 350°F. In a large bowl, beat the egg until it is light in color. Add the sugar and beat until smooth. Stir in the buttermilk. Mix the flour, baking soda, baking powder, and salt together in a medium-sized bowl. Then add the flour mixture to the buttermilk mixture, stirring until moistened. Melt the butter in a microwave or on top of the stove. Mix the walnuts and melted butter together. Stir the nut mixture into the batter. Pour the batter into greased miniloaf pans. Bake for 45 to 55 minutes.

Remove the loaves from the pans and cool on wire racks. Wrap tightly in plastic wrap and then in aluminum foil. Freeze the loaves until you're ready to take them on your trip.

AT CAMP

Slice the bread and butter it if desired.

Banana Breakfast Bars

Makes 10–12 servings

The problem with these bars is keeping them around long enough to take them on a trip.

AT HOME

Preheat the oven to 350°F. Mix the butter and sugar together in a medium-sized mixing bowl. Beat the egg and pour it in the bowl. Mash the bananas in a separate bowl, add them to the eggs, and mix well. Stir in the oats, salt, and milk powder, combining well. Add the walnuts and the raisins or chocolate chips and stir to combine.

Line the tops and sides of a 9-inch by 9-inch baking pan with a single piece of parchment paper. Then butter the top of the paper. Pour the batter into the pan. Bake at 350°F for 1 hour. After the slab has cooled, cut it into bars and wrap them in waxed paper. Place the wrapped bars in a ziplock freezer bag. These bars freeze very well for several months.

TIP

To make the parchment paper easier to manage, place a little butter in the bottom of your pan and then place the parchment paper in the pan. The butter underneath with hold the paper in place, making it easier for you to butter the top of the paper.

½ cup butter, softened

⅔ cup brown sugar

1 egg

3 ripe bananas

3½ cups rolled oats

½ teaspoon salt

¼ cup malted milk powder, such as Ovaltine, or chocolate-flavored protein powder

¾ cup chopped walnuts

1 cup raisins or chocolate chips (or ½ cup of each)

½ teaspoon cinnamon

¼ teaspoon ground ginger

⅛ teaspoon nutmeg

½ cup canola or vegetable oil

½ cup honey

1½ teaspoons vanilla extract

1 egg

2 cups rolled oats

1 cup all-purpose flour

½ teaspoon salt

½ cup wheat germ

¾ cup lightly packed dark brown sugar

¼ cup dried pears, chopped

¼ cup dried apples, chopped

¼ cup dried cranberries

½ cup walnuts, chopped

Harvest Oatmeal Bars

Makes 16 servings

This is another one of those make-at-home recipes where the bars seem to disappear before the trip.

AT HOME

Preheat the oven to 350°F. Mix the spices and liquid ingredients together in a small bowl. Combine all of the dry ingredients in another larger bowl. Add the liquid ingredients to the dry ingredients and mix until the liquid mix is distributed evenly throughout the dry ingredients.

Lightly butter the bottom of a 9-inch by 13-inch non-stick baking pan and then line it with parchment paper. Lightly oil the top of the parchment paper. Press the mixture firmly into the pan. Bake for 25 to 30 minutes or until the edges start to turn golden brown.

Place the pan on a wire rack and cool completely before removing the bars from the pan. Turn the bars out onto a board. Cut into 16 bars and wrap each in waxed paper. Package the bars in a ziplock. Freeze them if you aren't going to use them right away.

Cereal Bars

Makes 10 servings

This fruity and sweet bar is made from cornflakes, tart fruit, and crunchy nuts.

AT HOME

Oil a 9-inch by 13-inch pan and set aside. Mix together cornflakes, nuts, dried fruit, coconut, and pepitas in a large bowl. Set aside. Melt the butter on medium-high heat in a saucepan. Add the brown sugar and corn syrup and stir until the sugar is dissolved and the mixture starts to bubble. Remove the sweet mixture from the heat, add the vanilla extract, and pour it into the cereal mixture. Stir with a wooden spoon until the flakes are well coated.

Put the mixture into the prepared pan. Butter the bottom of a large drinking glass and use it to push the mixture firmly into the pan. Put the pan in the refrigerator and allow the mixture to set for about an hour.

Remove the hardened mixture from the pan and cut it into 10 bars. Individually wrap the bars in waxed paper and put them in a freezer ziplock bag. Store the bars in the freezer, for up to three months, until you're ready to use them.

TIP

Pepitas are shelled pumpkin seeds. If you can't find pepitas, you can use sunflower seeds instead.

6 cups cornflakes

¼ cup walnuts, chopped

¼ cup almonds, slivered

¼ cup dried apples, chopped

¼ cup dried cherries

¼ cup shredded coconut

¼ cup pepitas

¼ cup butter

⅓ cup dark brown sugar

⅓ cup golden or dark corn syrup

½ teaspoon pure vanilla extract

Quinoa Bars

Makes 10 servings

2 tablespoons butter

¾ cup quinoa

2 egg whites

¼ cup honey

½ cup brown sugar

1 teaspoon cinnamon

½ teaspoon pure vanilla extract

¼ teaspoon pure orange extract

¾ cup rolled oats

½ cup wheat germ or oat bran

¼ cup shredded coconut, toasted

A seed the ancient Inca used, quinoa, pronounced keen-wa, *contains amino acids and has a nutty taste when toasted. Because it has a bitter coating to deter birds and other animals from consuming it, you must rinse it well before cooking it.*

AT HOME

Preheat oven to 350°F. Line a 9-inch by 9-inch pan with parchment paper so that the paper goes up the sides of the pan as well. Butter the parchment paper. Rinse the quinoa in a fine strainer under cold water for at least 3 minutes. In a nonstick frying pan toast the quinoa, stirring frequently. As soon as some of the seeds start to pop remove the quinoa from the pan and set it aside to cool.

Beat the egg whites in a large bowl. Melt 2 tablespoons of butter and add it to the egg whites. Mix in the honey, brown sugar, cinnamon, and vanilla and orange extracts. Add the rolled oats, wheat germ, and the toasted quinoa. Stir until well combined. Pour the mixture into the pan and spread it into the corners. Bake for 35 to 45 minutes, until the center is set and the edges are browned.

Remove the pan from the oven and place it on a wire rack to cool. When the slab is cool, turn the pan upside down and dump bars onto a large cutting board. With a sharp knife cut the slab into 10 bars. Individually wrap the bars in waxed paper and put them all together in a ziplock freezer bag. Store the bars in the freezer, for up to three months, until you're ready to use them.

TIP

To make the parchment paper easier to manage, place a little butter in the bottom of your pan and then place the parchment paper in the pan. The butter underneath will hold the paper in place, making it easier for you to butter the top of the paper.

Cinnamon Walnut Buns

Makes 3–4 servings

These buns are adapted from a Swedish tea ring recipe that is a holiday breakfast tradition in my family.

At Home

Place a freezer ziplock bag of yeast dough mix and its instructions into a large freezer ziplock bag along with the nuts and sultanas. Mix the brown sugar and cinnamon together; wrap it in plastic wrap and place it in the larger ziplock containing the yeast dough mix. Add the butter to what you will take on your trip.

At Camp

Add nuts and sultanas to the dry ingredients for the yeast dough. Prepare the dough and let rise according to the recipe directions. If the weather is cold, you can place the ziplock inside your jacket to aid in rising. Once the dough has risen, press it out into a rectangular shape.

Butter the dough, keeping the butter 1 inch away from the edges. Sprinkle with the sugar and cinnamon mixture, followed by the nuts and raisins and roll it up starting on one of the long sides. Moisten the long edge with a bit of water and press to seal the roll. Cut into 6 pieces.

Place the buns in an Outback or reflector oven and bake for 10 to 12 minutes after the oven is preheated. Once the buns are cooked through and golden, remove them from the heat and let them cool for a few minutes so that the sultanas do not burn your mouth.

Tip

An easy way to roll out the dough is to put it in a freezer ziplock and use your water bottle as a rolling pin. Then all you have to do is cut off one side of the bag and add the filling. If you don't want to go to the trouble of rolling the dough out, just pull off little balls of dough, coat them with soft butter, and then sprinkle them with the sugar, cinnamon, nuts, and sultanas.

1 recipe *Basic Yeast Dough*
    (page 212)

⅛ cup chopped walnuts

⅛ cup dried sultanas (optional)

3 tablespoons brown sugar

1 teaspoon cinnamon

2–3 tablespoons softened butter

⅛ cup vegetable oil

1 tablespoon butter

¾ cup flour

½ teaspoon baking soda

⅛ teaspoon salt

¼ cup rolled oats

½ teaspoon cinnamon

⅛ teaspoon ground ginger

½ cup brown sugar

¼ cup flaked coconut, plus 2 tablespoons for topping

¼ cup walnuts, chopped

¼ cup dried sultanas

2 chai tea bags or equivalent loose tea

½ cup water

Chai Tea Breakfast Cake

Makes 4–6 servings

Chai tea is a combination of spices and black tea usually brewed in milk. This breakfast cake is similar in texture to a coffee cake and is spiced with the flavors of chai. Even though you can prepare this cake at home and then bring it with you, I prefer to bake it at camp and devour it while it's still slightly warm.

At Home

Pack the oil in with any other vegetable oil and the butter in with any other butter you will take on your trip. Mix the flour, baking soda, salt, oats, cinnamon, ginger, and brown sugar together and put in a medium ziplock freezer bag. Wrap 2 tablespoons of coconut in plastic wrap and put the bundle into a small bag. To that bag add the rest of the coconut, as well as the walnuts and raisins. Put the small bag and 2 chai tea bags in the medium bag with the dry ingredients.

At Camp

Boil ½ cup water and pour into a mug with the chai tea bags. Allow to steep for 5 or 10 minutes. Remove the plastic wrap bundle of coconut for the topping from the bag with the nuts, coconut and raisins. Mix the nuts, coconut, and raisins in with the other dry ingredients. Once the tea has steeped and is strong, add the ⅛ cup of vegetable oil to the tea and stir. Then mix it in with the dry ingredients. Be careful if the liquid is still hot.

Grease a baking pan with 1 tablespoon butter or line it with buttered parchment paper. Pour the batter in the pan. Place the pan in an Outback or reflector oven (after it has preheated) and then bake for 25 to 35 minutes.

Tip

This recipe also works well with flavored chai teas such as vanilla chai or orange chai. If you use orange chai, substitute cranberries for the raisins.

Breakfast Bread Pudding

Makes 2–3 servings

Because this recipe requires baking, it is best for a rest day or one with moderate travel.

AT HOME

Package the bread in a large ziplock freezer bag. In a smaller ziplock freezer bag, mix egg powder, sugar, spices, and powdered milk together and then place it in the larger bag. Bundle up the raisins in a piece of plastic wrap. Put the mixed dried fruit in small ziplock freezer bag. Put these in the larger bag with the bread.

AT CAMP

Add a little hot water to the bag of mixed dried fruit and allow it to rehydrate while you prepare the other ingredients. Cut or tear the bread into 1-inch pieces and put them in the bottom of a pot. Add 1 cup of water to the bag containing the powdered ingredients and mix well. Drain the rehydrated fruit and add it and the raisins to the bread. Pour the liquid ingredients on top of the bread mixture.

Bake in a preheated Outback or reflector oven for 30 minutes or until a toothpick or knife inserted in the center comes out clean.

TIP

If you are using an Outback Oven, you may want to line the pot or pan with parchment paper to make cleanup easier.

2–3 slices multigrain bread

2 servings powdered scrambled egg mix

¼ cup vanilla sugar

¼ teaspoon cinnamon

⅛ teaspoon nutmeg

⅓ cup nonfat powdered milk

¼ cup raisins

½ cup mixed dried fruit (peaches, pears, and cherries)

1 cup water

1 tablespoon orange zest

4 tablespoons nonfat
   powdered milk

2 tablespoons powdered
   whole egg

1 cup flour

3 teaspoons baking powder

½ teaspoon salt

1 tablespoon vanilla sugar

¼ cup dried cranberries

2 tablespoons vegetable oil

Butter (optional)

Maple syrup (optional)

¾–1 cup water

Orange Cranberry Pancakes

Dehydration Time: 2–5 hours
Makes 2 servings

The flavors of oranges and cranberries work well together. Dried fruit cooked in a little orange juice is a delicious topping alternative to syrup.

AT HOME

Using a fine grater or zest tool, scrape off only the orange part off the rind of a navel orange. Dry the zest on lined dehydrator trays for 2 to 5 hours. Mix the powdered milk, powdered egg, flour, baking powder, salt, and vanilla sugar together in a large ziplock freezer bag.

Wrap the cranberries and orange zest separately in plastic wrap and place the bundles in the freezer bag with the dry ingredients. Add the butter and vegetable oil to what you will take on your trip. Pack the syrup in a leakproof bottle.

AT CAMP

Add a small amount of hot or boiling water to the orange zest in your camp mug. Allow to rehydrate for 5 to 10 minutes and then drain. Add the cranberries and orange zest to the dry ingredients. Mix ¾ cup of water into the dry ingredients. Stir to moisten and add extra water as necessary to obtain a pancake consistency. Do not overmix or the pancakes will be tough.

Pour a little vegetable oil into a frying pan and heat over a medium flame. Pour in ¼ of the batter and cook until the edges appear dry. Then flip and cook until the underside is golden. Repeat until you have 4 pancakes, adding more oil to the pan between each pancake as necessary. Serve with a little butter and syrup if desired.

TIP

The batter is easy to manage if you make it in the ziplock freezer bag. Then simply cut off a corner of the bag and squeeze it into the pan. Between pancakes, be careful to situate the bag so that the batter doesn't spill out of the cut corner.

4 tablespoons nonfat
  powdered milk

2 tablespoons whole
  powdered egg

1 cup flour

3 teaspoons baking powder

½ teaspoon salt

1 tablespoon sugar

¼ cup dried blueberries

1 chai tea bag or enough
  loose tea to make 1 cup

2 tablespoons vegetable oil

Butter (optional)

Maple syrup (optional)

¾–1 cup water

Chai Tea Pancakes

Makes 2 servings

The spice of chai tea perfectly complements the blueberries in this pancake.

At Home

Mix the milk powder, powdered egg, flour, baking powder, salt, and sugar together in a large ziplock freezer bag. Wrap the blueberries in plastic wrap and place them, along with the chai tea bag, in the freezer bag with the dry ingredients. Add butter and vegetable oil to what you will take on your trip. Pack the syrup in a leakproof bottle.

At Camp

Add ½ cup boiling water to the chai tea bag and let steep for 3 to 5 minutes. Allow the tea to cool for a few minutes and then add ½ cup cool water. Add the blueberries to the dry ingredients. Add ¾ cup of the chai mixture to the dry ingredients in the large ziplock bag. Stir to moisten and add extra water as necessary to obtain a pancake consistency. Do not overmix or the pancakes will be tough.

Place a little vegetable oil in a frying pan and heat over a medium flame. Pour in ¼ of the batter and cook until the edges appear dry. Then flip and cook until the underside is golden. Repeat until you have 4 pancakes, adding more oil to the pan between each pancake as necessary. Serve with a little butter and syrup if desired.

Tip

The batter is easy to manage if you make it in the ziplock freezer bag. Then simply cut off a corner of the bag and squeeze the batter into the pan. Between pancakes, be careful to situate the bag so that the batter doesn't spill out of the cut corner.

Cheesy Mushroom Pancakes

Makes 2 servings

This recipe grew out of a debate my husband and I had while on a wilderness camping trip. We disagreed about whether it was possible to make a savory pancake. He was skeptical but now admits that this breakfast is among his favorites.

AT HOME

Wrap the cheese. Place the dried onion and mushrooms in a small ziplock freezer bag. Mix the milk powder, egg powder, flour, baking powder, salt, basil, and pepper together in another small ziplock freezer bag. Place everything in a larger ziplock freezer bag. Add butter and vegetable oil to what you will take on your trip.

AT CAMP

Add a small amount of hot or boiling water to the mushrooms and onions. Allow to rehydrate for 5 to 10 minutes and drain. Mix ¾ cup air-temperature water into the dry ingredients. Stir to moisten and add extra water as necessary to obtain a pancake batter consistency.

   Place a bit of vegetable oil in a frying pan and heat on medium. Pour in ¼ of the batter and cook until the edges appear dry and then flip. Cook until the underside is golden. Repeat until you have 4 pancakes, adding more oil to the pan between each pancake as necessary. Serve with a little butter if desired.

TIP

The batter is easy to manage if you make it in the ziplock freezer bag and then simply cut off a corner of the bag and squeeze it into the pan. Between pancakes, be careful to situate the bag so the batter doesn't spill out of the cut corner.

1-inch x 1-inch x 3-inch block old cheddar cheese

1 tablespoon dried onion

1 tablespoon dried porcini mushrooms, crumbled

4 tablespoons nonfat powdered milk

2 tablespoons whole powdered egg

1 cup flour

3 teaspoons baking powder

½ teaspoon salt

¼ teaspoon basil

½ teaspoon pepper

2 tablespoons vegetable oil

Butter (optional)

¾–1 cup water

Egyptian Bean Breakfast

1 small onion, chopped

½ cup tomato sauce

½ teaspoon cumin

¼ teaspoon ground coriander

¼ teaspoon cayenne pepper

1 cup canned fava beans, drained and rinsed

2 tablespoons lemon juice

2 whole wheat pitas

Dehydration Time: 6–10 hours
Makes 2 servings

Similar to a traditional Middle Eastern breakfast called Fool Mudammes, *this is a hearty meal that makes a great lunch as well.*

AT HOME

Sauté chopped onion in a medium-sized nonstick frying pan until it starts to caramelize. If you do not have a nonstick pan, then spray a regular pan with cooking spray. Add the tomato sauce and spices. Stir for about 5 minutes until the sauce thickens. Mash the fava beans with a fork and add them to the pan. Heat the beans through and add the lemon juice. Allow the mixture to cool. Spread it on lined dehydrator trays and dry for 6 to 10 hours or until thoroughly dry.

Put a piece of parchment paper between the pitas and package them in a large ziplock freezer bag, removing as much air as possible. Place the dried bean mixture in a ziplock freezer bag.

AT CAMP

Rehydrate the bean mixture using equal parts of boiling water and dried mix. When the beans are rehydrated, reheat them if necessary. Serve with pita bread.

Spicy Potato Cakes

Dehydration Time: 5–8 hours (optional)
Makes 2–3 servings

These are hearty and filling with a little kick from the Cajun spice.

At Home

Spread chili sauce on a lined dehydrator tray and dry for 5 to 8 hours. Package the potatoes and chives in a large ziplock freezer bag. Put the flour, spices, milk powder, and baking powder in another bag. Place the chili sauce in a third bag and wrap the cornmeal in plastic wrap. Put the bag with the flour mixture, the cornmeal bundle, and the bag with the chili sauce into the potato bag. Add some oil to what you already plan to take on your trip.

At Camp

Boil ½ cup water; pour a small amount into the chili sauce and the rest into the potato and chive mixture. When the potatoes are cool enough to handle, add the flour mixture and combine well. Open the cornmeal bundle and place it on a flat surface.

Make several small pancakes from the potato and flour mixture, and then dip both sides of each pancake in the cornmeal. Fry over medium heat in an oiled pan until golden. Serve topped with a little chili sauce.

Tips

Be sure to use potatoes that require you to add water only.

If you are only going for a weekend, you can take the chili sauce in a Nalgene bottle or another suitable leakproof container.

Salsa with grated Monterey Jack cheese works well as an alternative topping.

⅓ cup chili sauce or mild salsa

½ cup instant mashed potatoes (dry measurement)

½ teaspoon dried chives

¼ cup flour

½ teaspoon Cajun spice

¼ teaspoon black pepper

¼ cup nonfat powdered milk

1 teaspoon baking powder

⅓ cup cornmeal

Oil for frying

½ cup water

Black Bean Cakes

1 cup canned black beans, drained and rinsed

½ teaspoon mustard powder

1 tablespoon dried onion

¼ teaspoon dried sage

½ teaspoon dried thyme

½ cup rolled oats

Salt and pepper to taste

2 tablespoons olive oil

Dehydration Time: 5–9 hours
Makes 2 servings

These have a meaty taste and texture that makes for a hearty breakfast. Serve these with a small dollop of your favorite traditional or soy mayonnaise.

AT HOME

Dry the black beans on lined dehydrator trays for 5 to 9 hours or until dried through. Place the beans in a ziplock freezer bag along with the mustard powder and dried onion. Roll up the thyme and sage in a piece of plastic wrap and put the bundle in the bag with the beans. Measure the oats into a ziplock freezer bag and put that bag inside the bean bag. Add the oil to the other olive oil that you will take on your tip.

AT CAMP

Add boiling water to the bean mixture, in a ziplock freezer bag, using a little less than 1 part water to 1 part dried ingredients. Let sit for 5 to 10 minutes and add a little more water if necessary. Add the spices and oats to the bean mixture in the freezer bag. Be careful as the liquid may still be hot. Let the air out of the bag, close it tightly and knead it to mix everything together.

Heat the olive oil in a frying pan. Cut one corner off the bag, Squeeze ¼ of the mixture into the frying pan and then flatten into a patty. Fry the patties for approximately 4 minutes turning occasionally. Season with salt and pepper to taste.

Huevos Rancheros

Dehydration Time: 7–9 hours
Makes 2 servings

Sometimes I like to use Monterey Jack cheese that already has hot peppers in it, which adds another layer of spice.

At Home

Dehydrate the ½ cup salsa on lined dehydrator trays for 7 to 9 hours and then place in a ziplock. Pour the egg powder in a small ziplock with a note about how much water to add. Put the package of powdered scrambled egg mix into the bag containing the salsa. Place a piece of parchment paper between the tortillas and place them in a large freezer ziplock. Wrap the cheese. Pack some hot sauce in a leakproof container. Put the bag with the salsa and the bag with the cheese in with the tortillas. Add the butter or oil to what you will take on your trip.

At Camp

Rehydrate the salsa using equal parts of boiling water and dried mix and let it sit for about 15 minutes. Combine scrambled egg mix with water as indicated on the note you enclosed and beat well with a fork. Add hot sauce to taste and stir. Melt a little butter or oil in the bottom of a pot or frying pan, and add the eggs and cook as you would for scrambled eggs. Season the eggs with salt and pepper.

Place a tortilla on each plate, and scoop half of the egg mixture into the center of each one. Top with salsa and the grated cheese. Roll up each tortilla and serve.

½ cup salsa

2 servings powdered scrambled egg mix

Enough water to reconstitute the powdered eggs

2 flour tortillas

½ cup grated Monterey Jack or Pepper Jack cheese

Hot sauce to taste

Butter or vegetable oil

Salt and pepper to taste

Breakfast Wrap

½ cup canned, flaked ham

½ teaspoon dried onion

2 servings powdered scrambled egg mix

Enough water to reconstitute the scrambled eggs

1-inch x 1-inch x 3-inch block of Swiss cheese

2 flour tortillas

Butter or vegetable oil

Dehydration Time: 7–9 hours
Makes 2 servings

I like to use Swiss cheese in this recipe because of the mild, nutty flavor it imparts, but you can substitute your favorite cheese. The filling is also tasty on bannock or biscuits.

AT HOME

Dehydrate the ½ cup ham for 7 to 9 hours, and place it in a freezer ziplock. Add the onion to the bag with the ham. Put the egg powder in a ziplock with a note about how much water to add. Add the package of powdered scrambled egg mix to the bag containing the ham. Place a piece of parchment paper between the tortillas and place them in a large freezer ziplock. Wrap the cheese. Add the butter or oil to what you will take on your trip.

AT CAMP

Mix equal parts of boiling water and ham and onion flakes, and let it rehydrate for about 15 minutes. While the ham is rehydrating, thinly slice or grate the cheese. Combine scrambled egg mix with water as indicated on the note and beat well with a fork. Add hot sauce to taste and stir. Drain off any excess water from the reconstituted ham and onions.

Put a pat of butter or some oil in the bottom of a pot or frying pan. Once it has melted, add the eggs and cook as you would for scrambled eggs. Add the ham and cheese to the pan and stir until the cheese is melted and the ham is warmed. Place a tortilla on each plate and scoop half of the egg mixture into the center of each one. Roll up each tortilla and serve.

Breakfast Frittata

Dehydration Time: 7–9 hours
Makes 2 servings

Frittatas are delicious as breakfast or even dinner. Change the vegetable combinations to create different flavors.

At Home

Dehydrate the mixed vegetables for 7 to 9 hours and place in a ziplock. Put the scrambled egg mix in a small freezer ziplock with a note about how much water to add to reconstitute. Add the package of powdered scrambled egg mix to the bag containing the vegetables. Wrap the Parmesan cheese. Add the butter or oil to what you will take on your trip.

At Camp

Combine equal parts of boiling water and dried mixed vegetables to reconstitute. Let sit for about 15 minutes. In a separate container, mix scrambled egg powder with water as indicated on the note you enclosed, and beat well with a fork.

Put a little butter or oil in the bottom of a pot or frying pan. Add ¼ cup of Parmesan cheese to the egg mixture and pour into the preheated pan. Top with the rehydrated vegetables and cook on medium to low heat until the egg mixture is cooked. Add salt and pepper. Remove the frittata from the pan, cut it into two servings, and sprinkle each with 1 tablespoon of grated Parmesan.

Tip

If a little egg mixture remains uncooked in the center, just tilt the pan slightly and let the uncooked egg move to the outer edges.

---

1 cup frozen mixed vegetables

2 servings powdered scrambled egg mix

Water as directed on the powdered egg package

¼ cup grated Parmesan cheese, plus 2 tablespoons for topping

Butter or vegetable oil

Salt and pepper to taste

Ham and Swiss Rollups

½ can (3 ounces) flaked ham

1 recipe *Basic Biscuits* (page 210)

1-inch x 1-inch x 3-inch block of
    Swiss cheese

1 tablespoon butter

Dehydration Time: 7–10 hours
Makes 2–3 servings

This recipe was what I call a happy accident. I had planned ham and cheese wraps for one of my family's meals while we were hiking a rugged freshwater coastline. We ended up not eating the meal and used it one morning for breakfast. In cooler weather, my family and I bake these the night before so that we can have breakfast on the go.

At Home

Dehydrate the flaked ham for 7 to 10 hours. Place the biscuit mix in a large ziplock. Put the ham in a small ziplock bag and place in the larger bag with the biscuit mix. Wrap the cheese. Add the butter to the other butter you are taking. Be sure to bring the directions below as well as those for the *Basic Biscuits* recipe.

At Camp

Rehydrate the ham using equal parts of boiling water and dried mix and place in a cozy for about 30 minutes. Follow the *Basic Biscuits* recipe to create the biscuit dough. Instead of making biscuits, however, put the dough inside a large ziplock bag and lay it on a flat surface.

Using a water bottle (or your hands) roll the dough inside the bag. Break the cheese into small pieces. Cut one full side of the ziplock bag off and then sprinkle the dough with the ham and cheese bits. Roll the dough up and then slice it into 6 rounds.

Place the rounds on a baking pan lined with parchment paper. Bake them for 20 minutes. If you are cooking these in a frying pan, do so until they're golden on the bottom, then flip, and cook until done.

Tips

This recipe is good for a layover day or for when you have a shorter hiking day planned. It also makes for a hearty lunch or dinner along with your favorite soup.

You can vary this recipe by using different cheeses or adding your favorite herbs.

Breakfast Pizza

½ cup spaghetti sauce

5 thin tomato slices

2 Greek-style whole wheat pitas

½–1 cup sliced Swiss cheese

¼ cup precooked bacon bits or
   vegetarian "bacon" bits

1 tablespoon olive oil

Salt and pepper to taste

Dehydration Time: 7–10 hours
Makes 2 servings

Pizza for breakfast—why not? My family and I had some spaghetti sauce and pitas left over from the day before and were out of eggs so we made a pizza.

AT HOME

Dry ½ cup of spaghetti sauce and 5 thin tomato slices on separate lined dehydrator trays for 7 to 10 hours. The sauce, when it's dry, will have a texture similar to fruit leather. Place a piece of parchment paper between the pitas and package in a large ziplock freezer bag. Wrap the cheese. Package the bacon, tomato slices, and sauce separately in small ziplock bags and place the packages and the cheese in a freezer ziplock bag. Add the oil to the rest of the oil you will take on your trip.

AT CAMP

Combine the spaghetti sauce and tomato slices, in separate containers, with equal parts of hot water and dried ingredients, and let rehydrate for 20 minutes or until fully rehydrated. Line the bottom of your frying pan with parchment paper. Put a little olive oil on the parchment paper and then place the pita on top. Lightly oil the top of the pita. Spread half the spaghetti sauce over the "dough" and follow it with half the tomato slices, bacon bits, and crumbled cheese. Lightly sprinkle with salt and pepper.

   Cover the frying pan with a lid (an upside-down pot works well in a pinch), and cook on low until the cheese melts and the toppings are hot, being careful not to burn the bottom. Repeat for the second pita.

Sausage and Potato Breakfast

Dehydration Time: 7–10 hours
Makes 3–4 servings

This is a simple, hearty, and warming dish—breakfast comfort food.

AT HOME

Remove the ½ cup of sausages from their casings, and fry them on medium-high heat until cooked through, about 10 minutes. Rinse off the fat with hot water and fry the sausage again. Repeat until the fat has been removed. Dehydrate for 7 to 10 hours on lined dehydrator trays until dry or about the consistency of gravel. Blot the meat with paper towels occasionally during the drying process.

Put the package of instant potatoes in a large freezer ziplock along with powdered milk if the potato instructions require it. Place the dried sausage and powdered scrambled egg mix separately in small freezer ziplocks and put them in the bag with the potatoes. Pack the butter with the other butter that you will take on your trip. Pack some extra oil or butter if you plan to fry the mixture.

AT CAMP

Rehydrate the sausage using equal parts of boiling water and dried sausage. Add the powdered eggs and milk to the dry potato flakes. Add boiling water according to the potato package directions. Stir in the sausage and butter once the potatoes are ready. If desired, put the potato mixture into a frying pan and fry in a little oil or butter until golden.

½ cup garlic sausage

1 package instant mashed cheese potatoes

Enough powdered milk to make the milk required for potatoes

2 tablespoons powdered scrambled egg mix

1 tablespoon butter

Enough water to make the instant potatoes

French Toast

4 slices bread

2 servings powdered scrambled egg mix

1½ teaspoons vanilla sugar

2 tablespoons nonfat powdered milk

Vegetable oil

Maple syrup or freeze-dried berries

¾ cup water

Makes 2 servings

You might as well flatten the bread at home because it will get squashed in your pack; my son always gets a real charge when I ask him to squish the bread for me. The bread comes back nicely when cooked.

AT HOME

Put the bread in a large ziplock freezer bag and compress the slices until they are somewhat flattened. Pour the eggs, vanilla sugar, and powdered milk in a smaller ziplock freezer bag. Put some of your favorite syrup in a small leakproof bottle, or put freeze-dried berries into a small plastic bag. Seal the smaller bag and syrup bottle (or bag of berries) inside the larger bag. Add a little vegetable oil to what you will take on your trip.

AT CAMP

Remove the bag with the egg and milk mixture from the large ziplock freezer bag and dump it in a pot. Add ¾ cup of water and combine well. Put a little vegetable oil in your frying pan and preheat it over medium heat. Dip a piece of bread into the egg mixture and fry it, flipping once, until golden. Repeat with the remaining slices. Serve with a drizzle of your favorite syrup or rehydrated freeze-dried berries.

TIP

For the best results, use powdered scrambled egg mix and not powdered whole eggs.

Trail Yogurt

Makes 2–3 servings

8 tablespoons nonfat powdered milk

1 teaspoon yogurt culture powder

1¾ cups water

Honey or vanilla sugar (optional)

Making homemade yogurt is very easy to do on the trail. You will need a 2-cup, high-quality, very clean, stainless steel thermos for this, and it is one of those recipes that actually works better with powdered milk. It is best to make yogurt in the late afternoon the day before as it takes the culture some time to do its job. You should probably test this recipe at home first to get the hang of it. Once you do, you'll be making fresh yogurt on many of your trips.

At Home

Measure the milk powder accurately and put in a small zip-lock freezer bag. Put the culture in a snack-sized sandwich bag and place that in the bag with the milk powder. Be sure to include a copy of the directions below.

At Camp

Boil ¼ cup of water and pour it in your thermos to warm the metal. Mix 1¾ cup water and the powdered milk together in a pan. Scald the milk by heating it until the edges start to bubble and it reaches the boiling point. Be careful not to boil though. Remove the milk from the heat and cool until the milk is warmer than body temperature but not overly hot. If the milk is too hot, you will kill the culture; and if it's too cool, the yogurt will not set.

Discard the now cooled water out of the thermos. Then put the yogurt culture in the thermos and add a little bit of the warm milk. Stir until the powder has dissolved. Then pour the remaining milk into the thermos. Stir well and secure the lid tightly. Put the thermos in a large ziplock bag and then inside a cozy.

At bedtime take it into your sleeping bag with you. If you are a restless sleeper, wrap the cozy in some clothing and set it beside you where you won't knock it over. Avoid disturbing it as much as possible; do not shake or stir. By morning, you will have yogurt. If you don't like unsweetened yogurt, add a little honey or vanilla sugar to it before serving.

Tips

You need as much milk powder as you would normally use to make 2 cups of milk even though you will only be making 1¾ cups. These extra milk solids make for a richer and better texture.

The yogurt may not incubate if you use old culture.

Freeze-dried berries go well with yogurt, and it makes a great topping for a bowl of granola.

Chapter 6
LUNCHES

What outdoors people eat during the day and around lunchtime varies by activity. Most thru-hikers tend to graze, or munch on a series of snacks throughout the day, rather than have a more extravagant lunch. Recipes for grazers are found in Chapter 7. That said, I have met backpackers and paddlers who prefer something a little more substantial. It can be nice to have bigger lunches when time permits, but on longer travel days munching along the way is often preferable. I recommend that you preplan your menu according to your route and try to stick to it. No matter which way you decide to handle midday eating, remember that it is important to refuel. Not only does your body need energy, but your campmates will appreciate it—most of us tend to get crabby when we are hungry.

When it comes to group situations, it's best to plan ahead for lunch, especially if there are beginners in the group. This break lets everyone recharge, which can go a long way in keeping group morale high. Stopping also gives you a few moments to add water to an ingredient that you might want to start rehydrating for dinner.

Weather is a consideration as well. It's a good idea to bring some extra grazing foods in case the weather is too nasty to stop and prepare lunch. The time of year also determines the lunch menu. If it is very cold out, you will probably prefer warmer fare. In the summer months though, you may prefer a smaller uncooked lunch such as a salad or a snack, especially on hotter days.

Uncooked Fare

Uncooked lunches are generally quicker and easier as they do not usually require a great deal of preparation or cleanup. Many items store well and are perfect for using in an uncooked lunch. Here are some suggestions:

- Antipasto
- Bagels
- Chicken
- Coleslaw
- Crackers
- Cream cheese
- Dips
- Dried or cured sausage such as salami, pepperoni, or summer sausage
- Fruit
- Hard cheese
- Honey
- Jam
- Leftovers
- Mayonnaise or Miracle Whip (in single-serving packets)
- Nut butters
- Pâté
- Pickles
- Pita bread
- Precooked bacon such as Ready Crisp
- Preserves
- Salmon
- Salsa
- Tortilla chips
- Trail sprouts
- Tuna
- Vegetables (choose sturdy types)
- Wraps

You could mix some fruit in with cream cheese and have it on a bagel. Salmon is also very nice on a bagel with cream cheese. Hard cheeses like cheddar and precooked bacon are a tasty combination. Chop an apple into some coleslaw or have some vegetables and dip. Salmon and tuna are great in a wrap; make it more interesting by adding some trail sprouts. Nut butters provide protein and are a good addition to a bagel or wrap. Some precooked bacon left from breakfast jazzes up a chicken wrap. You can also use leftovers from dinner, dessert, or breakfast. Leftover foccacia from dinner the night before makes a great base for antipasto, salami, or cheese.

Cooking on the Go

If you choose to cook for lunch, rely on your stove; you may not be in a place where you will have enough water to douse a cooking fire properly. Here are some tips for cooking on the go:

- Keep your pots and stove accessible.
- Start rehydrating your meal at breakfast.
- If you have a thermos, fill it with boiling water in the morning for a hot drink or instant soup.

- Do not block a trail or portage.

- Make sure you have enough water for cooking and cleanup.

- Bring extra ziplock bags in case you have leftovers.

- Be sure to clean up any garbage from your lunch spot.

   You should probably plan for cooked lunches that require the least amount of dishes and cleanup. One-pot meals such as soups or stews are preferred. Sometimes it is nice to toast your bagel or heat the filling for your wrap. You might not want to have anything too heavy on the stomach either.

Salad

⅓ cup roasted red peppers

1 cup of canned green lentils, well drained and rinsed

1 small carrot, coarsely grated

2 cloves garlic, minced

3 tablespoons celery leaves, chopped

⅛ cup fresh chives or scallions, chopped

⅛ cup fresh parsley, chopped

¼ teaspoon dried thyme

1 tablespoon lemon zest

Salt and pepper to taste

3 tablespoons feta cheese, crumbled

Dressing

⅓ cup extra virgin olive oil

1½ tablespoons lemon juice

⅛ teaspoon cayenne pepper

¼ teaspoon cumin

½ teaspoon dried sweet basil

Citrus Lentil Salad

Dehydration Time: 5–7 hours
Makes 2 servings

My family loves to have salads on the trail and this is one of our favorites. It appeared in Joy of Backpacking *by Brian Beffort.*

At Home

Roast the red peppers according to the instructions on page 6. Once they've cooled, peel them and chop them into ¼-inch pieces. Combine all the salad ingredients in a medium-sized bowl and toss. Spread out the salad mixture on lined dehydrator trays. If your unit has a temperature control, set it for 135°F. Dry the mixture for 5 to 7 hours.

Pour the olive oil and lemon juice into a leakproof container such as a small Nalgene bottle. Pack the cayenne, cumin, and basil in plastic wrap or a small ziplock bag. Put the salad, bottle of dressing, and spice packet inside a medium ziplock bag and seal, making sure to remove as much air as possible.

At Camp

Rehydrate the salad in the plastic bag using a formula of 1½ parts dried mix to 1 part water. Wait 5 to 10 minutes and then add a little more water if needed. If you accidentally use too much water, be sure to drain the salad well before adding the dressing.

While the salad is rehydrating, put the contents of the spice packet into the bottle containing the olive oil and lemon juice mixture. Shake vigorously. Pour the dressing on the rehydrated salad and stir gently to combine. Serve the salad with lightly toasted Greek pitas or stuff it into pitas.

TIP

If you plan to prepare this salad well ahead of your trip, wait to make the oil and lemon mixture until closer to your departure date. The dried ingredients will keep in the freezer for up to 6 months. Write the recipe name and date you made it on the outside of the freezer bag, using an indelible marker; be sure to write yourself a reminder on the bag about adding the dressing.

Garbanzo Bean, Tomato, and Thai Chili Salad

1½ tablespoons olive oil or vegetable oil

⅓ cup onion, chopped

1 clove garlic, minced

2 or 3 fresh Roma tomatoes, diced

1 or 2 green Thai chili peppers, seeds removed and minced

1 tablespoon fresh ginger, peeled and minced

2 cups canned chickpeas (garbanzo beans), drained and rinsed

1 tablespoon lemon juice

⅓ cup lime juice

1 tablespoon fresh cilantro, coarsely chopped

1 teaspoon black pepper, freshly ground

⅛ teaspoon kosher salt

Dehydration Time: 8–12 hours
Makes 2 servings

Garbanzo beans, or chickpeas, have a buttery texture. This hearty and flavorful salad can be served warm or cold and goes well with flatbread.

AT HOME

Heat the oil in a frying pan over medium to medium-high heat. Add the onion and sauté for a minute. Then add the garlic and tomatoes and simmer for a few minutes, until the tomatoes start to reduce. Add the peppers and ginger and cook for a few more minutes. Next add the chickpeas and lemon and lime juice. Simmer for a few minutes and then remove from the heat.

Stir in the cilantro, salt, and pepper. Allow the mixture to cool and then measure the amount you will dry. Write this measurement on a sticky note. Spread the salad on lined dehydrator trays to dry. When the salad is dry, package it in a ziplock freezer bag along with your note.

AT CAMP

Rehydrate the salad by adding enough boiling water to the mix to make it equal to the measurement on your sticky note. Do not add the water first or you will have too much liquid.

TIP

If you'd like to have this recipe for lunch, you can add cold water to the mixture at breakfast and let it rehydrate in your pack as you travel.

Jasmine Rice and Shrimp Salad

Dehydration Time: 6–12 hours
Makes 2 servings

As great looking as they taste, blood oranges complement shrimp well. This recipe uses Sriracha, pronounced see-RAH-cha, *a spicy chili sauce from Thailand.*

AT HOME

Write the cooking instructions from the rice package down on a piece of paper and place it in a freezer bag with the rice. Add the pouch of shrimp to the bag containing the rice. Put the coconut in a dry frying pan over medium heat and toast until golden.

Remove it from the heat and let cool. When it's cool, wrap the coconut and cashews in separate pieces of plastic wrap and place them in the rice bag. Combine the salt, parsley, and basil together in another piece of plastic wrap and put it in the bag.

Dry the mango, ginger, onion, and red pepper on separate lined dehydrator trays. When they're dehydrated, put them in a single ziplock freezer bag. Pour the chili sauce and red wine vinegar into a leakproof bottle. Add the bag of dried ingredients and the bottle of chili sauce and vinegar to the rice bag. Add the oil to the other vegetable oil that you will take on your trip. Pack the blood orange just before you leave.

AT CAMP

Add boiling water to the mango, ginger, onion, and red pepper mixture using equal amounts of dried ingredients and water. Allow to sit for 15 to 20 minutes or until rehydrated. While that rehydrates, cook the rice according to the directions you included in the bag. Allow the rice to cool. Add the mango mixture and the pouch of shrimp to the rice.

Cut the skin off the blood orange and remove 6 or 7 sections, leaving the membrane behind. Cut the orange sections

½ cup jasmine rice (uncooked measurement)

1 foil pouch (3½ ounces) cooked shrimp

1 tablespoon coconut, toasted

2 tablespoons cashews, chopped

½ teaspoon salt

¼ teaspoon dried parsley

¼ teaspoon dried basil

½ cup mango, chopped

1 teaspoon fresh ginger, minced

⅛ cup red onion, diced

⅛ cup red pepper, thinly sliced

¼–½ teaspoon Sriracha chili sauce to taste

1 tablespoon red wine vinegar

3 tablespoons vegetable oil

1 small blood orange

into thirds and add the pieces to the cooled rice. Squeeze 1 tablespoon of juice from the remaining bit of orange and mix it with 3 tablespoons vegetable oil and the spices, red wine vinegar, and the chili sauce. Combine well and pour over the salad. Mix gently until combined. Sprinkle with toasted coconut and cashews.

TIPS

If you don't want to stop on the trail at lunch, cook the rice at breakfast while you pack up your camp, and store it in a ziplock freezer bag until lunch. You can also precook the rice at home and dry it for 7 to 10 hours on lined dehydrator trays; rehydrate it using a ratio of equal parts dried rice and boiling water. If you combine the mango, ginger, onion, and red pepper mixture with cold water at breakfast, it will be reconstituted by lunchtime.

If you can't find shrimp in pouches, you can use canned shrimp. If weight is a consideration or you are traveling in an area that bans cans, then dehydrate it. It takes about 3 to 8 hours to dry through; be careful not to overdry it. Rehydrate the shrimp at camp by adding equal parts boiling water and dried ingredients.

Curried Tuna and Couscous Salad

Dehydration Time: 5–10 hours
Makes 2 servings

Quick cooking and versatile, couscous makes a good base for a salad. This flavorful dressing works well with tuna; to make it vegetarian use some of your favorite vegetables instead of the fish.

AT HOME

Preheat the oven to 350°F. Cut the tomatoes into halves or quarters and sprinkle with a little salt. Put them on an oiled baking sheet. Roast them for 30 to 40 minutes. Remove the tomatoes from the oven and allow them to cool. Dry the minced onions and cooked tomatoes on separate lined dehydrator trays for 5 to 10 hours or until dried thoroughly. Package in a ziplock freezer bag.

Place the couscous in a large ziplock freezer bag with a copy of the cooking instructions from the package. Add the pouch of tuna and the bag with the tomato mixture to the bag of couscous. Wrap the curry powder and almonds separately in plastic wrap. Pour the mustard, honey, and red wine vinegar in a leakproof container and place it in the bag of couscous along with the spice and almonds. Add the olive oil to the other oil that you will take on your trip.

AT CAMP

Add enough boiling water to the tomatoes and onions to barely cover them. Allow to sit for 15 to 20 minutes or until rehydrated. Prepare the couscous according to the directions you packed. Allow the couscous to cool.

Make the dressing by mixing the mustard, honey, and red wine vinegar with 2 tablespoons olive oil and the curry powder. When the couscous is done, mix in the tomatoes and onions and add the dressing. Sprinkle with sliced almonds and stir gently to coat.

Salad

⅓ cup roasted cherry or grape tomatoes

½ teaspoon salt

⅛ cup red onion, minced

½ cup instant whole wheat couscous

1 3-ounce pouch tuna

¼ cup sliced almonds

Dressing

¼ teaspoon curry powder

¼–½ teaspoon Dijon mustard to taste

½ teaspoon honey

1 tablespoon red wine vinegar

2 tablespoons olive oil

Tip

If you don't want to cook on the trail, prepare the couscous at breakfast and pack it in a ziplock freezer bag to use at lunchtime. If you combine the tomato and onion mixture with cold water at breakfast, it will be reconstituted by lunchtime.

Carrot Raisin Salad with Peanuts

Dehydration Time: 6–12 hours
Makes 2–3 servings

In this carrot raisin salad with an Asian twist, the shredded carrots rehydrate quickly and the dressing has a spicy kick.

AT HOME

Dry the grated carrot and red pepper slices on lined dehydrator trays for 6 to 12 hours or until they are leathery and dry throughout. Place the dried vegetables in a large ziplock freezer bag.

Wrap the peanuts and raisins in small pieces of plastic wrap and place them in the freezer bag. Wrap the cilantro and red pepper flakes in plastic wrap and put that in the bag as well. Pour the tamari sauce and honey into a leakproof container and place that in the bag with the vegetables. Pack an empty freezer bag in with the large bag of ingredients as well. Add the peanut butter to what you will take on your trip. Before you leave, be sure to put a fresh lime in the bag.

AT CAMP

Add just enough water to the carrots and sweet peppers to cover them. Allow to rehydrate for 15 to 30 minutes. Meanwhile pour the tamari and honey mixture into the empty freezer bag. Add ¼ cup of peanut butter and spices. Cut the lime in half and squeeze the juice from one half into the bag with the tamari mixture.

Compress the bag to remove as much air as you can and zip it closed. Knead the bag until the dressing is well mixed. Drain the carrot and pepper mixture well. Add the vegetables to the bag of dressing along with the peanuts and raisins. Let sit for about 10 minutes.

Salad
2 large carrots, peeled and shredded

1 sweet red pepper, thinly sliced

Dressing
2 tablespoons chopped peanuts

½ cup sultana raisins

½ teaspoon cilantro

⅛ teaspoon crushed red chillies

1½ tablespoons tamari sauce

1 teaspoon honey

¼ cup peanut butter

2 tablespoons fresh lime juice

Tip

If you are planning to have this for lunch on the trail, add cold water to the vegetable mixture at breakfast, and it'll be ready by the time you stop for lunch. You can also make the dressing in the morning and let the flavors infuse while you hike.

Chicken and Apple Slaw

Dehydration Time: 5–10 hours
Makes 3–4 servings

Cabbage dries incredibly well, reduces in size substantially, and rehydrates very quickly.

AT HOME

Cut the carrots in half and then cut them into ⅛-inch thick slices. Place on dehydrator trays to dry. Shred the two types of cabbages and dry them on separate dehydrator trays that have been lined or that include an additional mesh screen.

When the carrots and cabbage are dry, place them in a ziplock freezer bag. Add the freeze-dried chicken, dried apples, and red pepper flakes to the bag. Place the cider vinegar in a leakproof container and put that in the bag with the cabbage. Add the vegetable oil to the oil you will take with you on your trip.

AT CAMP

Shortly before you plan to eat the salad, rehydrate the dried ingredients with cold water using a ratio of 1 part dried mix to ⅔ part water. Check the salad after a few minutes and add a little more water as necessary.

Drain any excess water once the cabbage has reconstituted and then add apple cider vinegar and vegetable oil to suit your taste. Season the coleslaw with salt and pepper.

TIP

Don't let the slaw rehydrate in too much water or for too long or it will become soggy.

2 medium carrots

1½ cups savoy cabbage

1½ cups red cabbage

⅓–½ cup freeze-dried chicken

⅓ cup dried apple, diced

⅛ teaspoon red pepper flakes

1½ tablespoons apple cider vinegar

3 tablespoons vegetable oil

Salt and pepper to taste

Cranberry Raspberry Slaw with Almonds

1/3 cup sliced almonds

1 medium carrot

3 cups green cabbage

1/3 cup dried cranberries

1/8 teaspoon crushed black pepper

1 1/2 tablespoons raspberry vinegar

3 tablespoons vegetable oil

Salt to taste

Dehydration Time: 5–10 hours
Makes 3–4 servings

This colorful coleslaw combines tart and fruity flavors with a touch of pepper.

AT HOME

Toast the almonds in a dry frying pan until they start to turn golden. Remove them from the heat and let cool. When they are cool, scoop the nuts into a small ziplock bag. Shred the carrots and cabbage and dry on separate dehydrator trays that have been lined or include an additional mesh screen.

When the carrots and cabbage are dry, place them in a ziplock freezer bag. Add the cranberries, black pepper, and the bag of toasted almonds to the bag of vegetables. Pour the raspberry vinegar in a leakproof container and put that in the large bag as well. Add the vegetable oil to the oil you will take on your trip.

AT CAMP

Do not start to rehydrate the carrots and cabbage until shortly before you will eat the salad. Rehydrate with cold water using a ratio of 1 part dried mix to 2/3 part water. Check the salad in a few minutes and add a little more water as necessary. Drain any excess water once the cabbage has reconstituted. Then add raspberry vinegar and vegetable oil to suit your taste. Sprinkle the almonds on the coleslaw and season with salt.

TIP

Don't let the slaw rehydrate in too much water or for too long or it will become soggy.

Broccoli Carrot Slaw

Dehydration Time: 6–12 hours
Makes 3–4 servings

This recipe is a great way to use up broccoli stems.

At Home

Toast the sunflower seeds in a dry nonstick frying pan. Allow the sunflower seeds to cool, and then put the seeds and the bacon into small separate ziplock bags. Blanch the broccoli stems for 2 minutes in boiling water. Allow the stems to cool. Then cut the broccoli into matchstick-sized pieces. Shred the carrots. Place the broccoli and carrots on separate dehydrator trays that have been lined or include additional mesh screens.

When the carrots and broccoli are dry, place them in a ziplock freezer bag. Add the marjoram and the bags containing the bacon and sunflower seeds to the bag of vegetables. Pour the mango vinegar into a leakproof container, and put that in the bag with the broccoli and carrots. Add the vegetable oil to the oil you will take on your trip.

At Camp

Rehydrate the broccoli and carrots with cold water using a ratio of 1 part dried mix to ⅔ part water. Check them after 10 minutes and add a little more water as necessary.

Drain any excess water once they have reconstituted and then add mango vinegar and vegetable oil to suit your taste. Sprinkle the sunflower seeds and bacon on the slaw and season with salt.

¼ cup shelled sunflower seeds

⅓ cup shelf-stable bacon or vegetarian "bacon" bits (optional)

2 cups broccoli stems

2 medium carrots

⅛ teaspoon dried marjoram

1½ tablespoons mango or red wine vinegar

3 tablespoons vegetable oil

Salt and pepper to taste

Sunny Garlic Hummus

1 19-ounce can chickpeas, rinsed and drained

¼ cup orange juice

½ teaspoon lime juice

2 cloves garlic

1 heaping teaspoon orange zest

2 tablespoons tahini

Pinch of kosher salt

¼ teaspoon cracked black pepper

Dehydration Time: 5–7 hours
Makes 2–4 servings

Hummus is one of the easiest things to make for a trail lunch, and this one has the sunny flavor of oranges.

AT HOME
Combine and blend all the ingredients using a food processor or hand blender until you have a thick paste. Spread evenly on lined dehydrator trays, keeping the mixture about ¼ inch thick. Dry for 5 to 7 hours or until the mixture crumbles and is thoroughly dry. Store in a medium ziplock freezer bag.

AT CAMP
Rehydrate the hummus using a formula of 1½ parts dried mix to 1 part water. Wait 5 to 10 minutes and then add a little more water if it's too dry. Serve as a dip with Greek pitas or your favorite crackers or use as a spread in a wrap.

TIP
If you need to increase your fat intake for cold-weather hiking, drizzle a little olive oil on the hummus just before you eat it.

Roasted Red Pepper Hummus

Dehydration Time: 5–7 hours
Makes 2–4 servings

Roasted red peppers add a subtle sweetness to this hummus, which is excellent with chicken in a wrap.

AT HOME

Roast the red peppers according to the instructions on page 6. Once they've cooled, peel them and chop them into ¼-inch pieces. Combine all the ingredients in a food processor or large bowl if you're using a hand blender. Process them until you have a thick, smooth paste.

Spread evenly on lined dehydrator trays, keeping the mixture about ¼ inch thick. Dry for 5 to 7 hours or until the mixture crumbles and is thoroughly dry.

AT CAMP

Rehydrate the hummus using a formula of 1½ parts dried mix to 1 part water. Wait 5 to 10 minutes and then add a little more water if necessary. Serve as a dip with Greek pitas or your favorite cracker or use as a spread in a wrap.

TIP

Although many people think that capers are a product of the sea, they are actually the bud of the bush of the same name found in the Mediterranean.

1 19-ounce can chickpeas, rinsed and drained

3 tablespoons lemon juice

2 cloves garlic

½ teaspoon capers (optional)

2 tablespoons tahini

Pinch of kosher salt

⅓ cup roasted red peppers

Lemon Wasabi Hummus

1 19-ounce can chickpeas, rinsed and drained

¼ cup lemon juice

1 teaspoon lemon pepper

2 cloves garlic

1 tablespoon wasabi paste

2 tablespoons tahini

Pinch of kosher salt

Dehydration Time: 5–7 hours
Makes 2–4 servings

The heat of wasabi combines with tart lemon flavor to give this hummus a kick.

At Home
Combine all the ingredients in a food processor or a large bowl if you're using a hand blender. Process them until you have a thick, smooth paste. Spread evenly on lined dehydrator trays, keeping the mixture about ¼ inch thick. Dry for 5 to 7 hours or until the mixture crumbles and is thoroughly dry.

At Camp
Rehydrate the hummus using a formula of 1½ parts dried mix to 1 part water. Wait 5 to 10 minutes and then add a little more water if necessary. Serve as a dip with Greek pitas or your favorite cracker or use as a spread in a wrap.

Tip
If you need to increase your fat intake for cold-weather hiking, drizzle a little olive oil on the hummus just before you eat it.

Roasted Eggplant Spread

Dehydration Time: 7–10 hours
Makes 2–4 servings

Rye bread or rye crisps are the perfect accompaniment to this flavorful spread; it's also a nice condiment for wraps.

At Home

Preheat the oven to 350°F. Cut the eggplants into quarters lengthwise. Place the cut eggplant in a baking dish and drizzle with olive oil. Roast the eggplants for a half hour, turning once halfway through roasting. Remove eggplants from oven and let them cool. Peel them once they're cool enough to handle. Using a food processor or hand blender, combine all the ingredients until you have a well-blended purée.

Spread evenly on lined dehydrator trays, keeping the mixture about ¼ inch thick. Dry for 7 to 10 hours or until the mixture is thoroughly dry.

At Camp

Rehydrate the spread using a formula of 1½ parts dried mix to 1 part water. Wait 5 to 10 minutes and then add a little more water if necessary.

2 small eggplants

1–2 tablespoons olive oil

¼ cup plain yogurt

2 tablespoons lemon juice

1 tablespoon fresh parsley, chopped

3 cloves garlic, minced

2 teaspoons lemon zest

1½ teaspoons stone ground mustard

Salt and pepper to taste

1 19-ounce can black beans, drained and rinsed

2 cloves garlic, minced

1½ tablespoons onions, minced

½ tablespoon olive oil

1½ tablespoons salsa

2½ teaspoons lime juice

½ teaspoon black pepper, freshly ground

¾ teaspoon cumin

1 teaspoon cilantro, chopped

Pinch of salt

Black Bean Dip

Dehydration Time: 5–7 hours
Makes 2–4 servings

Black beans, also known as black turtle beans, have an earthy flavor and are a good source of protein and fiber.

AT HOME

Purée the black beans, garlic, onions, olive oil, salsa, and lime juice. Add the black pepper, cumin, cilantro, and salt and purée again. Dehydrate the purée on a lined dehydrator tray as you would for fruit leather. The dip takes between 5 and 7 hours to dry.

Once it is dry, you can grind it into a powder (a spice or coffee grinder works best for this). While it's not necessary to process it into a powder, this step greatly speeds up the rehydration process.

AT CAMP

Rehydrate the bean dip using a formula of 1½ parts dried mix to 1 part water. Wait 5 to 10 minutes and then add a little more water if necessary. Serve the hummus warm or cold with crackers, Greek pita wedges, or tortilla chips or as a spread in a chicken wrap.

White Bean, Walnut, and Pomegranate Dip

Dehydration Time: 5–7 hours
Makes 2–4 servings

Pomegranate juice gives this dip a pinkish color and a unique flavor.

AT HOME

Purée all the ingredients together in a blender or food processor. Dehydrate on a lined tray as you would for fruit leather. The dip takes between 5 and 7 hours to dry. Once it is dry, you can grind it into a powder using a spice or coffee grinder to make it easier to rehydrate.

AT CAMP

Rehydrate the bean dip using a formula of 1½ parts dried mix to 1 part water. Wait 5 or 10 minutes and then add a little more water if necessary. When you reach your lunch stop, you can warm the dip or enjoy it cold with crackers, Greek pita wedges, or tortilla chips. It is also good in a chicken wrap.

1 19-ounce can cannellini or white kidney beans, drained and rinsed

1 sprig fresh rosemary, stem removed

¼ cup walnuts

¼ cup pomegranate juice

¼ cup red onion, chopped

¼ teaspoon kosher salt

¼ teaspoon white pepper

Curried Bean Pâté

1 19-ounce can pinto beans

4 tablespoons liquid reserved from beans

1 tablespoon olive oil

2 tablespoons lemon juice

10 drops Tabasco sauce, more or less depending on your taste

1 tablespoon curry powder

¼ teaspoon parsley

Pinch of salt

Dehydration Time: 5–7 hours
Makes 2–4 servings

This dip is full of strong flavors, so be sure to dry it with similar dishes so the flavors don't transfer to and interfere with other foods in your dehydrator.

AT HOME

Drain the beans, reserving the liquid, and rinse them. Purée beans, 4 tablespoons reserved liquid, olive oil, lemon juice, and Tabasco sauce. If the mixture is too stiff, add more reserved liquid. Add the curry powder, parsley, and salt and purée again.

Dehydrate on a lined tray as you would for fruit leather. The pâté takes between 5 and 7 hours to dry. Once it is dry, you can grind it into a powder (a spice or coffee grinder works best for this). While it's not necessary to process it into a powder, this step greatly speeds up the rehydration process.

AT CAMP

Rehydrate the bean pâté using a formula of 1½ parts dried mix to 1 part water. Wait 5 or 10 minutes and then add a little more water if needed. Serve the dip warm or cold with crackers, Greek pita wedges, or tortilla chips or as a spread in a vegetable wrap.

Warm Crab and Artichoke Heart Dip

Dehydration Time: 8–12 hours
Makes 2–4 servings

This is a rich and decadent dip that takes only a few minutes to prepare. Serve with bagel chips or crackers.

AT HOME

Dry the artichoke hearts on dehydrator trays until thoroughly dehydrated. Wrap the grated Parmesan cheese. Place the dried artichokes and chives in a ziplock freezer bag along with the pouch of crab, bundle of grated cheese, and the mayonnaise packets.

Pack a lemon or add the lemon juice to any other lemon juice you will take on your trip. Pack the butter with the other butter you are taking. Pack hot sauce if desired.

AT CAMP

Cover the artichoke hearts and chives with boiling water to rehydrate. Set aside for 10 to 15 minutes and then drain off any excess water. Put a little butter in the bottom of your pot over medium heat. Pour in the artichoke mixture and sauté for a few minutes. Stir in the crab and heat for a few moments. Remove from the heat. Add the mayonnaise and cheese and combine well. Stir in the lemon juice and hot sauce.

TIPS

If you combine the artichoke and chive mixture with cold water at breakfast, it'll be reconstituted by lunchtime.

If you can't find crabmeat in small pouches, you can use canned crab. If weight is a consideration or you are traveling in an area that bans cans, then dehydrate the meat. Pour the crabmeat onto lined dehydrator trays and dry for 5 to 8 hours until dried through. Rehydrate at camp by adding equal parts boiling water and dried ingredients.

⅓ cup canned or jarred artichoke hearts, chopped

3 tablespoons Parmesan cheese, grated

2 teaspoons dried chives

1 pouch (3½ ounces) premium crabmeat

3 single-serving packets mayonnaise or whipped salad dressing

1 tablespoon lemon juice

1 tablespoon butter

Hot sauce to taste (optional)

Salt to taste

Chili con Queso

½ cup salsa

2½ tablespoons water

1-inch x 1-inch x 3-inch block of Monterey Jack cheese

1-inch x 1-inch x 3-inch block of old cheddar cheese

2 teaspoons Nestlé Nido or powdered whole milk

⅛ teaspoon cumin

2–3 cups tortilla chips

Dehydration Time: 5–7 hours
Makes 2–4 servings

My family and I like to make this for lunch when the weather is cool. It also makes a yummy dip for vegetables.

AT HOME
Dry the salsa on lined dehydrator trays for 5 to 7 hours. Wrap the cheese. Put the cumin in a piece of plastic wrap and put it in the ziplock bag. Add the Nido or milk powder to any other milk powder you will take on the trip. Package the tortilla chips in a rigid container.

AT CAMP
Rehydrate the salsa using a ratio of 1 part dried ingredients to 1 part water. When the salsa is rehydrated, unwrap the cheese and cut it into small cubes. Add 2 ½ tablespoons of water to a cool pot and then add 2 teaspoons of Nido or whole milk powder, stirring until combined. Place salsa, cumin, and cheese in a pot and then heat until the cheese melts and the mixture is warm. Serve with tortilla chips.

TIP
Start rehydrating the salsa at breakfast using a leakproof container, and by lunchtime the salsa will be ready to be eaten.

Water Bottle Sprout Garden

Makes 4–5 servings

2 tablespoons organic sprouting
  seeds

Potable water

*This recipe always makes me think of my preschool years—
do you remember putting a seed in a cup and watching
it come to life? Well this works on the same principle. A
variety of different sprouts can be used for this type of trail
gardening. Among my family's favorites are broccoli, adzuki
beans, peas, lentils, and alfalfa. Packed with nutrition and
flavor, they make great additions to salads, wraps, and sandwiches, and a delicious garnish on soups. You'll want to start
your sprouts 3 to 4 days before you plan to eat them.*

At Home
Pack a wide-mouth 32-ounce Nalgene water bottle with a
small carabiner attached to the lid strap. Place a few rubber
bands and four layers of cheesecloth cut about 2 inches larger than the size of the top of the bottle in a ziplock freezer
bag. Pack the sprouting seeds in another ziplock freezer bag
and place that in with the rubber bands and cheesecloth.

At Camp
One morning about three or four days before you want
to eat the sprouts, place 2 tablespoons of sprouting seeds
in your water bottle and add a cup of filtered water to the
seeds. Seal the bottle and let the seeds soak for 4 to 6 hours.
    Open the bottle and place two layers of cheesecloth over
the opening. Secure with a rubber band. Drain the seeds
well and if you are still on the move attach the bottle to the
outside of your pack with the carabiner.
    For the next few days all you need to do is rinse the seeds/
sprouts at breakfast and dinner. To rinse just pour in about
1 cup of potable water and gently swirl the sprouts in the
bottle. Then drain well. Carry the bottle with the top open
and the cheesecloth in place; replace the cloth if it gets dirty.

By the third or fourth day, depending on the type of seeds you're growing, you will have crunchy sprouts.

Tips

If you will be going on a short trip, you can start the sprouts at home a day or two before you leave.

If you have leftover sprouts, keep watering them and save them for the next day.

Chicken, Broccoli, and Yellow Pepper Wrap

Dehydration Time: 5–10 hours
Makes 2–4 servings

This wrap makes a hearty and filling lunch, but it could also double as a dinner dish.

At Home

Roast a whole sweet yellow pepper on a baking sheet, which has been sprayed with cooking spray, under the broiler until the skin turns black and bubbles. While the pepper is still warm, peel off the blackened skin and chop the pepper into pieces. Chop the broccoli into small pieces and then steam or boil until desired tenderness. Dehydrate broccoli and yellow pepper on separate trays for 5 to 7 hours. Drain the chicken and cut it into very small pieces. Dehydrate for about 7 to 10 hours, until completely dry.

Place the chicken in a ziplock freezer bag. Put the vegetables, chives, and oregano in a separate ziplock bag. Then put the vegetable bag and salad dressing packets inside the chicken bag. Package the wraps in a large ziplock freezer bag with a layer of parchment paper between each one.

At Camp

Rehydrate the chicken with a ratio of 1 part dried chicken to 1 part boiling water. In another container, rehydrate the vegetables and chives by covering with boiling water. Drain any excess water from the chicken and the vegetables. Place some chicken and veggies in each wrap and top with salad dressing, oregano, salt, and pepper. Roll it up and enjoy.

Tips

If you would prefer a vegetarian wrap, substitute your favorite raw vegetables for the chicken.

To save time, you can start rehydrating the chicken and vegetables at breakfast using cold water and keep them in leakproof containers as you travel. When you stop for lunch, drain off any excess water and enjoy your wraps.

¼ cup roasted sweet yellow pepper

¼ cup broccoli

1 cup canned chicken

¼ teaspoon dried chives

¼ teaspoon oregano

4 single-serving packages of ranch dressing or mayonnaise

Salt and pepper to taste

2 10-inch wraps

Roasted Red Pepper and Chipotle Chicken Wrap

⅓ cup roasted red pepper

½ chipotle pepper, chopped

1 cup canned or pouched chicken

1 piece smoked Gouda to taste

2 10-inch wraps

Salt and pepper to taste

Dehydration Time: 5–10 hours
Makes 2 servings

This wrap has a balance of sweet and smoky flavors with just a little bit of heat. To make the wrap vegetarian, substitute your favorite raw vegetables for the chicken.

AT HOME

Roast a sweet red pepper under the broiler until the skin turns black and bubbles. Peel off the skin while the pepper is still warm and discard. Chop the pepper into pieces. Mix the chopped chipotle and red peppers. Spread them on lined dehydrator trays and dry them for about 5 to 7 hours.

Drain the chicken and cut it into very small pieces. Dehydrate until completely dry, about 7 to 10 hours. Place the chicken in a large ziplock freezer bag and the pepper mixture in a small ziplock bag. Put the pepper bag inside the chicken bag.

Wrap the Gouda. Package the wraps in a large zippered freezer bag with a layer of parchment paper between each one.

AT CAMP

Rehydrate the chicken using equal amounts of chicken and boiling water. In another container, rehydrate the pepper mixture by covering with boiling water. Drain any excess water from the ingredients. Chop the Gouda. Split the chicken and pepper mixture between the two wraps and top each with the smoked Gouda, salt, and pepper. Roll them up and enjoy.

TIP

You can start rehydrating the chicken and the pepper mixture, in separate containers, at breakfast using cold water. When you stop for lunch, drain off any excess water and enjoy your wrap.

Apple Peanut Salad Wrap

Makes 2 servings

½ cup peanut butter

¼ cup dried apples

⅛ cup dried blueberries

⅛ cup sunflower seeds

2 10-inch wraps

Kids and adults alike enjoy this fast lunch on the trail.

AT HOME
Put the peanut butter in a leakproof tube or container or mix it with the other peanut butter you will take on your trip. Put the apples, raisins, and sunflowers seeds in a small ziplock freezer bag. Package the wraps, separated by a layer of parchment paper, in a large ziplock freezer bag.

AT CAMP
Mix the fruit, seeds, and peanut butter together and spread it on the wraps. Roll them up.

Tuna Teriyaki Wrap

4 10-inch tortillas

1 tablespoon liquid teriyaki sauce

2 3-ounce foil pouches tuna

¼ teaspoon dehydrated onion

1 tablespoon dried mushrooms, finely chopped

Crushed red chilies to taste

6 baby carrots

Salt and pepper to taste

1–2 tablespoons water for rehydration

Makes 2 servings

Fresh baby carrots add some crunch and sweetness to this wrap.

At Home

Place a piece of parchment paper between each wrap and put them in a ziplock freezer bag. Pour the teriyaki sauce into a small Nalgene bottle. Place the bottle in a large ziplock bag with the other ingredients.

At Camp

Rehydrate the onion and mushrooms in a small amount of water for about 10 to 15 minutes. While the onions and mushrooms are rehydrating, cut the baby carrots up into matchstick-sized pieces and set aside.

In a pot or bowl, combine the tuna, red chilies, teriyaki marinade, and the rehydrated onion and chopped mushroom mixture. Stir well. Place ¼ of the mixture in a wrap and top with carrot matchsticks. Roll it up and enjoy.

Tuna Bagel with Black Bean and Corn Salsa

Dehydration Time: 5–10 hours
Makes 2–4 servings

Bagels survive well in a backpack. The hint of lime in the salsa complements the tuna; chicken would also work well in this wrap.

At Home

Mix corn, lime juice, salsa, and black beans together. Spread the mixture on lined dehydrator trays and dry for 5 to 10 hours. Place the dried salsa in a ziplock bag with the pouches of tuna. Wrap and pack two bagels in plastic wrap, and place them in the ziplock bag with the other ingredients.

At Camp

Remove the tuna pouches from the ziplock bag. Add warm water to the salsa mixture, using a little less water than dried mix. Once rehydrated, add the tuna to the salsa mixture and place ¼ of the mixture on each half of the bagel. Serve open faced.

Tip

If you are planning to have this for lunch on the trail, add cold water to the salsa mixture at breakfast, and it'll be ready by the time you stop for lunch.

¼ cup frozen corn, thawed

1 tablespoon lime juice

½ cup salsa

¼ cup canned black beans, drained and rinsed

2 foil pouches tuna, approximately 3 ounces each

2 multigrain bagels

2 tablespoons lime juice

½ cup crushed pineapple, drained well

¾ cup plum tomatoes, drained and chopped

⅛ teaspoon cumin

¼ teaspoon kosher salt

¼ teaspoon dried cilantro

1 tablespoon green onion, chopped

½ clove garlic, minced

¼ teaspoon (or to taste) chipotle pepper sauce

Tropical Salsa

Dehydration Time: 7–12 hours
Makes 2 servings

This salsa combines sweet and spice with a hint of smokiness; it's delicious served with toasted tortillas or tortilla chips or added to a chicken or turkey wrap.

AT HOME

Combine all the ingredients together in a large bowl. Dry on lined dehydrator trays for 7 to 12 hours or until the pieces are dried through. Break the salsa into small pieces and place it in a ziplock freezer bag.

AT CAMP

Add warm water to the salsa mixture using a little less water than dried mix. Add more water if necessary.

TIP

If you are planning to have this for lunch on the trail, add cold water to the salsa mixture at breakfast, and it'll be ready by the time you stop for lunch.

Cream of Potato and Roasted Garlic Soup

Makes 2 servings

Hungarian hot paprika gives this dish a little heat. Enhance the flavor of this soup by adding a little smoked Gouda or chicken.

AT HOME

Combine dry ingredients and place in a zippered freezer bag with the camp instructions.

AT CAMP

Put 2¼–2½ cups of water in a pot to boil. The less water you use, the thicker the soup will be. When the water comes to a boil, turn off the heat and add the bag of dry ingredients. Stir for a few moments. Add more water if necessary to reach the desired consistency.

TIP

If you are growing water bottle sprouts (see page 91 for the recipe) on your trip, use a few to garnish the soup and add some crunch.

1 tablespoon dried chives

1 teaspoon roasted garlic

⅔ cup instant potato flakes

½ teaspoon dried parsley

¼ teaspoon dried thyme

⅓ cup nonfat powdered milk

½ teaspoon Hungarian hot paprika

½ teaspoon salt

¼ teaspoon cracked black pepper

2 ¼–2 ½ cups water

Lentil Soup

Dehydration Time: 8–10 hours
Makes 2–4 servings

1 cup dried red lentils

2 cups vegetable stock

¼ cup onion, finely chopped

⅛ cup carrot, coarsely grated

⅛ teaspoon cayenne (optional)

½ teaspoon parsley

Salt and pepper to taste

When I was little, my mother used to make lentil soup with ham stock and serve it with mashed potatoes. This is my vegetarian version.

AT HOME

Rinse and drain lentils. Bring vegetable stock to a boil and add onions, lentils, grated carrot, and seasonings. Let soup simmer until it is thick and the lentils are cooked. Place the soup on lined dehydrator trays. Dry for 8 to 10 hours or until completely dry. Tear into small pieces and place in a ziplock bag.

AT CAMP

Rehydrate the soup mixture using equal parts dried mix and boiling water. When the mixture is rehydrated, re-heat it if necessary. If the lentils aren't fully rehydrated, let it simmer for a few minutes when reheating. Serve with crackers or pita. Add a dash of Tabasco sauce for a little extra kick.

TIP

You can rehydrate this with cold water if you start first thing in the morning and store it in a leakproof container. Then when you stop for lunch, you can just heat it up.

Masoor Dal

Dehydration Time: 8–10 hours
Makes 2 servings

Masoor dal is a pink lentil dish that cooks very quickly, but I use red lentils because they are easier to find. The toasted cumin seeds add a peppery flavor and nuttiness to the dish.

At Home

Rinse the lentils and check them over for any foreign matter. Bring the water to a boil and add the lentils. Reduce the heat to medium and simmer for about 18 minutes, until most of the water is gone and the lentils are cooked.

Toast the cumin seeds in a large frying pan until they become fragrant. Remove them from the pan and set aside. In that same pan, sauté the onion in the sunflower oil until it softens. Then add the garlic and sauté for about another minute, being careful not to overcook it. Add the ginger, turmeric, and tomato and cook for about 10 minutes over medium heat. Stir in the cooked lentils, salt, and toasted cumin seeds.

Allow the mixture to cool and then measure it. Write this measurement on a sticky note. Spread on lined dehydrator trays to dry. When the dal is dry, package it in a ziplock freezer bag along with the sticky note.

At Camp

Rehydrate the dal by adding enough boiling water to the mix to equal the measurement on your sticky note. Be sure to account for and add your dried ingredients to the rehydration container prior to adding the water. You can always add more water if you need to. Reheat the rehydrated dal if it's not warm enough. This recipe goes well with flatbreads such as pita or chapati.

Tip

To save time, you can rehydrate this recipe by adding cold water to the mixture at breakfast and then reheating it when you stop for lunch.

2 cups water

1 cup dried red lentils

⅛ teaspoon cumin seeds

1½ tablespoons sunflower oil

⅓ cup onion, diced

2 cloves garlic, minced

1 tablespoon fresh ginger, peeled and minced

½ teaspoon turmeric

1 tomato, chopped

½ teaspoon kosher salt

Chapter 7

Snacks

Sometimes munching is more practical than lunching. Snacking keeps your body fueled throughout the day and can save time, which is important if you have a long way to travel. There are so many ideas for snacking on the go:

- Gorp (good old raisins and peanuts)
- Meat, fish, or tofu jerky
- Fresh fruit
- Dried fruit
- Granola or cereal bars
- Fruit leather
- Wasabi peas
- Root vegetable chips
- Dark chocolate (It does not melt as much in the heat.)
- Pumpkin or sunflower seeds
- Sesame snaps (a cracker made of sesame seeds and honey)
- Baked goods left over from the night before
- Vegetable leather

Snack Storage

It is a good idea to store snacks in single-serving sizes for each day. If you are traveling in a group, make sure each person has his or her own bag. This precaution can prevent contamination of the food from hands that might not be too clean. If you are using fresh fruit as a snack, protect it from bruising by wrapping it in a few paper towels or placing it in a hard-sided container, and use it early in your trip. If you use a hard-sided container, you should open it at camp to let out any excess moisture.

Blueberry Banana Energy Bars

⅓ cup dried banana chips

⅓ cup honey

⅓ cup brown sugar

⅓ cup peanut butter

2 cups high-energy cereal or cereal made of strong flakes, crushed

½ cup dried blueberries

⅓ cup slivered almonds

⅓ cup white chocolate chips

Makes 10 servings

These no-bake energy bars are very simple to make.

AT HOME

Break the banana chips into smaller pieces and set aside. Heat the honey and brown sugar in a large pot and let simmer for 1 minute. (Boiling too long will make the bars brittle.) Remove the pan from the heat and add the peanut butter. Stir until the peanut butter is well incorporated. Add the crushed cereal, blueberries, almonds, and banana and chocolate chips and combine well.

Coat the bottom and sides of an 8-inch square pan with vegetable oil. Scoop the mixture into the pan and pack down evenly. Freeze for 30 minutes. Transfer the pan contents to a cutting board. Allow to return to room temperature and then cut into 10 bars. Wrap bars in waxed paper and store in ziplock bags. The bars will keep in the freezer for up to 3 months.

Cranberry Macadamia Energy Bars

Makes 10 servings

The tart cranberries add a contrast of flavors to these bars.

At Home

Heat the honey and brown sugar in a large pot and let simmer for 1 minute. (Boiling too long will make the bars brittle.) Remove the pan from the heat and add the peanut butter. Stir until the peanut butter is well incorporated. Add the crushed cereal, cranberries, nuts, and chocolate chips and combine well.

Coat the bottom and sides of an 8-inch square pan with vegetable oil. Scoop the mixture into the pan and pack down evenly. Freeze for 30 minutes. Transfer the pan contents to a cutting board. Allow to return to room temperature and then cut into 10 bars. Wrap bars in waxed paper and store in ziplock bags. The bars will keep in the freezer for up to 3 months.

⅓ cup honey

¼ cup brown sugar

¼ cup peanut butter

2 cups high-energy cereal or cereal made of strong flakes, crushed

½ cup dried cranberries

½ cup macadamia nuts, chopped

⅓ cup white chocolate chips

⅓ cup honey

¼ cup brown sugar

¼ cup peanut butter

2 cups high-energy cereal or cereal made of strong flakes, crushed

½ cup dried currants

⅓ cup hazelnuts, chopped

½ cup milk chocolate chips

Hazelnut Currant Energy Bars

Makes 10 servings

Milk chocolate, currants, and hazelnuts make this energy bar a yummy treat.

AT HOME

Heat the honey and brown sugar in a large pot and let simmer for 1 minute. (Boiling too long will make the bars brittle.) Remove the pan from the heat and add the peanut butter. Stir until the peanut butter is well incorporated. Add the crushed cereal, currants, hazelnuts, and milk chocolate chips and combine well.

    Coat the bottom and sides of an 8-inch square pan with vegetable oil. Scoop the mixture into the pan and pack down evenly. Freeze for 30 minutes. Transfer the pan contents to a cutting board. Allow to return to room temperature and then cut into 10 bars. Wrap the bars in waxed paper and store in ziplock bags. These bars will keep in the freezer for up to 3 months.

TIP

When you purchase hazelnuts that have been removed from the shell, their skins are often still intact. To remove the skins, place the nuts in a metal colander or sieve and roll them around with your hands. The friction will remove the skins.

Chocolate Hazelnut "No Bake" Fudge

Makes 6–8 servings

¼ cup butter, softened

⅓ cup Nutella chocolate hazelnut spread

¾–1 cup icing or confectioners sugar

⅛ cup hazelnuts, chopped

This no-cook fudgelike confection is very easy to make and tastes like fine hazelnut chocolate truffles.

AT HOME
Combine butter and hazelnut spread in a medium-sized bowl. Add ¾ cup icing or confectioners sugar and mix well, adding more icing sugar as needed. You may have to knead the mixture with your hands. Shape it into a rectangle and top it with chopped hazelnuts. Push the hazelnuts down so they adhere to the fudge. Wrap tightly in plastic wrap or waxed paper and place in a ziplock freezer bag.

AT CAMP
Break or slice the fudge into pieces and enjoy.

TIPS
When you purchase hazelnuts that have been removed from the shell, their skins are often still intact. To remove the skins, place the nuts in a metal colander or sieve and roll them around with your hands. The friction will remove the skins.

If you can't find chocolate hazelnut spread, you can substitute peanut butter and replace the hazelnuts with peanuts.

Ginger Cashew Bark

Makes 3–4 servings

Candied ginger gives this bark a spicy bite, and the cashews add some extra energy.

1 cup milk chocolate, broken into pieces

⅓ cup dried, candied ginger chunks

⅓ cup whole cashews, unsalted

AT HOME

Heat water in a double boiler, making sure it doesn't touch the top section. If you don't have a double boiler, fill a pot about ⅓ of the way with water and place a metal bowl on top. The bowl should fit snugly. Make sure the water does not touch the bottom of the bowl. Bring the water to a boil and reduce the heat to medium-low to keep the water simmering.

Put the chocolate in the top section or bowl and stir it until it has melted. Shut the heat off and add the ginger and cashews, stirring to coat. Spread the mixture on a cookie sheet lined with waxed paper and let set. When it has hardened, break it into large pieces and pack them in a ziplock freezer bag.

Strawberry Bark

Dehydration Time: 5–10 hours
Makes 3–4 servings

You can use any dried fruit you prefer in this bark, but the strawberries are divine with the white chocolate.

AT HOME

Arrange the strawberry slices on lined dehydrator trays, and dry for 5 to 10 hours.

After the strawberries are dehydrated, heat water in a double boiler, making sure it doesn't touch the top section. If you don't have a double boiler, fill a pot about ⅓ of the way with water and place a metal bowl on top. The bowl should fit snugly. Make sure the water does not touch the bottom of the bowl. Bring the water to a boil and reduce the heat to medium-low to keep the water simmering.

Put the chocolate in the top section or bowl and stir it until it has melted. Shut the heat off and add the strawberries, stirring to coat. Spread the mixture on a cookie sheet lined with waxed paper and let it set. When it has hardened, break it into large pieces and pack them in a ziplock freezer bag.

⅓ cup strawberries, cut into ¼-inch slices

½ cup white chocolate chips

1 cup dark chocolate, broken into
   pieces

⅓ cup dried cherries

⅓ cup whole almonds

Cherry Almond Bark

Makes 3–4 servings

*I used to make this bark as a gift for family and friends
when I was a university student on a tight budget. I re-
ceived a lot of complaints when I was no longer a starving
student and started buying gifts instead. I still use this recipe as a welcome snack on the trail, and the dark chocolate
fairs better in the heat.*

At Home

Heat water in a double boiler, making sure it doesn't touch
the top section. If you don't have a double boiler, fill a pot
about ⅓ of the way with water and place a metal bowl on
top. The bowl should fit snugly. Make sure the water does
not touch the bottom of the bowl. Bring the water to a boil
and reduce the heat to medium-low to keep the water simmering.

   Put the chocolate in the top section or bowl and stir it
until it has melted. Shut the heat off and add the cherries
and almonds, stirring to coat. Spread the mixture on a
cookie sheet lined with waxed paper and let it set. When it
has hardened, break it into large pieces and pack them in a
ziplock freezer bag.

Chocolate-Covered Coffee Beans

Makes 6 servings

½–¾ cup milk chocolate

⅓ cup flavored coffee beans

I make this recipe with pecan-flavored coffee beans, but you can use whatever flavor you prefer. It also works well with espresso beans. Eat these as a snack, or drop one or two into your morning cup of coffee or a cup of hot chocolate.

AT HOME

Heat water in a double boiler, making sure it doesn't touch the top section. If you don't have a double boiler, fill a pot about ⅓ of the way with water and place a metal bowl on top. The bowl should fit snugly. Make sure the water does not touch the bottom of the bowl. Bring the water to a boil and reduce the heat to medium-low to keep the water simmering.

Put the chocolate in the top section or bowl and stir it until it has melted. Shut the heat off and add the coffee beans, stirring to coat. Drop the covered beans one by one onto waxed paper and let set. Put the chocolate-covered beans in a ziplock freezer bag.

Teriyaki Jerky

1 pound flank steak, thinly sliced

1 tablespoon ginger, freshly grated

1 tablespoon crushed red chilies

½ cup teriyaki sauce

¼ cup dark soy sauce

Dehydration Time: 8–12 hours
Makes 10 servings

Choose a lean cut of meat such as round or flank steak; get your butcher to slice it for you if you can.

At Home

Cut meat into 2-inch by 5-inch by ¼-inch pieces. Mix the ginger, chilies, and teriyaki and soy sauces together in a shallow pan. Place the meat in the pan, turning to coat. Marinate for 24 hours in the refrigerator. Remove the meat from the refrigerator and drain the marinade.

Place the meat strips about ½ inch apart on lined dehydrator trays. Dry at 160°F for 8 to 12 hours. The jerky is done when the meat is dry and cracks easily when bent; it should resemble leather. Package it in ziplock freezer bags, and store it in the freezer until you are ready to leave.

Tip

It's easier to slice meat for jerky if it is slightly frozen.

Chipotle Jerky

Dehydration Time: 8–12 hours
Makes 10 servings

The smokiness of chipotle peppers works really well in a jerky marinade.

At HOME

Cut the meat into 2-inch by 5-inch by ¼-inch pieces. Mix the chipotle pepper, sugar, onion, tomato juice, hickory smoke, and tamari sauce together in a shallow pan. Place the meat in the pan, turning to coat. Marinate in the refrigerator for 24 hours. Remove the meat from the refrigerator and drain the marinade.

   Place the meat strips about ½ inch apart on lined dehydrator trays. Dry at 160°F for 8 to 12 hours. The jerky is done when the meat is dry and cracks easily when it is bent; it should resemble leather. Package it in ziplock freezer bags and store in the freezer until you are ready to leave.

1 pound flank steak, thinly sliced

½ a chipotle pepper, minced

¼ cup brown sugar

1 tablespoon red onion, minced

½ cup tomato juice

2 teaspoons liquid hickory smoke

¼ cup tamari sauce

Smoked Salmon Jerky

1 pound smoked salmon, thinly sliced

¼ cup brown sugar

1½ tablespoons black pepper, freshly cracked

½ cup red grapefruit juice

2 teaspoons liquid hickory smoke

¼ cup tamari sauce

Dehydration Time: 8–12 hours
Makes 10–12 servings

Citrus and hickory flavors make this a delicious alternative to beef jerky. Try to choose a piece of salmon that isn't too fatty.

At Home

Cut fish into 2-inch by 5-inch by ¼-inch pieces. Mix the brown sugar, pepper, grapefruit juice, hickory smoke, and tamari sauce together in a shallow pan. Place the fish in the pan, turning to coat. Marinate in the refrigerator for 24 hours. When seasoned, remove the pan from the refrigerator and drain the marinade.

Place the meat strips about ½ inch apart on lined dehydrator trays. Dry at 160°F for 8 to 12 hours. The jerky is done when the fish is dry and cracks easily when it is bent; it should resemble leather. Package it in ziplock freezer bags and store in the freezer until you are ready to leave.

Spiced Dried Pears and Apples with Walnuts

Dehydration Time: 6–15 hours
Makes 4 servings

Harvest time comes to mind with this simple trail snack.

AT HOME

Soak the chopped apples and pears in lemon juice in a medium-sized bowl for 5 minutes. Drain and sprinkle with ginger and cinnamon. Spread the fruit chunks on a lined dehydrator tray. Dehydrate for 6 to 15 hours, until the fruit is leathery.

Toast the walnuts in a dry frying pan until they become fragrant. Package the fruit and walnuts together in a ziplock freezer bag, and store the bag in the refrigerator until your trip. This snack will keep for up to 6 months if refrigerated and about 4 weeks without refrigeration.

2 Fuji or Royal Gala apples, chopped

2 d'Anjou pears, chopped

½ cup lemon juice

⅛ teaspoon ground ginger

¼ teaspoon cinnamon

¼ cup walnuts

Crunchy Berry Yogurt Leather

1 cup low-fat mixed-berry-flavored yogurt

⅓ cup granola

Dehydration Time: 6–15 hours
Makes 4 servings

Sometimes my family gets bored with fruit leather on the trail; this is a great alternative with a bit of crunch.

At Home

Spread the yogurt about ¼ inch thick on lined dehydrator trays. Sprinkle with your favorite granola and let it dehydrate until the yogurt is dry and pliable like leather. Cut into pieces, wrap it in plastic wrap, and store it in the refrigerator until your trip. This snack will keep about 6 months if refrigerated and for about 6 weeks at room temperature.

Pumpkin Pie Leather

1 cup cooked canned pumpkin

½ teaspoon cinnamon

¼ teaspoon ginger

Dehydration Time: 6–15 hours
Makes 4 servings

Portable pumpkin pie! Okay it isn't quite the same, but it still tastes really great.

At Home

Mix the pumpkin and spices together. Spread the mixture about ¼ inch thick on lined dehydrator trays. Let it dry for 6 to 15 hours—the timeframe depends upon the consistency of the canned pumpkin, which varies by brand—until it is pliable like leather. Cut it into pieces, wrap it in plastic wrap, and store it in the refrigerator until your trip. This snack will keep for up to 6 months if refrigerated and for 6 to 8 weeks without refrigeration.

Cantaloupe Strawberry Leather

Dehydration Time: 6–15 hours
Makes 4 servings

1 cup cantaloupe

½ cup strawberries

This leather is tasty and interesting looking. The melon and strawberries pair nicely, but you could switch it up by using different fruit combinations.

AT HOME

Purée the cantaloupe and strawberries separately. Strain the strawberry purée through a fine mesh sieve. Spread the cantaloupe purée about ¼ inch thick on lined dehydrator trays. Then pour the strawberry purée in a ribbon on top of the cantaloupe purée. Run a toothpick or skewer back and forth through the purées, making a swirl pattern.

Let the fruit dry for 6 to 15 hours (depending on the moisture content and ripeness of the fruit) until it is pliable like leather. Cut it into pieces, wrap it in plastic wrap, and store it in the refrigerator until your trip. This snack will keep for up to 6 months if refrigerated and for 6 to 8 weeks without refrigeration.

¼ cup cornflakes

⅛ cup mini-chocolate chips

⅛ cup dried banana chips

⅛ cup walnuts

⅓ cup peanut butter

Monkey Gunk

Makes 2–3 servings

This gunk is chunky and tasty and somewhat like peanut butter balls.

AT HOME
Break the banana chips into pieces. Mix the dry ingredients and pour them in a ziplock freezer bag. Put the peanut butter in a small leakproof container or add it to other peanut butter you will take on your trip.

AT CAMP
Mix ⅓ cup peanut butter with the ingredients in the freezer bag. Make into 4 balls.

---

1 cup honey mustard and onion pretzels

⅓ cup smoked almonds

¼ cup dry roasted peanuts

⅓ cup dried root vegetables

¼ cup pepitas (hulled pumpkin seeds) or sunflower seeds

¼ cup salted cashews

Honey Mustard Gorp

Makes 6–8 servings

Once when I was headed out on a backpacking trip and wanted a savory trail mix with a hint of sweetness, I came up with this.

AT HOME
Mix all of the ingredients together in a medium-sized bowl. Package in ziplock freezer bags.

Pizza Gorp

Makes 6–8 servings

Even though you make the majority of this gorp ahead of time, it requires a moment of preparation on the trail.

AT HOME

Toast the pine nuts in a dry nonstick frying pan. Allow the pine nuts to cool. Mix all of the ingredients except the pepperoni sticks together in a medium-sized bowl. Package each serving in a ziplock freezer bag. Put an individually wrapped pepperoni stick in each bag.

AT CAMP

When you are ready to enjoy your gorp, take a short break and cut up a pepperoni stick into the bag of gorp. Continue your hike and enjoy your snack.

¼ cup pine nuts

1 cup mini-cheese-flavored crackers

¼ cup freeze-dried tomatoes, chopped

¼ cup dry roasted peanuts

⅛ teaspoon oregano

6 small individually wrapped dried pepperoni sticks (shelf-stable variety)

Chocolate Blueberry Gorp

Makes 6–8 servings

Once my family and I stopped at a local bakery near a trailhead, and it had chocolate-covered blueberries. Although we haven't seen them since, every time I eat this mix I am reminded of those berries.

AT HOME

Mix all of the ingredients together in a medium-sized bowl. Package it in ziplock freezer bags.

¼ cup honeyed or plain sunflower seeds

⅓ cup dried blueberries

⅓ cup mini-chocolate chips

¼ cup walnuts

¼ cup pretzels

Spicy Gorp

½ cup corn chips

⅓ cup barbeque-flavored peanuts

¼ cup sunflower seeds

⅓ cup dried wasabi peas

¼ cup pepitas (shelled pumpkin seeds)

¼ cup raisins

¼ cup sesame sticks

Makes 6–8 servings

Wasabi peas and barbeque-flavored peanuts make this gorp a little spicy.

AT HOME

Mix all of the ingredients together in a medium-sized bowl. Package in ziplock freezer bags.

Chapter 8

DINNERS

After a long day of outdoor activities, most people are famished. When it is very hot, I tend to eat smaller portions throughout the day and have a more substantial dinner. If the weather is a little dicey or my husband and I arrived at camp late, one of us will set up the tent while the other works on filtering water and preparing dinner. I take a variety of dinners on a trip along with a printed copy of my meal plan. During inclement weather, I switch to an easier dinner. Having the meal plan written up means that I have an accurate inventory of what remains in the food pack.

Try to get all of your cooking and eating finished and your food pack hoisted before dark if possible. Cleanup is easier when it is still daylight. In addition, critters seem more plentiful at night. Rodents and raccoons can be especially bothersome. Of course if you are above the tree line, you will need to use an approved bear canister.

At home, you might consider dehydrating leftovers from supper. Thick stews and soups are especially wonderful for this; just be sure to chop it into small pieces and separate the meat, beans, and vegetables because all of them dry at different rates. Oftentimes I double a dinner recipe—we have the meal for dinner, and then I dry the rest. This approach saves time and effort by doing the work for two meals at once. Hot spices seem to lose their heat a bit during the dehydration and reconstitution process so you might take a little extra spice along on your trips to add more at mealtime if desired.

Thicker pastas don't cook well at higher altitudes. If you are traveling in these areas, replace regular pasta such as spaghetti with much finer pasta such as angel hair (capellini d'angelo) or rice pasta. You can also precook and dry pasta and rice to reduce cooking time on the trail. Cook the rice or pasta but not all the way. Stop about 2 minutes before it is cooked. The quickest way to stop the pasta from cooking is to pour a glass of cold water into the pot. For rice you can stop the cooking by sitting the pan in a sink of cool water making sure the water level is not higher than the pan. Then spread it on dehydrator trays and dehydrate for 6 to 10 hours until thoroughly dry. At camp add hot or boiling water and let the food sit in a pot cozy for about 15 minutes or until reconstituted.

Vegetables and Side Dishes

Vegetables are easy to dehydrate for reheating in the outdoors; frozen or drained, canned vegetables work well dried on screens or fruit leather dehydrator trays. Canned corn, especially the peaches and cream variety, dehydrates and rehydrates beautifully. Fresh vegetables such as squash and turnips are best cooked through and mashed before dehydration. Use frozen peas or you'll end up with mush. Frozen hash browns dehydrate very well, too. Instant mashed potatoes are great for longer trips, and you can jazz them up with a little creativity. A variety of freeze-dried fruits and vegetables are available from companies online such as Just Tomatoes, Etc. at www.justtomatoes.com. These products are almost instant and have a good flavor. That said, I still like to dehydrate my own vegetables. If you are using fresh vegetables such as corn, potatoes, green beans, asparagus, carrots, broccoli, cauliflower, or brussels sprouts for dehydration purposes, it is best to blanch them in boiling water for a few minutes before drying. The more delicate items like peppers, spinach, and tomatoes do not need to be blanched nor do shredded carrots or cabbage.

If you decide to take a fragile food like mushrooms, I recommend drying them instead of taking them fresh. Mushrooms turn to mush in a day or so. If you do not feel like drying your own, look for the dried kind in your supermarket or Asian market. I have been able to find everything from white mushrooms to shitakes and portabellas already dried; although they're expensive, a little goes a long way.

Garlic bread, biscuits, dumplings, or focaccia make a great side dish, especially when your meal includes sauce. I often toast garlic bread over the campfire. Leftover dip makes a great appetizer; sometimes I bring a dip intending to use it this way.

Casseroles and Skillet Dishes

Casseroles and skillet dishes are easy, filling, and tasty. Since the final dish is cooked in one pot or pan, preparation is a little simpler. I generally try to combine vegetable, protein, and starch components. Some great bakes are potpies, macaroni and cheese, shepherd's pie, and lasagna. I also like to do what I call skillets, which do not require baking. This is great for stir-frying and for pasta dishes. Just make your sauce and vegetable mixture and then add rice, quinoa, or pasta. If you have a large group, however, you may require more than one stove and pot for these types of dinners.

Packaging Meals

Each recipe includes guidelines for packaging the meals. Keep in mind that if you are not using the sauces and such right away then you should freeze them. Do not freeze the pastas, rice, tortillas, pitas, couscous, or such—only freeze the items that you have dehydrated. Be sure to write the name of the recipe, number of servings, date, and predehydration measurements on a note, and put it inside the bag. You might also write the page number of the recipe on the note as well—that will make it easy for you to find the camp instructions when you are getting ready for your trip. At camp instructions can also be found for download at www.WildernessPress.com or www.AForkintheTrail.com.

Pastas such as fusilli (corkscrews), farfalle (bowties), or penne lisce (smooth tubes) travel best and stand up to quite a bit of abuse. If you do take spaghetti or angel hair pasta, wrap it tightly with plastic wrap and place it in an empty paper towel tube to prevent the noodles from breaking.

If you will be traveling in a situation where you won't use all the servings in a single meal, simply split the recipe into single-serving portions when packaging it. Be sure to label the packages, and insert a note with each serving so that you know how much water to add back into the food. If you forget to add the note, add just enough water at camp to cover the ingredients.

3 tablespoons vegetable oil

1 pound stew beef

1 small onion, chopped

⅔ of a medium green pepper, chopped

1¼ cups tomato juice

½ teaspoon salt

¼ teaspoon freshly ground black pepper

2 teaspoons hot or sweet Hungarian paprika

¼–⅓ cup flour

¼–⅓ cup water

2 cups broad egg noodles (uncooked measurement)

Hungarian Goulash

Dehydration Time: 7–10 hours
Makes 3–4 servings

My husband spent a few months in Hungary and came back with some Hungarian paprika that had been ground and sun-dried by a friend's grandmother. He asked me to make goulash with it and said this tasted exactly like what he had eaten in Budapest.

At Home

Remove all visible fat from the beef and then cut it into ½-inch pieces. Pour the vegetable oil in a large pot over medium heat and then add the meat. Brown the meat and add the chopped onion and green pepper. Cook until the onions are soft. Then add the tomato juice, salt, pepper, and the paprika. Cover and simmer for 1½ hours. Stir occasionally, checking to make sure there is enough liquid to prevent the meat from sticking to the pot.

Scoop out the meat and vegetables and set them aside. Bring the sauce to a boil. While that's simmering, pour equal amounts of flour and water in a jar with a lid. Screw the lid shut and shake well. This flour mixture is known as slurry. Stir the sauce constantly while you pour a little slurry into the pot. Continue to stir. If the sauce is not as thick as you would like, add a little more slurry. Allow it to cook for a few minutes while still stirring constantly. When the sauce has reached a gravylike thickness, remove the pot from the heat.

Measure the goulash, and write this measurement on a sticky note. Separate the vegetables from the meat. Place the meat, sauce, and vegetables on separate lined dehydrator trays. Dehydrate the meat for 7 to 10 hours until it looks like large gravel, and dehydrate the sauce and vegetables for 6 to 8 hours or until they are dried thoroughly. Put the uncooked egg noodles in a large ziplock freezer bag. Package the meat, vegetables, and sauce in one ziplock freezer bag. Put the sauce bag inside the noodle bag along with the sticky note.

At Camp

Add enough boiling water to the meat, sauce, and vegetable mix to equal the measurement on your sticky note. Be sure to account for and add your dried ingredients to the rehydration container prior to adding the water. You can always add more water if you need to.

Once all the ingredients are rehydrated, boil the noodles. Once they're done, drain them carefully. Cover the noodles and set them aside. Pour the meat and sauce into a second pot and bring to a boil. Pour the sauce into the noodles, stir, and serve. If desired, add a little sprinkle of paprika once served.

Tips

Do not use Spanish paprika—it does not have the same depth of flavor as Hungarian paprika.

This goulash recipe is also nice served over potatoes. If you prefer, you can use textured vegetable protein instead of meat.

It is important to allow dried meat a little more time to come back. If the meat for this recipe doesn't rehydrate all the way soaking in boiling water, simmer it for a few minutes.

Chicken Mushroom Maggi

1 cup canned chicken

½ 10-ounce can cream of mushroom soup

½ cup frozen green beans

2 cups farfalle (bowtie) pasta (uncooked measurement)

3–4 tablespoons mixed, dried mushrooms

2 tablespoons Maggi seasoning

1-inch x 2-inch x 3-inch block mozzarella cheese

Dehydration Time: 5–10 hours
Makes 3–4 servings

Made from vegetable protein, Maggi seasoning enhances the earthy flavor of mushrooms.

At Home

Dehydrate the chicken and soup separately on lined trays for 7 to 10 hours. Dehydrate the frozen green beans for 5 to 7 hours. Put 2 to 3 servings of noodles in a large ziplock freezer bag. Add the soup and chicken to a second bag, and put the mushrooms and green beans in a third bag. Pour the Maggi seasoning in a small Nalgene or other leakproof bottle. Wrap the cheese. Place the cheese and the bag of vegetables in the bag with the chicken and soup.

At Camp

Place the soup and chicken together in a Nalgene bottle or pot. Add just enough boiling water to cover the ingredients and allow to rehydrate. Add boiling water to the mushrooms and green beans in the ziplock freezer bag and allow to rehydrate. Once they are rehydrated, drain any excess water from the vegetables.

Once all the ingredients are rehdyrated, boil water and cook the pasta. Meanwhile mix the sauce, chicken, veggies and 2 tablespoons of Maggi seasoning together in another pot. Cut the cheese into small cubes and set it aside. When the pasta is cooked, remove it from the heat and drain well. Replace the lid and set the pot aside.

Heat the sauce in your second pot over the stove. Once the sauce is hot, add the cheese and stir until it has melted. Remove the sauce from heat. Place the drained pasta back on the heat, pour the sauce onto the pasta, and stir until heated through. Serve and sprinkle with a little more Maggi seasoning if desired.

Tips

It is important to allow dried chicken a little more time to come back. If the meat for this recipe doesn't rehydrate all the way soaking in boiling water, simmer it for a few minutes.

If you don't want to dehydrate canned chicken, then bring a 7-ounch foil pouch of chicken and add it to the rehydrated soup, vegetables, and Maggi seasoning.

1 pouch or can (7 ounces) cooked
chicken

1 10-ounce can of condensed
cream of chicken or cream of
celery soup

1½ cups frozen mixed vegetables
(carrots, peas, and corn)

1 recipe *Basic Biscuits* (page 210)

Chicken Potpie
with Biscuits

Dehydration Time: 5–10 hours
Makes 2–3 servings

*This hearty dish is great for a layover or a day when you
will arrive in camp early.*

AT HOME
Dehydrate the chicken and soup for 5 to 10 hours separately on lined trays. Dehydrate the frozen mixed vegetables
for 5 to 7 hours.

AT CAMP
Rehydrate the soup in a Nalgene bottle or ziplock bag.
Rehydrate the vegetables and chicken in separate ziplock
freezer bags. Use enough water to barely cover the dried
ingredients. Once the vegetables have rehydrated, drain the
excess water from them. Mix the chicken, soup, and vegetables together in a pot. Top with the biscuit dough and
bake in an Outback or reflector oven for 30 minutes, until
the dough is cooked through.

TIPS
While this recipe is better when all the ingredients are
baked together, you can make it without a backpacker's
oven. Just fry-bake the biscuit dough in one large slab as
explained in the *Basic Biscuits* recipe. Cook the filling over
your stove for about 15 minutes or until it's hot all the way
through. Spread the cooked biscuit slab on top of your
chicken mixture.

   If weight is not a consideration, you can take a pouch of
chicken without having to dehydrate it first.

Salmon Cakes

Makes 2–3 servings

This recipe was inspired by a good friend while we were on a weeklong trip together. On one of those damp and windy days that chill you to your core, the mood was sullen until she served her salmon cakes.

At Home

Put the mayonnaise and dried onion in separate small ziplock bags. Put the stuffing in a large ziplock bag. Pour the lemon juice into a small leakproof container. Put the mayonnaise packs, dried onion, lemon juice, and a pouch of salmon in the large bag. Wrap the mozzarella cheese.

At Camp

Cut or grate the cheese as finely as you can. Add a little boiling water to the onion and allow it to rehydrate for about 10 minutes. Drain it and mix all ingredients together in a large bowl or pot. Add 4 tablespoons water and let it set for 10 minutes. Shape the mixture into patties and cook them on a greased frying pan until golden on both sides, about 3 to 4 minutes per side.

Tip

A nice side of vegetables complements this dish well.

½ package stuffing mix for poultry

1½ teaspoons lemon juice

3–4 single-serving packages of mayonnaise

1½ teaspoons dried onion

1 pouch or can (3¾ ounces) red sockeye or wild salmon

1-inch x 2-inch x 3-inch block mozzarella cheese

4 tablespoons water

6 lasagna noodles

14-ounce package instant mashed
    potatoes or enough to make 2
    cups of potatoes

6 slices precooked bacon
    (optional)

2 teaspoons dried chives

Nonfat powdered milk (if the
    potatoes require milk)

2 tablespoons sour cream powder
    (optional)

1-inch x 2-inch x 3-inch block old
    cheddar cheese

Pseudo Perogies

Makes 2–3 servings

*When I was a child, I woke up on the last Saturday of each
month to the comforting smell of cheese and potatoes. I'd
sneak out to the kitchen and watch my father make a big
batch of perogies from scratch. This recipe reminds me of
that and is, at least to me, the ultimate comfort food.*

AT HOME

Break the lasagna noodles into large pieces. Keep the
potatoes and optional bacon in their packaging. Place the
potatoes, bacon, and broken noodles into a large ziplock
freezer bag. Package dried chives in a small piece of plastic
wrap and place it in the bag with the other items.

If powdered milk is required, put it in a small bag. If
you are taking sour cream powder, put it in a small bag as
well. Put these bags in the bag with the other ingredients.
Wrap the mozzarella cheese.

AT CAMP

Add boiling water to the chives in a Nalgene bottle or cup
and allow to rehydrate for 5 minutes. Drain them and set
aside. Chop up the bacon, warm it in a frying pan, and
then set it aside. Cook the lasagna noodles in boiling water
until they are tender and set them aside. Cut up the cheese
and set it aside.

If you're using sour cream powder, mix it with the potato flakes. Boil water for the potatoes. Add the potato flakes
and stir, adding powdered milk if the potatoes require it.
Add the chives, bacon, noodles, and cheese. Stir over low
heat until the cheese melts.

Pizza

Dehydration Time: 5–15 hours
Makes 2 servings

When my family became bored with pita pizzas, I created a homemade pizza on the trail—it was surprisingly easy.

AT HOME

Prepare the yeast dough mix per the instructions on page 212 and put it in a small ziplock freezer bag. Put the yeast dough mix and its instructions along with any herbs you might want to use in the crust into a large ziplock freezer bag.

Slice or chop the vegetables as appropriate and place them on dehydrator trays. Dry them for 5 to 15 hours, depending on the vegetables you've chosen. Also dry ¼ to ½ cup of your favorite pizza sauce. Package the vegetables and sauce in separate ziplock freezer bags and place both bags in with the dough mix. Wrap the cheese. Leave the pepperoni in its packaging and pack it with the other ingredient. Add the oil to what you are taking.

AT CAMP

Using an equal amount of boiling water and dried ingredients, add water to the bag containing the vegetables, being careful not to burn yourself. Add boiling water to the sauce bag, using a little less water than dried sauce. Prepare the dough according to the recipe directions and rub a little olive oil onto it before letting it rise. If the weather is cold, you can place the ziplock bag inside your jacket to aid in rising.

Once the dough has risen, press it out into a pan. Slice the cheese and pepperoni if you are using it. Drain any excess water from the vegetables. Spread with sauce and then layer the cheese and other toppings. Bake the pizza in the oven for 10 to 12 minutes, allowing a few minutes for the oven to preheat with the pizza in it before you start timing. Once the cheese is melted and the crust is golden, remove it from the heat and let it cool for a few minutes before eating it.

1 recipe *Basic Yeast Dough* (page 212)

½ cup assorted vegetables (peppers, mushrooms, onions, and tomatoes)

¼–½ cup pizza sauce

¼–½ pound block mozzarella cheese

10–20 slices shelf-stable pepperoni (optional)

2–3 tablespoons olive oil

Tips

If you will be keeping the cheese for a long time without refrigeration, wrap it in vinegar-soaked cheesecloth and dip it in paraffin.

With these basic instructions you can make all kinds of variations: chicken, broccoli, and roasted red peppers; spinach, tomato, and feta cheese; beef, provolone cheese, roasted garlic, and green peppers; ham, mushrooms, zucchini, and Knorr alfredo sauce mix instead of tomato-based sauce; vegetarian bacon and cheddar; and many more. The only limit is your imagination.

Cheese Fondue

Makes 2–4 servings

This classic fondue is quick and easy to make in the back-country. My family and I like to dip raw broccoli and French bread cubes in it—no double dipping!

At Home

Wrap the Gruyere. Put the white wine in a small leakproof container. Wrap the clove of garlic and flour separately in pieces of plastic wrap and put both packets in a larger bag. Pack the items that you will dip in the fondue separately.

At Camp

Prepare the items you will dip in the fondue. Cut the cheese into small cubes and return them to the ziplock bag. Put 1 tablespoon of flour into the bag with the cheese, close the bag and shake so that the flour coats the cubes. Cut the garlic clove in half.

Add the garlic and ½ cup of wine or juice to a pot and bring to a boil. Add half of the cheese and stir constantly over medium heat until the cheese is melted. If the cheese is sticking turn the heat down to medium-low. Then add the other half of the cheese. Stir until all cheese is melted and warmed through, being careful not to burn the cheese.

Reduce the heat to the lowest possible setting. Use a fork to remove the pieces of garlic. Pierce your bread or other dipping items with a fork and dip them in the cheese mixture. If the cheese starts to set up too much for dipping, just melt it again over low heat stirring constantly.

Tips

A teaspoon of dill weed is a nice addition to the fondue.

You can dip all sorts of things in cheese fondue. Cubes of French or pumpernickel bread are a good choice—it doesn't matter if the bread goes a little stale as the warm cheese will

8 ounces Gruyere cheese

½ cup white wine

1 clove garlic

1 tablespoon all-purpose flour

Items for dipping (see Tip below)

soften it. Some other options are bread sticks, crackers, toasted tortillas, Melba toast, cured sausage, raw vegetables, shrimp or clams (the kind in the foil pouches), and apples and pears (dried or fresh). If weight isn't a consideration, you can even take some baby new potatoes, boil them, and dip them in the fondue.

Chipotle Pork with Toasted Tortillas

Dehydration Time: 7–12 hours
Makes 3–4 servings

Preparing this dish in a slow cooker keeps the meat moist and tender. Do not use a picnic pork shoulder as it is too salty.

AT HOME

Mix all of the ingredients except the meat, tortillas, and cheese and place them in the crock of a slow cooker. Trim the pork shoulder of all visible fat and cut it into two pieces. Add the boneless pork shoulder to the slow cooker. Turn the pork in the cooker so that it becomes well coated with the sauce. Cook on high for six hours or until the meat is so tender that you can easily shred it. Don't remove the lid until the cooking is complete.

When the meat is cooked, use two forks to shred it. If any gristle or fat is still present, remove it. Return the shredded meat to the sauce and stir well. Taste to see if more seasoning is required, adding as necessary, and remove the bay leaf.

Measure the pork mixture and write this measurement on a sticky note. Spread the meal on lined dehydrator trays and dry it for 7 to 12 hours. Place the dried mix, along with the sticky note, in a ziplock freezer bag. If you are taking cheese, wrap it. Package the tortillas in a large ziplock freezer bag, separating them with sheets of parchment paper.

AT CAMP

Add enough boiling water to the pork mixture in a pan to equal the measurement on your sticky note. Be sure to account for and add your dried ingredients to the rehydration container prior to adding the water. You can always add

1 small onion, diced

½ teaspoon oregano

1 bay leaf

1 teaspoon kosher salt

1 teaspoon black pepper, freshly ground

1 tablespoon chipotle pepper purée or ½ of a chipotle pepper, chopped

14 ounces canned, crushed tomatoes

8 ounces canned, diced tomatoes, drained

1 pound boneless pork shoulder

6–8 flour or corn tortillas

1-inch x 1-inch x 3-inch piece of cheddar cheese (optional)

more water if you need to. Allow it to rehydrate for 20 to 30 minutes or until fully rehydrated.

While it's rehydrating, grate the cheese if you're using it. Once the mixture is reconstituted, heat it up on a stove, being careful not to burn it. Remove the mixture from the heat and cover it with a lid. Meanwhile, toast several tortillas. Place a generous scoop of the pork mixture on each plate. Garnish with the toasted tortillas and grated cheese as desired.

Tips

If you don't have a slow cooker, simmer the ingredients in a heavy pot over low heat for 2 or 3 hours, stirring occasionally.

It is important to allow dried meat more time to come back. If your meat dish doesn't rehydrate all the way soaking in boiling water, simmer it over medium heat for a few minutes.

Curried Chicken with Raisins and Currants

Dehydration Time: 7–10 hours
Makes 4–6 servings

This fragrant dish is inspired by the flavors of India. Be sure to dry it with similar dishes as the flavors could transfer to other foods on your dehydrator.

AT HOME

Pour a handful of flour into a shallow bowl. Pat the chicken dry with paper towels and dip each piece in the flour. Melt most of the butter in a large pot over medium-high heat until it starts to brown. Place half of the chicken thighs in the bottom of the pan and cook until they are golden on all sides. Remove the cooked chicken, place it on a plate, and set it aside. Melt some more butter in the pan and cook the remaining chicken. Set this batch of chicken aside with the other chicken.

Add the green pepper and onions to the pan and cook them until the onions start to caramelize. Add the spices and stir for a few moments. Then add the tomatoes, raisins, currants, lemon juice, sugar, garlic, chicken stock, and chicken. Cover and simmer for an hour.

Remove the chicken and vegetables from the pot and allow the sauce to reduce by simmering for 5 to 10 minutes, stirring occasionally. Meanwhile, shred the chicken with two forks. Return the shredded chicken and vegetables to the pot. Remove the pot from the heat and let it cool.

Measure the amount you will dry and write the measurement on a sticky note. Place the meal on lined dehydrator trays and dry for 7 to 10 hours. Put the basmati rice in a large ziplock bag. Package the chicken mixture in a medium ziplock freezer bag and put that in a larger bag of rice. Don't forget to include instructions for cooking the rice and the sticky note.

A handful of flour

4 tablespoons butter

1½ pounds boneless chicken thighs

1 green pepper, chopped

2 medium onions, chopped

½ teaspoon thyme

¼ teaspoon ground cloves

¼ teaspoon cracked peppercorns

½ teaspoon cinnamon

⅛ teaspoon nutmeg

½ teaspoon kosher salt

2 cups canned, diced tomatoes

¼ cup golden raisins

½ cup dried currants

3 tablespoons lemon juice

1½ tablespoons demerara or raw sugar

3 cloves garlic, minced

⅔ cup chicken stock

1 cup basmati rice (uncooked measurement)

At Camp

Add enough boiling water to the curry mixture in a pot to equal the measurement on the sticky note. Be sure to account for and add your dried ingredients to the rehydration container prior to adding the water. You can always add more water if you need to. Allow it to rehydrate for an hour in a pot cozy. Add more water when it's almost finished if necessary.

When the chicken is fully rehydrated, boil some water in a separate pot for the rice. Cook the rice according to the instructions you brought. Allow the rice to sit a few minutes in the pot while you heat the chicken mixture. Serve the chicken over the rice.

Tips

If the chicken isn't fully rehydrated after an hour, simmer it over medium heat for about 5 minutes to soften it further. You can make instant rice by precooking your basmati rice at home and drying it for 5 to 7 hours. At camp add boiling water to rehydrate it.

To make this vegetarian use vegetable stock in place of the chicken stock and add 2 cups of vegetables such as broccoli and cauliflower and 1 cup of textured vegetable protein, or TVP.

Bruce's Chili con Carne

Dehydration Time: 7–10 hours
Makes 3–4 servings

My brother Bruce was an avid backpacker and loved to play around in the camp kitchen. This was his favorite chili recipe, and he would cook it over the campfire on the late fall camping trips that we shared when I was a kid. I've modified it to make it backpacker friendly. This chili is delicious served with cornbread, biscuits, or toasted tortillas.

AT HOME

Cook the meat in a large pot over medium-high heat until browned. Drain the fat, rinse the meat with boiling water, and return it to the pot. Add the rest of the ingredients, seasoning to taste, and simmer for an hour or more.

Remove the chili from the heat and allow to cool. Measure the chili and write this measurement on a sticky note. Place on lined dehydrator trays and dry for 7 to 10 hours. Place the dried chili in a ziplock freezer bag along with the sticky note.

AT CAMP

Add enough boiling water to the chili mix in a pot to equal the measurement on your sticky note. Do not add the water first or you will have too much liquid. Once the chili has rehydrated you might have to reheat it.

1 pound ground beef

1 small onion, chopped

1¼ cups canned, diced tomatoes

5 ounces or ½ can condensed tomato soup

2 cups canned dark red kidney beans

2 tablespoons chili powder

¼ teaspoon cayenne

Salt and pepper to taste

Bean and Mushroom Chili

1 small onion, chopped

1¼ cups canned, diced tomatoes

5 ounces condensed tomato soup

½ cup black beans

½ cup navy beans

½ cup pinto beans

½ cup assorted mushrooms

1 small green pepper, chopped

2 cups canned dark red kidney beans

2 tablespoons chili powder

1 teaspoon cumin

Salt and pepper to taste

Dehydration Time: 5–8 hours
Makes 3–4 servings

This chili includes four types of beans. Try adding a tablespoon of cocoa powder to enhance the flavors.

AT HOME

Put all of the ingredients in a large pot over medium heat, seasoning to taste. Simmer for an hour or more. Remove from heat and allow to cool.

Measure the chili and write this measurement on a sticky note. Pour onto lined dehydrator trays and dry for 5 to 8 hours. Place the dried chili and the sticky note in a ziplock freezer bag.

AT CAMP

Add enough boiling water to the chili mix in a pot to equal the measurement on your sticky note. Be sure to account for and add your dried ingredients to the rehydration container prior to adding the water. You can always add more water if you need to. Once the chili has rehydrated, you might have to reheat it.

TIP

This chili is delicious served with cornbread, biscuits, or toasted tortillas.

Basic Italian Pesto

Dehydration Time: 5–7 hours
Makes 2–4 servings

I like to make pesto by drying fresh herbs, usually from my garden, because the final product is better. Use it on hot or cold pasta, in a wrap with chicken, on a piece of bread, or in a pita. It also makes a great substitute for pizza sauce.

AT HOME

Preheat oven to 350°F and spread the pine nuts on a non-stick baking sheet. Toast them until golden. Remove them from the oven, let them cool, and roll them up in plastic wrap.

Fill a large bowl with ice water. Put a pot of water on to boil and put the basil and parsley into a fine strainer or sieve. When the water reaches a boil, dunk the sieve into the water for 10 to 15 seconds and then put the strainer full of herbs into the ice water to stop any cooking. Drain well. Place the herbs in a blender with garlic, lemon juice, salt, and pepper. Blend well.

Transfer the mixture onto lined dehydrator trays and dehydrate for 5 to 7 hours. Allow to cool and place the mix in a ziplock bag. Wrap the Parmesan cheese. Put the pine nut bundle into the ziplock bag. Pack the olive oil with any other olive oil that you will take with you on your trip.

AT CAMP

Add ½ part water to 1 part dried mix and allow to rehydrate, adding water a little at a time if necessary. Add ¼ cup of olive oil to the bag, close the bag and knead with your hands until combined. Shave the Parmesan with your knife or cut it into small pieces and crumble with your fingers. Add the cheese and the pine nuts to the bag and mix again, or, if you are having this with pasta, toss the pasta with the pesto and sprinkle the cheese on top.

1 tablespoon pine nuts, lightly toasted

1 ½ cups fresh basil, coarsely chopped

½ cup Italian parsley, coarsely chopped

1 clove garlic, minced

1 teaspoon lemon juice

¼ teaspoon salt

⅛ teaspoon black pepper, freshly ground

1-inch x 1-inch x 3-inch block Parmesan cheese

¼ cup olive oil

Orecchiette with Clams

1 tablespoon lemon juice

¼ cup dry white wine

2 tablespoons butter

2 tablespoons extra virgin olive oil

1-inch x 1-inch x 3-inch block
    Parmesan cheese

1 tablespoon dried parsley

1 clove garlic

½ pound orecchiette or linguini
    (uncooked measurement)

2 pouches (3 ½ ounces each)
    whole baby clams

Salt and pepper to taste

Makes 2–3 servings

Italian for "little ears," orecchiette has a shell-like appearance and holds delicate sauces well. If you cannot find it in your grocery store, you can use baby shells or linguini.

AT HOME

Put the lemon juice and wine in separate small leakproof bottles. Package the butter with the other butter you will take, and do the same with the olive oil. Wrap the cheese. Package the parsley and garlic individually in small pieces of plastic wrap. Put the bottles, parsley and garlic bundles, loose pasta, and clam pouches in a large ziplock freezer bag.

AT CAMP

Chop garlic finely. Shave Parmesan cheese. Set both aside. Boil salted water and cook the pasta until al dente. Drain the water, put the pot in a cozy, and set it aside. In another pot or frying pan, heat 2 tablespoons each of butter and olive oil. Add the garlic and cook for a few moments, over medium heat, being careful not to brown it.

Add ¼ cup white wine and lemon juice. Let simmer for about 5 minutes. Add the clams and parsley and heat through. Season the mixture with salt and pepper to taste. Pour the sauce over the pasta and stir gently to coat. Garnish with shaved Parmesan.

TIP

If you can't find clams in small pouches, use canned clams. If weight is a consideration or you are traveling in an area that bans cans, you can dehydrate the clams. Pour them onto lined dehydrator trays and dry for 5 to 8 hours until they are dried through. Rehydrate at camp by adding as much boiling water as you have dried ingredients and letting it sit for 20 to 30 minutes or until fully rehydrated.

Tomato Basil Sauce

Dehydration Time: 7–10 hours
Makes 6–8 servings

This basic Italian pasta sauce is a great base for many pasta dishes.

AT HOME

Pour olive oil in a large pot over medium heat. Add the onion and garlic and sauté, being careful not to brown the garlic. Add the tomatoes and spices. Simmer the sauce for 2 to 3 hours, until it thickens, stirring occasionally. Let cool slightly.

Measure ⅓ of the sauce and write this measurement on 3 sticky notes. Pour all the sauce lined dehydrator trays, spreading about ¼ inch thick, and dry for 7 to 10 hours. The sauce is done when it is dry and leatherlike. Divide the leather back into 3 portions (2 servings per portion) and package each portion in separate ziplock freezer bags along with your notes.

AT CAMP

Add enough boiling water to the dried sauce to equal the measurement on your note. Be sure to account for and add your dried ingredients to the rehydration container prior to adding the water. You can always add more water if you need to. Once the sauce has rehydrated, reheat and serve over your favorite pasta.

TIP

The day you plan to have the sauce for dinner, start rehydrating it at lunchtime by mixing the leather with cold water in a leakproof container. The sauce will be fully rehydrated at dinnertime.

¼ cup extra virgin olive oil

1 small onion, finely chopped

3 cloves garlic, crushed or minced

1 cup canned, diced tomatoes

5 cups plain canned tomato sauce

1 teaspoon dried sweet basil

1 teaspoon salt

1 teaspoon pepper

1 teaspoon crushed red chilies

Farfalle Arrabbiata with Red Sauce

2 servings dried *Tomato Basil Sauce* (page 143)

1 teaspoon crushed red chillies

Small block Parmesan cheese

2 cups farfalle (bowtie) noodles (uncooked measurement)

Dehydration Time: 7–10 hours
Makes 2–3 servings

Arrabbiata is Italian for "spicy hot." Accordingly, this pasta has a little nip.

AT HOME

Prepare and dehydrate the *Tomato Basil Sauce* according to the instructions on page 143. Package two servings of the dried sauce in a ziplock bag. Wrap the cheese. Wrap the crushed red chillies in plastic wrap. Place the cheese, red pepper, and sauce in a large ziplock freezer bag with the pasta.

AT CAMP

Shave the Parmesan cheese. Add enough boiling water to the dried sauce to equal the measurement on your sticky note. Be sure to account for and add your dried ingredients to the rehydration container prior to adding the water. You can always add more water if you need to.

Boil salted water in a separate pan. Cook the pasta in it and then drain. Place the covered pot with the pasta in a cozy and set aside. Heat the reconstituted sauce in another pot. Pour the sauce on the pasta and garnish with Parmesan shavings.

TIPS

You may substitute penne noodles for the farfalle if you prefer.

If you don't want to make pasta sauce from scratch, dehydrate your favorite store-bought sauce, following the drying instructions in the *Tomato Basil Sauce* recipe on page 143.

Linguini with Red Clam Sauce

Dehydration time: 7–10 hours
Makes 2–3 servings

2 servings dried *Tomato Basil Sauce* (page 143)

½ teaspoon dried lemon zest

2 pouches of whole baby clams (3½ ounces each)

½ pound linguini (uncooked measurement)

Linguini with clams is an Italian classic.

At Home

Prepare and dehydrate the *Tomato Basil Sauce* according to the instructions on page 143. Zest one lemon, spread it on a lined dehydrator tray, and dry for approximately 5 hours. Package 2–3 servings of the sauce in a ziplock bag with ½ teaspoon of the dried lemon zest. Reserve the remaining lemon zest for use in other recipes. Put the loose pasta, clam pouches, and bagged sauce in a large ziplock freezer bag.

At Camp

Add enough boiling water to the dried sauce to equal the measurement on your sticky note. Be sure to account for and add your dried ingredients to the rehydration container prior to adding the water. You can always add more water if you need to. Set the sauce aside to rehydrate for 30 minutes or until fully rehydrated.

Boil salted water in a pot. Cook the pasta and then drain the water. Place the covered pot containing the pasta in a cozy and set aside. Heat the sauce in another pot. Add the clams when the sauce is hot and heat for another minute. Pour the sauce on the pasta.

Tip

If you can't find clams in small pouches, use canned clams. If weight is a consideration or you are traveling in an area that bans cans, you can dehydrate them. To do so, pour the clams onto lined dehydrator trays and dry them for 5 to 8 hours until they are dried through. Rehydrate them at camp by combining equal parts boiling water and dried ingredients.

Ginger Mango Chicken with Cashews

1 tablespoon butter

¼ teaspoon kosher salt

½ teaspoon black pepper, freshly ground

3 boneless, skinless chicken breasts

1 small onion

2 teaspoons fresh ginger, grated

1 clove garlic, minced

½ cup sweet red pepper, cut into thin strips

2 teaspoons red wine vinegar

¼ cup mango chutney

1 tablespoon Dijon mustard

½ cup plain yogurt

1 green onion, chopped

¼ cup salted cashews, chopped

Dehydration Time: 7–10 hours
Makes 3–5 servings

At home I make this recipe with heavy cream, but since that doesn't work so well in the wilderness I use yogurt instead. You could also use sour cream. Serve this with chapati, bannock bread, or rice.

AT HOME

Melt the butter in a large skillet. Season the chicken with salt and pepper. Cook the chicken thoroughly in the skillet, turning once, until brown. Remove the cooked chicken from the pan and set aside. Put the onion, ginger, garlic, and red pepper in the pan. Cook for 1 minute.

Then stir in the red wine vinegar, chutney, mustard, and yogurt. Bring to a boil and then simmer over medium heat until the sauce thickens. Lower the heat and add the chicken and green onion. Season the sauce, to taste, with black pepper. Remove the pan from the heat and allow to cool. Remove the chicken from the sauce and cut it into ¼-inch pieces.

Measure the chicken and sauce and write the combined measurement on a sticky note. Arrange the chicken and sauce separately on lined dehydrator trays and dry for 7 to 10 hours. Wrap the cashews in a piece of plastic wrap. Put the cashew bundle and the dried ingredients in a ziplock freezer bag along with your sticky note.

AT CAMP

Remove the cashew bundle from the ziplock bag. Add enough boiling water to the chicken and sauce mixture to equal the measurement on your sticky note. Be sure to account for and add your dried ingredients to the rehydration container prior to adding the water. You can always add more water if you need to.

Keep the meal in a cozy until it is reconstituted (about an hour or until fully hydrated). If the meat is not completely rehydrated after soaking in the boiling water, simmer it gently over medium-low heat for several minutes. Sprinkle with cashews just before eating.

Tuna with Salsa, Lime, and Pasta

1 ⅓ cups chunky, medium-heat salsa

¼ cup vegetable juice mixture cocktail (such as V8)

1 tablespoon lime juice

2 pouches (3 ounces each) tuna

2 cups smooth penne (uncooked measurement)

Dehydration Time: 7–10 hours
Makes 2–3 servings

Lime complements tuna, and vegetable juice freshens up the flavor. Monterey Jack cheese makes a tasty topping for this pasta dish.

AT HOME

Mix the salsa, vegetable juice, and lime juice together. Measure the amount that you will dehydrate and write this measurement on a sticky note. Spread the salsa mixture on lined dehydrator trays. Dry for 7 to 10 hours or until any chunks are thoroughly dry.

Pour the salsa mixture in a small ziplock freezer bag along with the sticky note. Put the bag with the salsa mixture, pouches of tuna, and pasta in a large ziplock freezer bag.

AT CAMP

Add enough boiling water to the salsa mixture in a pan to equal the measurement on your sticky note. Be sure to account for and add your dried ingredients to the rehydration container prior to adding the water. You can always add more water if you need to. Set the salsa aside for 15 minutes or until fully rehydrated.

Once the salsa is rehydrated, boil salted water in a separate pan. Cook the pasta, drain, and place the covered pot with the pasta in a pot cozy. Heat the salsa mixture and stir in the tuna. Pour the sauce over the pasta, stir, and serve.

Pasta with Italian Sausage and Sweet Peppers

Dehydration Time: 6–10 hours
Makes 2–3 servings

Preparing the sausage for this dish takes a little effort, but it is well worth it.

At Home

Prepare the *Tomato Basil Sauce* according to the instructions on page 143. Remove the Italian sausages from their casings. Fry the sausage on medium heat until it is browned. In the meantime, bring a medium-sized pan of water to a boil. Pour the cooked meat into a metal colander and rinse it with boiling water.

Wipe the cooled frying pan out with a paper towel. Add the sausage back to the pan and fry it again. Rinse the sausage with boiling water one more time. Reseason it with salt, the chopped red peppers, and the crushed chilies. Put the sausage on paper towels to allow any residual fat or water to drain.

Place the sausage and chopped sweet peppers on separate lined dehydrator trays. Dry the peppers for 6 to 8 hours and the sausage for 7 to 10 hours. While the sausage is drying, occasionally pat it dry with paper towels to ensure that the fat is absorbed. The sausage will be the consistency of gravel when dried.

Place the sauce in a large ziplock freezer bag. Put the sausage and peppers in separate ziplock freezer bags and place those bags in with the sauce. Wrap the cheese. Place the sauce and loose pasta in a large ziplock freezer bag.

At Camp

Add just enough boiling water to the sausage and peppers in their separate ziplock freezer bags to cover the dried ingredients. Be very careful not to burn yourself. Add enough boiling water to the dried sauce in a large pot to equal the

2 servings dried *Tomato Basil Sauce* (page 143)

3 Italian hot sausages (about 6 inches long and 1½ inches thick)

¼ teaspoon crushed red chillies

⅛ teaspoon kosher salt

½ cup mixed, sweet peppers, chopped

Small piece of Parmesan cheese (optional)

2 cups fusilli (uncooked measurement)

measurement on your sticky note. Be sure to account for and add your dried ingredients to the rehydration container prior to adding the water. You can always add more water if you need to.

Boil salted water and cook the pasta. Drain the water and place the covered pot containing the pasta in a cozy. Drain any excess liquid from the rehydrated sausage and peppers and add them to the sauce. Heat up the sauce. Pour the heated sauce on the pasta and garnish with Parmesan shavings if desired.

Chai Tea Breakfast Cake
page 48

Cinnamon Walnut Buns
page 47

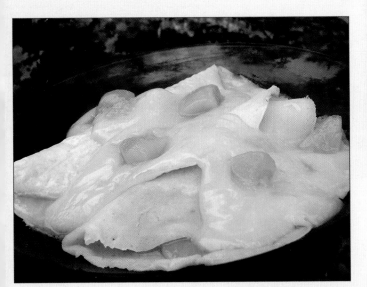

Maple Peach Crepes with Custard
page 41

Monte Cristo
page 251

Chicken and Apple Slaw
page 79

**Sunny Garlic Hummus, before *(top)*
and after *(bottom)* dehydration**
page 82

Water Bottle Sprout Garden
page 91

Lunches

Garbanzo Bean, Tomato, and Thai Chili Salad
page 72

Warm Crab and Artichoke Heart Dip
page 89

Citrus Lentil Salad
page 70

Tropical Salsa
page 98

Dinners

Chipotle Sweet Potatoes
after being dehydrated
page 179

Bruce's Chili con Carne
page 139

Hungarian Goulash
page 124

Steak and Strawberries
with Balsamic Reduction
page 256

Pizza
page 131

Moroccan Chicken with Sweet Potatoes
page 158

Orecchiette with Clams
page 142

Quinoa and Spinach Soup
page 170

Treats and Snacks

Winter Maple Candy
page 244

Chocolate Hazelnut "No Bake" Fudge
page 107

Roslyn Bullas

Nutty Monkey Fry Cookies
page 199

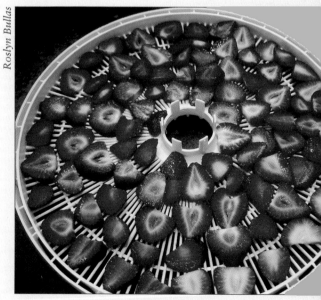

Strawberries arranged on a dehydrator tray
page 14

Baked Goods and Desserts

Basic Yeast Dough stuffed with some dried fruit
page 212

Blueberry-Orange Tea Cake
page 186

Key Lime Pie
page 267

Cinnamon pecan buns made using Basic Yeast Dough
page 212

Box and Reflector Ovens

Setting up a box oven
pages 246–247

Cooking a turkey in a box oven
pages 246–247

Turkey that was baked in a box oven
pages 246–247

A loaf of Basic Yeast Dough
baking in a reflector oven
pages 4 and 212

Pasta Carbonara

Makes 2 servings

This quick and simple recipe is perfect for long days on the trail.

At Home

Package the garlic and parsley separately in plastic wrap. Put the dried onion and egg mix in separate small ziplock bags. Wrap the spaghetti tightly in plastic wrap. Wrap the Parmesan. Put the noodle bundle in a large ziplock freezer bag with the bundles of parsley, egg mix, and dried onion. Leave the bacon bits in their store-bought packaging or wrap them in plastic wrap. Place them in the large ziplock bag as well. Package the oil with other olive oil you are taking.

At Camp

Pour some boiling water in with the dried onion. Then drain it and set it aside. Mince the clove of garlic. Add water to the egg mix, according to the mix's directions and set aside. In a pot or frying pan, sauté the bacon and onion until the bacon is warm and the onion starts to brown. Add the 2 ½ tablespoons olive oil to the pan. Remove it from the heat and pour in the minced garlic. Set the pan aside.

Boil salted water and cook the pasta. While waiting for the pasta to cook, shave or crumble the Parmesan cheese in a separate container. When the pasta is cooked, remove it from the heat and drain the water.

Add the bacon mixture to the pasta in the pot and stir. Immediately add the egg and cheese. Stir quickly to evenly distribute the egg mixture and coat the pasta.

Tip

If you are going to use this recipe a week or more into a trip, substitute ½ teaspoon dried garlic for the garlic clove to avoid spoilage.

1 clove garlic

1 teaspoon parsley

1 teaspoon dried onion

3 tablespoons scrambled egg mix

½ pound spaghetti (uncooked measurement)

1-inch x 1-inch x 3-inch block of Parmesan cheese

½ cup bacon bits or vegetarian "bacon" bits

2½ tablespoons olive oil

Enough water to reconstitute the egg mix

Garlic Shrimp with Orange and Balsamic Sauce

1 tablespoon butter

1½ tablespoons balsamic vinegar

¼ teaspoon kosher salt

½ teaspoon black pepper, freshly ground

1 clove garlic

6 saffron threads

1 medium navel orange

2 pouches (3 ½ ounces each) cooked shrimp

1 cup jasmine rice (uncooked measurement)

Makes 2 servings

My family and I often have this for dinner at home because it takes very little time to prepare and has delicious flavors.

AT HOME

Add the butter to any other butter you are taking. Pour the balsamic vinegar in a small leakproof container. Package the salt and pepper and clove of garlic in separate pieces of plastic wrap. Make another bundle of the saffron threads in plastic wrap. Write down instructions for the rice from the package it came in.

Put the shrimp packets, rice, vinegar, and bundles of saffron, garlic, and salt and pepper in a large ziplock freezer bag. Add the note about the rice. Write a reminder about packing an orange on the outside of the large bag so that you will remember.

AT CAMP

Cut the orange in half crosswise and set one half aside. Use a fork to extract the juice from the remaining half into a bowl. Add the saffron threads. Let this infuse for a few minutes. Use the juice and saffron infusion as part of the liquid requirement for the jasmine rice.

While the rice is cooking, put the 1 tablespoon butter and the salt, pepper, and balsamic vinegar in a frying pan or small pot along with the shrimp. Mince the garlic and add that to shrimp mixture. Using a fork, juice the other half of the orange into the shrimp.

When the rice is cooked, remove the pot from the heat and set it aside in a pot cozy. Warm up the shrimp mixture for 2 or 3 minutes until heated through. Divide the rice into 2 servings and pour half of the sauce over each serving.

Tip

If you can't find shrimp in small pouches, use canned shrimp. If weight is a consideration or you are traveling in an area that bans cans, you can dehydrate them. To do so, pour the shrimp onto lined dehydrator trays and dry for 3 to 8 hours until they are dried through, being careful not to overdry them. To rehydrate the shrimp at camp, combine equal parts boiling water and dried ingredients.

Bean and Corn Tostada

4 10-inch tortillas

1 cup ground beef

¼ teaspoon salt

¼ teaspoon black pepper,
   freshly ground

½ teaspoon cumin

⅛ teaspoon cayenne

1 tablespoon chili powder

¾ cup black beans, drained and
   rinsed

¾ cup canned corn, drained

⅓ cup salsa

½ cup quick-cooking rice

1-inch x 1-inch x 3-inch block
   Monterey Jack cheese

Dehydration Time: 6–10 hours
Makes 2 servings

Mexican-inspired cuisine adapts well for backpacking, but you'll need a plate for this one.

At Home

Stack 4 tortillas, placing a piece of parchment paper between each. Place the stacked tortillas in a large ziplock freezer bag.

If using ground beef, season the meat with salt and pepper. Fry the meat over medium heat until browned. In the meantime, boil some water in a medium-sized saucepan. Pour the cooked meat into a metal colander and rinse it with boiling water.

Wipe out the cooled frying pan with paper towels. Pour the meat back in the frying pan and cook it again. Rinse it a second time with boiling water in a colander. Reseason it with salt and pepper. Spread it on lined dehydrator trays and dry for 7 to 10 hours.

Mix the spices, beans, corn, and salsa together in a large bowl. Measure the mixture and write this measurement on a sticky note. Pour it on lined dehydrator trays and dry for 6 to 8 hours.

Put the rice, dried salsa mix, and beef in separate small ziplock bags. Place those bags in the large bag with the tortillas. Write down instructions for cooking the rice on a piece of paper and include that in the bag along with the sticky note for the salsa mix. Wrap the cheese.

At Camp

Cover the meat with boiling water in a pan and allow it to rehydrate. Add enough boiling water to the salsa mix to equal the measurement on your sticky note. Be sure to account for and add your dried ingredients to the rehydration container prior to adding the water. You can always add more water if you need to. When the meat and salsa are rehydrated, boil salted water in a separate pot and cook the rice according to the instructions you brought.

While the rice is cooking, break or cut the cheese into very small pieces. Remove the rice from the heat and allow it to sit for 5 minutes. Meanwhile, toast each tortilla in your frying pan until crisp. Add the salsa and meat to the pan of rice and mix. Put each toasted tortilla on a plate and then pour ¼ of the mixture on top of each. Top with ¼ of the cheese.

TIPS

Because there are 2 tostadas for each person, it is easier to prepare one for each of you, eat that, and then prepare seconds.

Textured vegetable protein, or TVP, can replace ground beef in this dish. If you omit the meat but don't want to use textured vegetable protein, increase the beans and corn by ¼ cup each.

Baja Chicken with Pinto Beans and Rice

2 teaspoons vegetable oil

4 boneless, skinless chicken thighs

⅓ cup onion, chopped

1 teaspoon chili powder

½ small jalapeño pepper, minced

1 clove garlic, minced

¼ teaspoon oregano

¼ teaspoon cilantro

1 cup canned, diced tomatoes

1 cup canned pinto beans

¼ teaspoon salt

¼ teaspoon pepper

1 cup rice

½ cup tortilla or corn chips

Dehydration Time: 6–10 hours
Makes 2–3 servings

Pinto beans have a mottled appearance and a texture similar to a kidney bean. I was interested to learn that beans related to the pinto bean were found in caves once inhabited by the Ancestral Puebloan (or Anasazi) in the southwestern United States. The beans in these caves were found to be thousands of years old.

AT HOME

Cut the chicken into 1-inch pieces. Pour the oil into a large frying pan over medium heat. Once the oil has warmed up, add the chicken pieces and onion and sauté for 5 minutes or until the chicken browns. Add the chili powder, jalapeño pepper, and garlic. Stir for a minute. Then add the oregano, cilantro, tomatoes, and beans and season with salt and pepper. Bring to a boil, turn down the heat, cover, and let simmer 30 minutes or until the chicken is very tender.

When the meal is finished cooking, allow it to cool. Measure the chicken and sauce separately and write those measurements on a sticky note. Remove the chicken from the pot. Shred it and place it on a lined dehydrator trays to dry for 7 to 10 hours. Spread the sauce on lined dehydrator trays and dry for 6 to 10 hours.

Package the sauce and chicken in separate ziplock freezer bags. Put those bags in a larger bag along with the rice. Be sure to include instructions for cooking the rice and the measurement sticky note. Package the tortilla or corn chips in a small crushproof container or put them in a ziplock freezer bag and wrap the bag in a few paper towels—it doesn't matter if they break.

AT CAMP

Add enough boiling water to the chicken and sauce mix separately to equal the measurements on your sticky note. Be sure to account for and add your dried ingredients to the rehydration container prior to adding the water. You can always add more water if you need to.

Once the chicken and sauce are reconstituted, boil water in a pot and cook the rice according to the note you included in the bag. When the rice is cooked, remove it from the heat and place it in a pot cozy. Mix the chicken and sauce together in a pan and heat it through over medium heat. Serve the rice and top with the sauce and finally the tortilla or corn chips.

TIP

Minus the chips, this dish makes a great wrap filling.

1 tablespoon olive oil

3 boneless, skinless chicken breasts

1 medium sweet potato

1 small onion

1 large carrot

1¼ cups chicken stock

3 fresh plum tomatoes

1 small yellow zucchini

1 small green zucchini

6 dried apricots

1 inch fresh ginger root

1 cup canned chickpeas

2 tablespoons lemon juice

1 tablespoon honey

⅛ teaspoon cayenne pepper

5 saffron threads

¼ teaspoon cinnamon

¼ teaspoon cumin

¼ teaspoon turmeric

Salt and pepper to taste

Moroccan Chicken with Sweet Potatoes

Dehydration Time: 7–10 hours
Makes 4–6 servings

One of my first wilderness cooking students lived in Morocco part of her life and shared some interesting stories with me. Her experiences inspired this dish.

At Home

Cut the chicken into small chunks. Dice the sweet potato, mince the onion, and chop the carrots. Put the olive oil in a heavy pot on medium heat. Add chicken chunks and brown them. Add the sweet potato, onion, and carrot. Then pour in the chicken stock to cover. Let simmer for 30 minutes.

While that is simmering, chop the tomatoes, zucchini, and apricots. Grate the ginger. Drain and rinse the chickpeas. Add all these ingredients, as well as the lemon juice, honey, and seasoning. Let simmer for another 30 minutes. Remove the meal from heat and let cool.

Measure what you will dry and write this measurement on a sticky note. Place the food on lined dehydrator trays and dry for 7 to 10 hours. Put the dried ingredients and the note in a ziplock freezer bag.

At Camp

Add enough boiling water to the chicken mixture in a pot to equal the measurement on your sticky note. Be sure to account for and add your dried ingredients to the rehydration container prior to adding the water. You can always add more water if you need to. Put the pot in a cozy and let sit for at least an hour or until fully rehydrated. When it is fully rehydrated, reheat it. Serve with French bread or pitas, if desired.

TIPS

It is important to allow chicken more time to come back. If the chicken doesn't rehydrate completely soaking in boiling water, simmer it over medium heat for a few minutes before serving.

If you prefer to make this vegetarian, you can substitute vegetable stock and omit the chicken. Then increase the vegetables by 1½ cups or add ¾ cup textured vegetable protein, or TVP.

Minestrone

Dehydration Time: 7–10 hours
Makes 4–6 servings

This hearty and flavorful minestrone has been one of my family's favorites for years. Serve it with a piece of garlic bannock.

AT HOME

In a large pot sauté the pancetta in olive oil until it is crisp. Remove the pancetta and set aside. Pour the onions, carrots, potatoes, and celery in the pot and stir. Cook until the onions are translucent. Add the celery leaves and garlic and sauté for another minute. Add the tomatoes, parsley, rosemary, and cheese rind and let simmer for about 10 minutes.

Add the Swiss chard and 2 cups of the stock. Purée half of the beans with the ½ cup remaining stock in a blender or food processor. Pour into the pot and simmer until the potatoes are cooked. Then add the remaining whole beans to the pot and heat through. Remove the cheese rind and the rosemary sprig. Allow the soup to cool.

Measure the soup and write this measurement on a sticky note. Pour the soup onto lined dehydrator trays and dry for 7 to 10 hours or until no moisture remains. Put the dried soup in a ziplock freezer bag along with the sticky note.

AT CAMP

Add enough boiling water to the soup mix to equal the measurement on your sticky note. Do not add the water first or you will have too much liquid. Once the soup has rehydrated, heat it through and serve. Garnish the soup with some shaved Parmesan.

TIP

To make this vegetarian, simply omit the pancetta.

1 tablespoon olive oil

5 thin slices pancetta, chopped

1 onion, chopped

2 medium carrots, chopped

1 russet potato, peeled and cubed

1 celery stalk, chopped

2 tablespoons celery leaves, chopped

2 garlic cloves, minced

2 cups canned diced tomatoes (with juice)

1 tablespoon parsley

1 sprig fresh rosemary

1-ounce rind of Parmesan cheese

1 pound Swiss chard, stemmed and chopped

2 cups plus ½ cup low-sodium beef or vegetable stock

2 cups cannellini or white kidney beans, drained and rinsed

Salt and pepper to taste

Parmesan cheese (optional)

Cuban Pork Stew

Dehydration Time: 7–12 hours
Makes 2 servings

Cuban cooking is something my family and I enjoy. When I first prepared this stew, I was surprised by how well bananas work in a savory meal—their sweetness contrasts nicely with the spices in this dish.

AT HOME

Remove all visible fat from the tenderloin and cut it into 1-inch pieces. Put the flour in a shallow bowl and add the pork, tossing the meat with your fingers to coat it in the flour. Heat the vegetable oil in a large heavy pot over medium heat. Add the pork and cook for 5 minutes, stirring to brown it on all sides. The flour may stick to the bottom of the pot a little.

Add the onion and green and jalapeño peppers. Cook until the onion starts to become translucent. Add the garlic and cook for another minute or so. Stir in the cumin, chili powder, cilantro, black pepper, juice or wine, chicken stock, and lime juice. Cover and simmer for 5 minutes.

Then add the chopped tomatoes. Bring the stew to a boil. Reduce heat and let simmer for 10 to 15 minutes or until the pork is tender when forked. Remove the stew from the heat and allow it to cool. Remove the pork from the rest of the stew and use two forks to shred it. Return the shredded meat to the sauce and stir well.

Measure the stew and write this measurement on a sticky note. Spread the meal on lined dehydrator trays and dry for 7 to 12 hours. Place the dried mix and note in a ziplock freezer bag. Add the rice and cooking instructions to another ziplock freezer bag. Place the bananas in a ziplock freezer bag. Put the bags containing the bananas and the rice into the one with the stew.

½ pound pork tenderloin

4 tablespoons flour

2 tablespoons vegetable oil

1 small onion, chopped

1 medium green pepper, chopped

1 jalapeño pepper, minced

2 cloves garlic, minced

½ teaspoon cumin

½ teaspoon chili powder

½ teaspoon dried cilantro

¼ teaspoon black pepper

½ cup white grape juice or white wine

1 cup chicken stock

1 tablespoon lime juice

¾ cup freeze-dried banana slices

2 plum tomatoes, peeled and chopped

1 cup rice

Salt to taste

At Camp

Add enough boiling water to the pork mix to equal the measurement on your sticky note and set aside to reconstitute for 30 minutes or until fully rehydrated. Be sure to account for and add your dried ingredients to the rehydration container prior to adding the water. You can always add more water if you need to. While the stew is reconstituting, make the rice and place it in a pot cozy to keep it warm. Then reheat the stew, being careful not to burn it.

Meanwhile, rehydrate the bananas with a little cool water. Mix them into the stew and stir to heat through. Serve the stew with the rice.

Tip

You can substitute a fresh banana cut into chunks or dehydrated banana slices for the freeze-dried banana slices. To make them, let the fresh banana chunks or slices soak in lime juice for about five minutes. Then dry them for 6 to 12 hours. Dehydrated banana slices take longer to rehydrate than freeze-dried bananas do; I recommend using boiling water to help speed up the process.

Harvest Pork and Apple Stew

Dehydration Time: 7–10 hours
Makes 4–6 servings

The inspiration for this stew came to me while my family and I were hiking among the old stone foundations of a hill-side farm and near an abandoned orchard one autumn. Rice or egg noodles are a great accompaniment for this dish.

AT HOME

Cut the meat into 1-inch pieces. Heat the vegetable oil in a large pot over medium heat. Coat the meat chunks in flour and then place them carefully in the pot, being careful not to splash oil on yourself. Brown the pork. Add the onions and celery, cooking until the onions wilt and become translucent.

Add the mushroom soup, honey, mustard, Worcestershire sauce, thyme, apples, mushrooms, apple juice, and pepper. Simmer, uncovered, over low heat for an hour or more until the meat is tender when forked. Remove the pan from the heat and allow the stew to cool. Remove the pork and shred it with two forks.

Measure the stew and write this measurement on a sticky note. Put the pork and sauce on separate lined dehydrator trays and dry for 7 to 10 hours. Place all the dried ingredients in a ziplock freezer bag along with the sticky note. Pack rice or bread if desired.

AT CAMP

Add enough boiling water to the dried stew to equal the measurement on your sticky note. Be sure to account for and add your dried ingredients to the rehydration container prior to adding the water. You can always add more water if you need to. Let the stew rehydrate for 30 to 40 minutes. Add more water if necessary. If the meat does not fully rehydrate, simmer it for about 5 minutes on your camp stove.

TIP

If you prefer, you can cook this meal "At Home" in a slow cooker.

---

1 tablespoon vegetable oil

1 pound pork tenderloin

A handful of flour

1 onion, diced

1 stalk celery, sliced

1 can (10 ounces) condensed golden mushroom soup

1 teaspoon honey

1 tablespoon whole-grain mustard

1 tablespoon Worcestershire sauce

½ teaspoon thyme

2 tart apples, cored, peeled, and diced

¼ cup fresh mushrooms, quartered

⅓ cup apple juice

¼ teaspoon ground white pepper

Rice or bread (optional)

Stew

1 pound stewing beef

Vegetable oil

A handful of all-purpose flour

1 medium onion, chopped

1 cup rutabaga, diced

Enough water to cover the meat
   and vegetables

Red wine (optional)

1 tablespoon dried parsley

1 tablespoon black pepper,
   freshly ground

Salt to taste

4 large carrots, diced

4 medium potatoes, diced

Beef gravy thickener

Dumplings

1 cup all-purpose flour

2 teaspoons baking powder

2 tablespoons instant
   powdered milk

¼ teaspoon salt

½ cup water

Beef Stew with Dumplings

Dehydration Time: 7–10 hours
Makes 4–6 servings

I modified this recipe from an old family favorite. It was one of the first meals I ever dehydrated for a dinner on a backpacking trip.

AT HOME

Cut the beef into ½-inch pieces. Put a little vegetable oil in the bottom of a heavy pot over medium-high heat. Coat the beef pieces in flour and then place them in the pot, being careful not to splash oil on yourself. Brown the beef. Reduce the heat and add the onions to the pot, stirring to mix well. Cover the mixture with water and/or red wine. Add the seasonings and let simmer for 30 minutes.

Add the carrots and rutabaga and let simmer for another 30 minutes. Add the diced potatoes and cook for another 15 minutes or until the potatoes are tender. Add gravy thickener and let cook according to the package directions until the gravy is the desired consistency, adding more thickener as necessary. Remove the pan from the heat and let the mixture cool.

Measure the amount you will dehydrate and write this measurement on a sticky note. Separate the meat from the sauce and vegetables. Arrange the meat, sauce, and vegetables on lined dehydrator trays and dry them for 7 to 10 hours.

Put all of the ingredients and the measurement note into a ziplock freezer bag. Put the dumpling mix in a separate ziplock bag and place that in with the dried stew.

At Camp

In a pot that has a lid, add enough boiling water to the stew mix to equal the measurement on your sticky note. Be sure to account for and add your dried ingredients to the rehydration container prior to adding the water. You can always add more water if you need to. Allow to rehydrate for 30 to 50 minutes or until fully rehydrated. Add ½ cup water to the dumpling mix in the zipper bag.

Put the rehydrated stew on the heat and bring it to a boil. Make sure you have enough liquid in the pot so that it won't boil dry while you make the dumplings. You may want to add a little more water before you add the dumplings so that the stew doesn't become too thick and stick to the pot.

Cut the corner off the ziplock bag so you have about a 2-inch opening. Squeeze several dumplings, each about the size of an egg, onto the top of the stew. Cover the pot and cook undisturbed for 15 minutes on medium-high heat. The dumplings should be moist on the outside but cooked in the center.

Tip

It is important to allow dried meat more time to rehydrate. If your meat dish doesn't rehydrate completely soaking in boiling water, simmer it over medium heat for a few minutes.

African Chicken and Groundnut Stew

1 tablespoon plus 1 tablespoon canola or vegetable oil

2 boneless, skinless chicken breasts

1 onion, chopped

3 small carrots, chopped

2 tablespoons ginger, peeled and chopped

1 small habanero or Scotch bonnet pepper, seeded and chopped

1 bay leaf

½ teaspoon black pepper, freshly ground

⅓ cup peanuts

1 large russet potato, peeled and cubed

½ cup sweet potatoes, peeled and cubed

3 plum tomatoes, seeded and diced

2 cups baby spinach, stemmed

⅓ cup peanut butter

Salt to taste

Dehydration Time: 7–10 hours
Makes 3–4 servings

Groundnuts are also known as peanuts. This recipe is my backpacking version of a West African dish a friend made for me and my husband on a car camping trip many years ago.

AT HOME

Cut the chicken into 1-inch pieces and set aside. Put 1 tablespoon oil in a large, heavy pot and heat on medium. Add the onion, carrots, ginger, hot pepper, bay leaf, and black pepper and sauté until the onions are translucent. Add the chicken and cover with water. Bring to a boil and simmer over medium heat for 20 to 30 minutes.

Remove the stew from the heat and discard the bay leaf. Remove the chicken from the stew, put it in a bowl, and set it aside. Purée the remaining contents of the pot in a blender or food processor and set that aside.

In a frying pan over medium heat, toast the peanuts just until they start to become fragrant and slightly golden. Remove them from the pan and set aside to cool. Add the remaining 1 tablespoon oil to the frying pan. Sauté the russet and sweet potatoes over medium heat for about 12 minutes or until they start to brown. Add the chicken pieces to the frying pan and cook for about 8 minutes, until the chicken is golden.

Remove the chicken and potatoes from heat. Bring the vegetable purée to a boil. Add the chicken, tomatoes, and potatoes. Simmer for 5 minutes. Then add the spinach and stir into the stew until the leaves are wilted. Season the stew with salt to taste. Remove from the heat and allow to cool. Remove the chicken from the stew and use two forks to shred the meat.

Measure the chicken and the purée and write this measurement on a sticky note. Place the chicken and purée on separate lined dehydrator trays and dry for 7 to 10 hours. Put the peanuts in a piece of plastic wrap and place that in a large ziplock freezer bag. Put the peanut butter in a tube, ziplock bag, or leakproof container or add it to other peanut butter that you are taking. Place the dried chicken, purée, and your sticky note in the large ziplock freezer bag.

At Camp

Add enough boiling water to the stew ingredients to equal the measurement on your sticky note. Be sure to account for and add your dried ingredients to the rehydration container prior to adding the water. You can always add more water if you need to.

Once the stew has rehydrated, heat it through. Pour in the peanuts and stir in the peanut butter. Heat for a minute or until all the peanut butter has melted and been incorporated into the stew.

Couscous Primavera

½ cup cherry tomatoes, quartered

1 small green zucchini, chopped

4 garlic cloves, minced

1 carrot, diced

½ sweet red pepper, chopped

1 onion, chopped

2 tablespoons olive oil

Salt and pepper to taste

½ teaspoon thyme

½ cup frozen broccoli florets

¼ cup frozen peas

1 cup instant couscous

1-inch x 1-inch x 3-inch block of Parmesan cheese

1 tablespoon dried parsley

Enough water to make the couscous

Dehydration Time: 6–10 hours
Makes 3–4 servings

This quick and simple couscous has a fresh flavor reminiscent of spring.

AT HOME

Preheat the oven to 400°F. Place the tomatoes, zucchini, garlic, carrot, red pepper, and onion into a baking dish. Drizzle with just enough olive oil to coat the vegetables. Stir and season the mixture with salt, pepper, and thyme. Roast the vegetables for 35 minutes, stirring every 10 to 15 minutes. Remove the pan from the oven when they're done and set aside to cool.

Arrange the roasted vegetables on lined dehydrator trays and dry for 6 to 10 hours. Thaw the frozen broccoli and peas, and dry for 6 to 10 hours on lined dehydrator trays. Place all of the dehydrated vegetables in a ziplock freezer bag and then put the bag into a larger freezer bag along with the couscous. Be sure to include a note with cooking instructions for the couscous.

Wrap the Parmesan cheese. Place the parsley in a piece of plastic wrap and put it in the bag. Package 2 tablespoons of olive oil in with the other olive oil that you are taking.

AT CAMP

Cover the vegetables with boiling water and set in a cozy until they are reconstituted. Once they have rehydrated, drain off any excess water, add 2 tablespoons of olive oil and parsley, and set aside. Boil water and cook the couscous according to the package directions you brought. When the couscous is done, add the vegetables and stir over low temperature until heated through. Garnish with slivers of Parmesan cheese and serve.

TIP

If you eat meat, a pouch of crab or salmon is a welcome addition to this dish.

¾ cup quinoa

2 tablespoons olive or vegetable oil

1 clove garlic, minced

1 small jalapeño pepper, minced

Kosher salt to taste

½ teaspoon black pepper, freshly ground

¾ teaspoon cumin

⅔ cup baby red potatoes, peeled and diced

½ cup carrot, peeled and diced

5 cups vegetable stock

1½ cups frozen corn

3 cups fresh baby spinach

¼ cup lime juice

⅛ cup fresh or 1 teaspoon dried cilantro

½ cup green onions, chopped

½ cup feta cheese (optional)

Quinoa and Spinach Soup

Dehydration Time: 7–12 hours
Makes 4–6 servings

A grain used by the Incas, quinoa (pronounced keen-wa) is often used as an alternative to rice or couscous and is a great source of amino acids. Because it has a bitter coating, you must rinse it very well. This soup reminds me of chowder. You can replace the carrots, corn, and potatoes with other vegetables such as snap peas and parsnips. It's nice garnished with toasted tortilla wedges or pita bread.

AT HOME

Place the quinoa in a fine sieve and rinse for at least 3 minutes to remove the bitter coating. Drain and set aside. Put the oil in a large pot over medium heat. Add the garlic and jalapeño pepper and sauté for a few moments, being careful not to brown the garlic. Add salt, pepper, cumin, potatoes, carrots, and quinoa. Sauté until the quinoa starts to make popping noises. Pour the vegetable stock in the pan and simmer for 12 minutes. Then add the frozen corn and simmer for 5 to 7 minutes more. Add the spinach, lime juice, cilantro, and green onions and cook until the spinach wilts. Crumble the feta and add it to the soup. Remove the soup from the heat and allow it to cool.

Measure the stew and write this measurement on a sticky note. Spread the stew on lined dehydrator trays and dry for 7 to 12 hours or until no moisture remains. Put the soup and the sticky note in a ziplock freezer bag.

AT CAMP

Add enough boiling water to the soup ingredients in a pot to equal the measurement on your sticky note. Be sure to account for and add your dried ingredients to the rehydration container prior to adding the water. You can always add more water if you need to. Let rehydrate for 20 minutes or until fully rehydrated.

Once the soup has rehydrated, heat it through over a stove and serve. If the soup is too thick, add a little more water.

TIPS

Even though there is a jalapeño pepper in this soup, it is not spicy. If you want to make it hotter, add some of the seeds from the pepper or use a bit more pepper.

Feta cheese is usually packed in brine and therefore salty. If you decide to use it in this recipe you may want to reduce the amount of the salt you add accordingly.

Crabby Asparagus and Wild Rice Soup

½ cup fresh asparagus, bottoms removed

1 teaspoon lemon pepper

¼ teaspoon garlic powder or 1 clove fresh garlic

2 teaspoons dried chives

1 low-sodium chicken or vegetable bouillon cube or packet (enough to make 2 cups)

½ cup instant wild rice

1 pouch (3 ½ ounces) premium crabmeat

2 ½ cups water

Salt to taste

Dehydration Time: 3–10 hours
Makes 2 servings

Big on earthy flavor, this soup goes nicely with garlic bannock or another similar accompaniment.

AT HOME

Steam blanch the asparagus over boiling water for 3 minutes. Remove from heat and allow to cool. Then cut the asparagus into 1-inch pieces and place the pieces on dehydrator trays, leaving space between them. Dehydrate for 3 to 10 hours or until completely dry.

Place the asparagus in a large ziplock freezer bag. Package the lemon pepper, garlic powder, and chives together. Place the spice bundle and a chicken bouillon cube in the bag. Put the wild rice in another small bag and add that to the larger bag. Add the pouches or bag of dehydrated crab to the larger bag.

AT CAMP

Cover the pieces of asparagus with boiling water and set the pot in a cozy for about 15 to 20 minutes until the vegetable chunks have reconstituted. After the asparagus has rehydrated, drain off any excess water and set it aside. Bring 2 ½ cups of water to a boil. Add the chicken bouillon and stir until dissolved. Add the seasonings, garlic (minced if using fresh), chives, and wild rice. Simmer until the wild rice is cooked (about 10 minutes). Add the asparagus and crab and heat through.

Tip

If you can't find crabmeat in small pouches, use canned crab. If weight is a consideration or you are traveling in an area that bans cans, you can dehydrate the meat. To do so, pour the crabmeat onto lined dehydrator trays and dry for 5 to 8 hours until the lumps are dried through. Rehydrate at camp by combining equal parts boiling water and dried meat.

Thai Pumpkin Soup

Dehydration Time: 6–10 hours
Makes 2–3 servings

1 tablespoon vegetable oil

1 clove garlic, minced

2 teaspoons fresh ginger, minced

2 cups low-sodium vegetable or
  chicken stock

14-ounce can stewed pumpkin

2 tablespoons Sriracha chili sauce

2 ½ tablespoons coconut powder

Juice and zest of 1 lime

Salt and pepper to taste

1½ tablespoons fresh cilantro,
  chopped

1 pouch (3 ½ ounces) small
  shrimp (optional)

I found traditional pumpkin soup lacking something until I married it with the flavors of Thailand. This recipe uses Sriracha, pronounced see-RAH-cha, *a spicy chili sauce from Thailand.*

At Home

Heat the vegetable oil in a large pot over medium heat. Add the chopped garlic and ginger and sauté for about 30 seconds. Add the vegetable stock, pumpkin, Sriracha chili sauce, coconut powder, lime juice, lime zest, salt, and pepper. Stir well to combine, and cook over medium heat for 20 minutes, stirring occasionally. Add the cilantro and heat for a few more minutes. Remove from heat and allow the mixture to cool.

Measure the soup and write this measurement on a sticky note. Spread the soup evenly on lined dehydrator trays and dry for 6 to 10 hours. Put the soup, pouches of shrimp, and your note in a ziplock freezer bag.

At Camp

Add enough boiling water to the dried soup in a pot to equal the measurement on your sticky note. Be sure to account for and add your dried ingredients to the rehydration container prior to adding the water. You can always add more water if you need to. Once the soup has rehydrated, heat it through over a stove. Add shrimp if desired.

Tip

If you can't find shrimp in small pouches, use canned shrimp. If weight is a consideration or you are traveling in an area that bans cans, then you can dehydrate them. To do so, pour the shrimp onto lined dehydrator trays, and dry for 3 to 8 hours until they are dried through, being careful not to overdry them. Rehydrate at camp by combining equal parts boiling water and dried ingredients.

Smoked Salmon and Corn Chowder

Makes 2 servings

This is my twist on clam chowder. If you can't find smoked salmon in small pouches, use red sockeye salmon.

AT HOME

Place the corn in a ziplock freezer bag. Combine the chives, potato flakes, parsley, thyme, milk powder, lemon pepper, dill weed, and salt and place in a medium ziplock freezer bag with a copy of the "At Camp" instructions. Add a pouch of smoked salmon and the package of corn to the freezer bag of dry ingredients.

AT CAMP

Put 2 ½–2 ¾ cups of water in a pot to boil. Use the smaller amount of water for a thicker soup. When the water comes to a boil, add the corn and salmon and let simmer for a few minutes. Shut off the heat and add the bag of dry ingredients. Stir for a few moments. Add more water if necessary to reach the desired consistency.

½ cup freeze-dried corn

1 tablespoon dried chives

⅔ cup instant potato flakes

½ teaspoon dried parsley

¼ teaspoon dried thyme

⅓ cup nonfat powdered milk

½ teaspoon lemon pepper

¼ teaspoon dill weed, chopped

½ teaspoon salt

1 small pouch (4 ounces) smoked salmon

2 ½–2 ¾ cups water

Baked Clam Chowder

2–3 slices multigrain bread

2 servings powdered scrambled egg mix

½ teaspoon seafood seasoning

¼ teaspoon black pepper, freshly ground

⅓ cup nonfat powdered milk

½ cup freeze-dried, mixed vegetables (carrots, corn, peas, bell peppers, and tomatoes)

1 pouch (3½ ounces) whole baby clams

1 cup water

Makes 2 servings

Similar to a strata, this dish really does taste like chowder.

At Home

Package the bread in a large ziplock freezer bag. In a small ziplock freezer bag, mix the egg powder, spices, and powdered milk and place in the larger bag. Put the freeze-dried, mixed vegetables in a small ziplock freezer bag. Put this and the pouch of clams in the larger bag with the bread.

At Camp

Add a little hot water to the bag of freeze-dried vegetables and allow them to rehydrate for a few minutes while you prepare the other ingredients. Cut or tear the bread into 1-inch pieces. Put the bread chunks into a pot. Add 1 cup of water to the bag containing the powdered ingredients and mix well. Drain the rehydrated vegetables and add to the bread. Add the clams to the bread and vegetables and mix gently. Pour the liquid ingredients on top of the bread mixture.

Bake in an Outback or reflector oven for 30 minutes or until a toothpick or knife inserted in the center comes out clean. Allow the oven to preheat, with the food in it, for about 5 minutes before you start timing. An Outback Oven should be set on "Upper Bake," and a reflector oven should be quite hot.

Tips

If you are using an Outback Oven, lining the pot or pan with parchment paper will make cleanup easier.

If you can't find clams in small pouches, use canned clams. If weight is a consideration or you are traveling in an area that bans cans, you can dehydrate them. To do so, pour the clams onto lined dehydrator trays and dry for 5 to 8 hours until they are dried through. Rehydrate at camp by combining equal parts boiling water and dried ingredients.

Vegetable Crisp

Dehydration Time: 6–10 hours
Makes 2–4 servings

You can use any vegetable combination that you like in this twist on what is usually a dessert made with apples. I often make it with carrots, turnips, onions, broccoli, and red potatoes.

AT HOME

Preheat the oven to 400°F. Chop the vegetables into small pieces and toss them in oil. Season with salt and pepper to taste. Pour them in a shallow pan. Roast them in a shallow pan for 40 to 50 minutes or until they start to become golden, stirring them every 10 or 15 minutes. Remove the pan from the oven and let them cool.

Spread the vegetables on lined dehydrator trays and dry for 6 to 10 hours. Put the vegetables in a large ziplock freezer bag. Put the herbs in plastic wrap and put the herb package, salt, flour, and oats in a small ziplock bag. Put the small bag in the vegetable bag. Add the butter to any other butter that you are taking. If you are taking cheese, wrap it and carry it separately.

AT CAMP

Cover the vegetables with boiling water in a pot and rest in a pot cozy until reconstituted. Drain off any excess water and place the rehydrated vegetables back in the pot. Add the herbs and 2 tablespoons butter to the ziplock bag containing the flour, salt, and oats. Mix together in the bag until you have a crumbly topping mix. Add shaved Parmesan if desired. Sprinkle the topping on the vegetables.

Bake in an Outback or reflector oven for 30 minutes or until the top is golden. Allow the oven to preheat, with the food in it, for about 5 minutes before you start timing. Cool slightly and serve.

2 ½ cups roasted vegetables

2 tablespoons canola oil

Salt and pepper to taste

¼ teaspoon rubbed sage

½ teaspoon thyme

½ teaspoon kosher salt

¼ cup flour

¾ cup large flake rolled oats

2 tablespoons butter

Parmesan cheese (optional)

TIP

If you are using an Outback Oven, line the bottom and sides of the pan or pot with a single piece of parchment paper; it will make cleanup much easier.

Chipotle Sweet Potatoes

Dehydration Time: 8–10 hours
Makes 2 servings

Sweet potatoes are packed with nutrition and flavor. These can be accented with a little sprinkle of cinnamon before serving.

At Home

Place the potatoes in a pot of water and bring to a boil. Simmer until the potatoes are tender when forked, about 15 to 20 minutes. Drain the water and pour the potatoes back into the pot. Add the sour cream and lime juice and zest. Mash the potato mixture. Add the chipotle peppers, adobo sauce, salt, pepper, brown sugar, and mix well. Spread the sweet potato mixture on lined dehydrator trays and dry for 8 to 10 hours. When it is dry, it will be leathery.

Break the dried mixture into small pieces by hand and run it through a blender or coffee grinder until it has broken up into small flakes. Package the sweet potatoes in a ziplock freezer bag. Store the sweet potatoes in the freezer until your trip. Add 2 tablespoons of butter to any other butter you are taking. Pack some cinnamon in plastic wrap if you plan to use it, and add it to the freezer bag of potatoes before you leave.

At Camp

Add equal amounts of potato flakes and boiling water in a pot and let reconstitute for 10 to 15 minutes or until fully rehydrated. Add 2 tablespoons of butter and stir. Sprinkle with cinnamon if desired.

Tips

This dish can be eaten on its own but is great with chicken or pork.

To make this recipe into a soup, add a cup of chicken stock or milk made from nonfat powder.

2 medium sweet potatoes, peeled and cubed

¼ cup low-fat sour cream

1 tablespoon fresh lime juice

1 teaspoon lime zest

1 canned chipotle pepper, chopped

½ teaspoon adobo sauce from the can of peppers

½ teaspoon kosher salt

½ teaspoon black pepper, freshly ground

¼ cup light brown sugar

2 tablespoons butter

⅛ teaspoon cinnamon (optional)

Chapter 9
Desserts and Baked Goods

There is nothing better than enjoying the calm of early evening with a decadent dessert or topping off your favorite meal with a light and fruity offering. Whipping up a special dessert for your campmate's birthday or anniversary is a wonderful thing to be able to do. Also after seven or eight days in the wild, it is nice to have some baked goods. Here are some of the things you need to consider when it comes to desserts and baked goods:

- Type of travel (backpacking, hiking, paddling, or portaging)
- Time of year and weather
- Length of trip
- Fuel consumption
- Baking methods
- No-bake options
- Weight
- Dinner meal (you won't want a heavy dessert if you just had a huge meal)
- Altitude, which can affect baking times
- Size of group

Recipe Modification

Most people are surprised at how easy it is to modify their favorite recipes for backpacking and paddling. Of course some recipes modify better than others but with a little imagination and the following tips you'll be making things you hadn't thought possible before. When you experiment, be sure to try your creations at home first. You do not want to end up with a botched meal or dessert when you are on a trip.

You can easily substitute powdered eggs for fresh eggs or powdered milk for fresh milk in baking and replace fresh fruit with dried fruit. You can safely carry oil, shortening, or margarine for baking—just make sure that, if you are using margarine, you choose the solid kind because soft margarines contain too much water for baking.

You can easily modify prepackaged fare from the grocery store. Look for cake mixes that make only one layer; they generally come in pouches rather than boxes. Use powdered eggs in place of the fresh eggs, and bring a little butter and icing sugar to make a yummy cake. You can even add ingredients to the batter to jazz it up a little, for example, some black walnuts and white chocolate pieces. Commercial muffin mixes work well, too.

You can use commercial pizza dough mix, cornbread mix, or biscuit mix. I prefer to make my own though. The *Basic Biscuit* recipe in this chapter is a good example. Use the recipe as a basic dough and add anything you like. To make it savory, for instance, add some cheese, olives, or herbs. To make it sweet, add a teaspoon of sugar to the dry ingredients and add some raisins. If you use water instead of milk in biscuits, it will make them a little lighter and less rich.

Baking Methods

My preference for a camp oven is the Outback Oven because it works with my pot set and stove so I do not need to count on a fire. Be sure to use the riser; your food will burn in seconds without it. My second choice is a reflector oven. If you do a web search, you can find building instructions and other information about reflector ovens. Here are two links to get you started: www. waterwalker.ca/oven.html and www.blazingpaddles.ca/outdoor_cooking/reflector. If you don't want to make your own, Sproul's of Maine sells ready-made reflector ovens at www.campfirecookware.com. A Dutch oven is just too weighty, and the BakePacker essentially steam bakes food and so does not create that lovely golden crust on baked goods. Fry-baking is also a good method but does not work for all recipes.

It is important to use parchment paper when baking in a pot that is not the nonstick variety. It makes cleanup much simpler and makes it easier to remove your baked goods from the pan.

Simple aluminum foil pouches are good for baking some items. For example, to make a baked apple, core the fruit, fill the hole with cinnamon and brown sugar, wrap it in foil, and place it over the hot coals.

A ziplock freezer bag works great for mixing ingredients. This method is especially useful if you are using dough, which requires kneading. You can keep the dough warm on colder days by setting it close to the fire (but not close enough to melt the bag) or by putting it inside your jacket.

Baked and Fried Desserts

Fried desserts are generally higher in fat and need careful attention to prevent burning. Frying dessert is faster sometimes than baking can be and is a great way to make cookies, brownies, dessert tortillas, crepes, dessert pizza, and biscuit-based desserts. Fry-baking does not work so well, however, for pies or for some cakes. For fry-baking, you need a frying pan with a lid, preferably a nonstick pan.

Baking generally requires a longer time frame, extra equipment, and a little more fuel than frying but is more versatile. You can cook cobblers, cakes, pies, muffins, brownies, buns, biscuits—the list goes on as far as your imagination can take you. Baking, in my opinion, is an essential luxury.

Uncooked Desserts

When it comes to uncooked desserts, most people probably think of chocolate or fresh fruit, but there are many more possibilities. Puddings and mousses are easy to make in a wide-mouth Nalgene bottle. They will not be quite as thick as they would be if you made them at home and chilled them in a refrigerator, but they will be thick enough and have a good flavor. You can make dessert bars at home and bring them or buy a no-bake cheesecake from the grocery store to have on a trip. Pancakes left over from breakfast can be sprinkled with lemon juice and icing sugar or spread with jam. You can even make yogurt in a stainless steel thermos; see the breakfast section for instructions on making trail yogurt (page 65).

Baking Times

All baking times are approximate and vary, based on several factors including altitude, weather, heat source, cooking vessel, and size. Check items at the earliest suggested time to avoid overbaking or burning your food.

Caramel Apple Tortillas

1 teaspoon brown sugar

⅛ teaspoon cinnamon

2 small flour tortillas

6 bite-size caramel squares

1 fresh apple or ¼ cup dried
   apple slices

1 tablespoon butter

Makes 2 servings

This recipe came from digging in the food pack to see what I could make during a heavy rainstorm. Using a fresh or commercially prepared dried apple eliminates the need for a dehydrator.

At Home

Mix the brown sugar and cinnamon together, and pour it in a small ziplock bag. Put a sheet of parchment paper between the tortillas, and place them in a large ziplock freezer bag with the caramels. Put the bag with the sugar and cinnamon in the large bag and pack a fresh apple in a paper bag or some dried apple slices in a small ziplock bag. Pack the butter with any other butter you are taking on your trip.

At Camp

If you're using dried apples, pour a little boiling water over them. Let them sit until rehydrated and then drain. If using a fresh apple, cut it into thin slices.

Line your frying pan with parchment paper. Butter one side of a tortilla and place it butter side down on top of the parchment paper. Cover the tortilla with a single layer of thinly sliced apple. If you are using a fresh apple, nibble on the leftover apple with your campmates.

Unwrap the caramels and cut them into smaller pieces. Place the pieces randomly on top of the sliced apples. Butter the other tortilla and place it butter side up on top of the apples and caramels. Sprinkle the tortillas with cinnamon-sugar mixture. Put the pan on your stove with a moderately low flame and cover with a lid or foil.

Fry-bake until the apples are soft and the caramels are gooey. Slide out of the pan and onto a plate. Allow to cool slightly before cutting. Cut and serve the dessert on a plate because it can be a little gooey.

Peach Gingersnap Cake

Makes 3–4 servings

I adapted this recipe from one of my favorite childhood treats, my mom's hot water gingerbread. The peaches pair nicely with the spice, and using commercially prepared dried peaches eliminates the need for a dehydrator. A dollop of vanilla pudding is a delicious topping for this dessert.

At Home

Package the powdered egg in a small ziplock bag. Combine the remaining dry ingredients and pour them in another ziplock bag. Pour molasses in a small leakproof jar. Put the peaches slices into another freezer bag. Place the freezer bags and the jar of molasses in a larger ziplock bag. Pack the butter with the other butter you are taking on your trip.

At Camp

Chop the peaches into pieces and put them in a little boiling water. Let them sit until they're rehydrated and then drain. Meanwhile cream ⅛ cup of butter and ⅛ cup of sugar together. In a separate cup or bowl, mix the powdered egg and 1 tablespoon of water, stirring until all the lumps are gone. Add the egg and molasses to the butter mixture and then beat until well combined.

Give the dried ingredients in the ziplock bag a good stir and then add them to the butter mixture. Stir until combined. Slowly add ¼ cup hot water while stirring. When well combined add the drained peaches.

Line the bottom and sides of a pot or pan with parchment paper. Pour the batter in the pan. Bake for 25 to 35 minutes or until a toothpick or knife inserted in the center comes out clean. Let cool slightly before serving.

Tip

If you have leftovers, wrap them and eat them for breakfast the next day.

1 tablespoon powdered egg

⅛ cup white sugar

1 tablespoon water

½ cup all-purpose flour

½ teaspoon baking soda

⅛ teaspoon salt

¼ teaspoon ginger

⅛ teaspoon ground cloves

¼ teaspoon cinnamon

¼ cup dark molasses

½ cup dried peach slices

⅛ cup butter, softened

¼ cup hot water

Blueberry-Orange Tea Cake

Makes 3–4 servings

I've always loved the summery taste of blueberries. My family often hikes in areas that have a plethora of wild blueberries, but we like to leave the berries for the wildlife. Buying dried blueberries means that you won't have to dehydrate anything for this recipe.

Cake
½ cup all-purpose flour

¼ cup white sugar

¾ teaspoon baking powder

½ teaspoon salt

1 ½ tablespoons powdered egg

⅛ cup vegetable oil

1 fresh orange

2 tablespoons water

Topping
½ cup dried blueberries

¼ cup white sugar

AT HOME

Combine the flour, sugar, baking powder, and salt. Pour the mixture in a ziplock bag. Put the dried blueberries and sugar for the topping in another ziplock bag and place that in the bag with the dry ingredients. Put the powdered egg in a small ziplock bag, and put that bag in the bag of dry ingredients. Pack an orange and add the oil to what you are taking on your trip.

AT CAMP

Rehydrate the blueberries in a little boiling water. Let sit until rehydrated and then drain and set aside. In a small pot or large ziplock freezer bag, mix the powdered egg and 2 tablespoons of water, stirring until all the lumps are gone. Add ⅛ cup oil to the egg mixture. Juice the orange using a fork and add ¼ cup orange juice to the oil and egg mixture. Stir well.

Slice the orange peel into thin layers, being careful to avoid the pith. Sliver the orange rind and mix it in with the dry ingredients. Add the liquid mix and stir just enough to moisten.

Line the bottom and sides of a pot or pan with parchment paper. Place the blueberries on the parchment paper and sprinkle with sugar. Gently spread the batter on top of the blueberries. Bake for 25 to 35 minutes or until a toothpick or knife inserted in the center comes out clean. Let cool slightly.

Black Currant and Lemon Fry Cake

Makes 4 servings

Who says you need an oven to bake a cake? This spongy white cake has a nice lemon flavor and is simple to make.

AT HOME
Package the lemon zest in a small ziplock bag. Combine the remaining dry ingredients, mix well, and place them in a ziplock freezer bag. Put the black currant jam in a leakproof container, and add the butter to the other butter you are taking on your trip. If your frying pan does not have a lid, pack a piece of aluminum foil big enough to cover the top.

AT CAMP
Add 1 tablespoon of water to the lemon zest, and let soak for 5 minutes. Add the lemon zest mixture and ⅔ cup of water to the bag of dry ingredients. Mix well. Heat 1 tablespoon of butter in a frying pan over low heat. Pour in the batter. Drop the black currant jam by teaspoonfuls on top of the batter. Run a knife or spoon through the jam and batter on the top of the cake so that some of the batter covers the jam.

When the jam is distributed, cover the pan and fry-bake over low flame for 10 to 12 minutes or until the top begins to look dry. Using a spatula, carefully flip the cake in the pan and cook the top for 5 minutes. If you aren't comfortable flipping the cake in this manner, then turn the cake onto a camp plate or the pot lid and slide it, top side down, back into the fry pan.

TIP
Change the flavor of this recipe by substituting marmalade or cherry, peach, or pineapple jam for the black currant jam. Do not use calorie-reduced lemonade powder in this recipe because it gives an undesired result when baked.

1 tablespoon dried lemon zest

1 tablespoon powdered whole egg

1 tablespoon white sugar

1 tablespoon lemonade powder

1 cup all-purpose flour

2 teaspoons baking powder

⅓ cup nonfat powdered milk

⅔ cup, plus 1 tablespoon water

¼ cup black currant jam

1 tablespoon butter

1 package instant chocolate pudding (4-serving size)

1 pouch Dream Whip instant topping

1–2 teaspoons hazelnut-flavored instant coffee granules

⅓ cup instant nonfat powdered milk

2 ¼ cups water

Mocha Moosey Mousse

Makes 2–3 servings

The inspiration for this recipe's name came from my son. One of his favorite camping jokes is to ask "How do you call a moose?" The answer is "Here Moosey Moose!"

AT HOME
Package the pudding, Dream Whip, instant coffee, and milk powder in a ziplock freezer bag.

AT CAMP
Dump the dry ingredients into a wide-mouth Nalgene bottle or a ziplock freezer bag. Add 2–2 ¼ cups water. Close tightly and shake until the mousse is thick. Pour the dessert into camp cups or bowls. Let sit for a few minutes and enjoy.

Pear Berry Crumble

Makes 2–3 servings

A fruit crumble is the most comforting dessert to finish off a long, wet day of hiking. The flavors of pear and berry work very well together in this recipe. Using commercially prepared dried pears and berries eliminates the need for a dehydrator.

At Home

Mix flour and rolled oats together and place in a ziplock bag. Put brown sugar and salt in another smaller ziplock bag. Place 1 tablespoon of white sugar in a piece of plastic wrap and put it inside the brown sugar bag. Put the dried fruit in another bag. Then place all the small bags of ingredients inside the bag containing the flour. Pack the butter with any other butter you are taking on your trip.

At Camp

Cover the fruit with boiling water. Let sit until rehydrated and then drain and set aside. Line the bottom and sides of a pot or pan with parchment paper. Place the rehydrated fruit in the bottom of the pot and sprinkle it with the white sugar.

Add 2 tablespoons butter to the ziplock bag containing the brown sugar mixture, and knead until the sugar mixture and butter are creamed. Blend in flour and rolled oats. Sprinkle over the fruit mixture. Bake for 30 to 40 minutes until the top is golden. Allow to cool slightly and serve.

¼ cup all-purpose flour

¾ cup rolled oats

¼ cup brown sugar

Pinch of salt

1 tablespoon white sugar

1 ½–2 cups dried pears and dried
   berries, mixed

2 tablespoons butter

1 package instant banana cream
    pudding (4-serving size)

1 pouch Dream Whip instant
    topping

⅓ cup instant nonfat
    powdered milk

12 vanilla wafers

½ cup freeze-dried bananas

2 ¼ cups water

Banana Cream Pie

Makes 2–4 servings

*When you make this banana cream pie, don't use the hard
banana chips that you find in most gorp mixtures. Freeze-
dried bananas have more of the texture of a fresh banana
when they are rehydrated.*

AT HOME
Package the pudding, Dream Whip, and milk powder in
a ziplock freezer bag. Place the vanilla wafers in another
ziplock bag. Place the dried bananas in plastic wrap or
another ziplock bag. Put both bags in with the pudding
mixture.

AT CAMP
Add a little water to the freeze-dried bananas and allow
them to rehydrate. Break up the vanilla wafers and place
them in the bottom of a pan or divide among bowls. Dump
the pudding mixture into a wide-mouth Nalgene bottle or
a ziplock freezer bag. Add 2–2 ¼ cups cool water.
    Close tightly and shake until thick. Pour the pudding
mixture over the vanilla wafers. Top with the rehydrated
bananas. Let sit for a few minutes and enjoy.

Chocolate Cashew Pie

Makes 2–4 servings

Salty cashews and chocolate make a great combination.

AT HOME

Package the pudding, Dream Whip, and milk powder in a medium ziplock freezer bag. Place the chocolate wafers in a small ziplock bag. Place the cashews in plastic wrap or another small ziplock bag. Put both bags in with the pudding mixture.

AT CAMP

Break up the chocolate wafers and place them in the bottom of a pan or divide them among bowls. Dump the pudding mixture into a wide-mouth Nalgene bottle or a ziplock freezer bag. Add 2–2¼ cups cool water.

Close tightly and shake until thick. Pour over the chocolate wafers. Top with the cashews. Let sit for a few minutes and enjoy.

1 package instant chocolate or chocolate fudge pudding (4-serving size)

1 pouch Dream Whip instant topping

⅓ cup instant nonfat powdered milk

12 chocolate wafers

¼ cup salted whole cashews

2¼ cups water

Lemon and Blueberry Cream Pie

1 package instant lemon cream pudding (4-serving size)

1 pouch Dream Whip instant topping

⅓ cup instant nonfat powdered milk

6–8 graham crackers

½ cup dried blueberries

2 ¼ cups water

Makes 2–4 servings

This light dessert has a summery tartness.

AT HOME
Package the pudding, Dream Whip, and milk powder in a ziplock freezer bag. Place the graham crackers in another ziplock bag. Place the dried blueberries in plastic wrap or another ziplock bag. Put both bags in with the pudding mixture.

AT CAMP
Add a little hot water to the dried blueberries and allow them to rehydrate. Break up the graham crackers and place them in the bottom of a pan or divide them among the bowls. Pour the pudding mixture into a wide-mouth Nalgene bottle or a ziplock freezer bag. Add 2–2 ¼ cups cool water.

Close tightly and shake until thick. Pour the pudding over the crumbs. Top with the rehydrated blueberries. Let sit for a few minutes and enjoy.

Tastes like S'mores Pie

Makes 2–4 servings

Want s'more? This no-bake pie is great for kids.

AT HOME
Package the pudding, Dream Whip, and milk powder in a ziplock freezer bag. Place the graham crackers in another ziplock bag. Place the marshmallows in plastic wrap or another ziplock bag. Put both bags in with the pudding mixture.

AT CAMP
Break up the graham crackers and place them in the bottom of a pan or divide them among the bowls. Pour the pudding mixture into a wide-mouth Nalgene bottle or a ziplock freezer bag. Add 2–2 ¼ cups cool water.

  Close tightly and shake until thick. Pour the pudding over the graham crackers. Top with the marshmallows. Let sit for a few minutes and enjoy.

TIP
If you prefer to use large marshmallows, toast them before putting them on top of the pie.

1 package instant chocolate pudding (4-serving size)

1 pouch Dream Whip instant topping

⅓ cup instant nonfat powdered milk

6–8 graham crackers

⅓ cup miniature marshmallows

2 ¼ cups water

Backcountry Apple Pie

1 cup, plus ¼ cup all-purpose flour

¼ teaspoon salt

½ cup vegetable shortening

¼ cup brown sugar

¼ teaspoon cinnamon

1 ¼ cups dried apples

2–3 tablespoons water

Makes 3–4 servings

Yes, you can make pastry in the backcountry—all you need is a round water bottle for a rolling pin and a large ziplock freezer bag for rolling out the dough. It isn't messy, and freshly baked pie is a real treat. This recipe is best on a shorter day of hiking or a layover day because it takes some time to bake.

AT HOME

Mix the salt and 1 cup of flour together and place in a large ziplock freezer bag. Put the vegetable shortening in a leak-proof container. Combine the brown sugar and cinnamon in a small bag. Put the additional flour in a small bag. Put the small bags of sugar and flour inside the large bag with the flour mixture. Pack the dried apples.

AT CAMP

Cover the apples with boiling water and let sit for 15 minutes. Drain and set aside. In a large ziplock freezer bag, mix the shortening with the flour using your fingertips until the mixture looks like small beans.

Add 2 to 3 tablespoons of cool water, and mix until the pastry comes together. Do not knead. Form the dough into a ball and put a little of the additional flour in the bag, lightly coating the inside of the bag and the outside of the pastry. Lay the bag on its side and place the pastry ball in the center. Close the bag, being sure to remove as much air as possible. Use your water bottle as a rolling pin to flatten the bagged pastry. When the pastry is rolled out evenly and about ⅛ of an inch thick, cut one side off the bag.

Place a piece of parchment paper in your pot or pan. Turn the pastry over onto the parchment paper and peel off the rest of the ziplock freezer bag. Put the rehydrated apples in the center of the pastry, keeping the fruit about 2½ inches from the edge. Sprinkle with the brown sugar mixture.

Fold the pastry edges up and over the edge of the filling. The crust should extend on top of the filling about 1 inch toward the center of the pasty. Bake for 30 to 40 minutes, until the pastry is cooked and the filling is hot.

Crepe Flambé

Makes 3–4 servings

My family and I had hiked in to a beautiful lake, the sun was getting low and, while we had dinner planned out, we had no plans for dessert. Someone in our group asked me if I could come up with a dessert out of what we had, which wasn't much as we were nearing the end of a trip. The result was an impressive flambé.

AT HOME

Package dry ingredients for the *Basic Crepes* recipe in a ziplock freezer bag. Put the brown sugar in another freezer bag and place that in with the mix. Put the rum or liqueur in a leakproof container and pack the butter with the other butter you are taking on your trip.

AT CAMP

Ensure that you are at least 6 feet away from anything flammable—do not make this recipe under a tarp or near your tent. Make crepes according to instructions from the *Basic Crepes* recipe or use crepes left over from the day before. Slice the crepes into ½-inch-wide strips.

Melt the butter in a pot or frying pan. Add the sugar and cook until it's bubbling. Add the crepe strips and sauté until they start to become crisp and are well coated.

Leave the stove on but take the pan away from the flame and add the rum or liqueur. Put the pan back on the heat and carefully tilt the pan so that the alcohol catches fire. Alternatively turn off the stove and light the pan with a match—either way be very careful. When the flames die out, the crepes will be crispy and rich.

TIP

Premade crepes that will last about a week in a pack are available at some grocery stores.

½ recipe *Basic Crepes* (page 211) or 3–4 leftover crepes

¼ cup brown sugar

2 ounces rum or Grand Marnier

2–3 tablespoons butter

Cobbler

½ cup canned, sliced peaches, drained and chopped

½ cup frozen blackberries

¼ cup white sugar

⅔ cup water

Topping

1 cup all-purpose or unbleached flour

¼ cup brown sugar

¼ cup white sugar

1 teaspoon baking powder

½ teaspoon ginger

¼ teaspoon cinnamon

⅓ cup butter

Blackberry Peach Cobbler

Dehydration Time: 5–15 hours
Makes 2–3 servings

Blackberries and peaches are the highlight of this rich and saucy cobbler. The ginger brings out the flavor of the fruit.

AT HOME

Place the peaches and blackberries on separate lined dehydrator trays. Dry for 5 to 15 hours or until the fruit is leathery and no moisture remains. Package ¼ cup of white sugar with the dried fruit in a small ziplock freezer bag. Mix all the topping ingredients, except the butter, together and place the mixture in a ziplock freezer bag. Add the package of fruit to the bag of topping mix. Add the butter to the other butter that you are taking.

AT CAMP

Boil ⅔ cup of water. Cover the fruit and sugar mixture with the water and allow it to rehydrate for about 30 minutes. Add ⅓ cup butter to the dry ingredients and mix until is crumbly. When the fruit is soft, make sure that you have ⅓ cup of liquid remaining—if you don't, add a little more water.

Put the fruit mixture in a pot that has a lid. Heat the fruit until it starts to boil, stirring frequently. Reduce the heat, but make sure the fruit is still very hot. Put the crumbly mixture on top of the hot fruit. Cover and let cook, without stirring, on very low heat about 10 to 13 minutes, until the topping is cooked. Be sure to keep the heat very low so that the fruit does not boil dry.

Strawberry Chocolate Macaroons

Makes 2–4 servings

This is another one of those accidental recipes that came from the leftovers in my backpack. You could use blueberries, bananas, or raspberries in place of the strawberries.

AT HOME
Package the cookies and strawberries in separate ziplock freezer bags. Put the strawberry bag inside the cookie bag. Put the milk chocolate in a third bag and place that in the cookie bag.

AT CAMP
Add a little water to the strawberries and set them aside to rehydrate. Meanwhile break the cookies up in a pan, and press them down to form a crust.

Boil 1 cup of water and remove it from the heat. Place the freezer bag of chocolate into the hot water, and let it sit until the chocolate has melted. Meanwhile put the strawberries on top of the macaroon crust. Snip a corner off the ziplock bag of chocolate, and squeeze the chocolate on top of the strawberry layer. Allow to sit for several minutes, until the chocolate sets, before eating it.

8–10 chocolate coconut macaroon cookies

⅓ cup freeze-dried strawberries

⅓ cup milk chocolate chips or a 2-ounce milk chocolate bar

White Chocolate Macadamia Nut Cookies

1 cup all-purpose flour

¼ cup dark brown sugar

½ teaspoon baking soda

¼ teaspoon salt

½ cup white chocolate chips

⅓ cup macadamia nuts

5 tablespoons, plus 1 teaspoon vegetable oil

4 tablespoons water

Makes 12 cookies (3 per package)

This is a craveable combination of decadent white chocolate and macadamia nuts.

AT HOME
Combine the flour, brown sugar, baking soda, and salt. Add the white chocolate chips and macadamia nuts. Stir well. Divide into 4 equal parts, and place each part in a ziplock bag. Package the oil with the other vegetable oil you are taking on your trip.

AT CAMP
Combine 1 package of the mix with 1 tablespoon of oil and 1 tablespoon of water. Put an additional teaspoon of oil in a frying pan and heat on a medium-low flame. Divide the batter into thirds and drop the balls of dough into the frying pan. Gently press each cookie down with a spatula.

Cook for about 3 minutes until the bottom browns. Flip and cook the other side. Cool for a few minutes before eating because the chocolate and nuts will be very hot.

Follow these same steps for each of the other 3 bags of cookies when you're ready to eat them.

Nutty Monkey Fry Cookies

Makes 12 cookies (3 per package)

I first made this recipe on a hike with some friends, which paralleled the shores of Georgian Bay in the Great Lakes. The evening was cold, the winds high, and spirits low—that is until we started trying to find a name for this cookie.

At Home

Combine the flour, brown sugar, baking soda, and salt. Add chocolate chips, banana chips, and walnuts. Stir well. Divide into 4 equal parts, and place each part in a ziplock bag. Package the oil with the other vegetable oil you are taking on your trip.

At Camp

Combine 1 package of the mix with 1 tablespoon of oil and 1 tablespoon of water. Put an additional teaspoon of oil in a frying pan and heat on a medium-low flame. Divide the batter into thirds and drop the balls of dough into the frying pan. Gently press each cookie down with a spatula.

Cook for about 3 minutes until the bottom browns. Flip and cook the other side. Cool for a few minutes before eating because the chocolate and nuts will be very hot.

Follow these same steps for each of the other 3 bags of cookies when you're ready to eat them.

1 cup all-purpose flour

¼ cup dark brown sugar

½ teaspoon baking soda

¼ teaspoon salt

½ cup mini-chocolate chips

¼ cup banana chips, crushed

¼ cup chopped walnuts

5 tablespoons, plus 1 teaspoon vegetable oil

4 tablespoons water

Raspberry Almond Cookies

Makes 12 cookies (3 per package)

¾ cup all-purpose flour

¼ cup unsweetened cocoa powder

¼ cup dark brown sugar

½ teaspoon baking soda

¼ teaspoon salt

¼ cup white chocolate chips

¼ cup freeze-dried raspberries

¼ cup sliced almonds

5 tablespoons, plus 1 teaspoon vegetable oil

4 tablespoons water

Raspberries and chocolate are one of my favorite combinations, and they make this fry cookie a delicious treat.

AT HOME

Combine the flour, cocoa, brown sugar, baking soda, and salt. Add the white chocolate chips and sliced almonds. Stir well. Divide into 4 equal parts, and place each part in a ziplock bag. Package the freeze-dried raspberries into 4 snack-sized bags. Place a bag of raspberries in each of the bags of cookie mix. Package the oil with the other vegetable oil you are taking on your trip.

AT CAMP

Put 1 bag of the raspberries in a ziplock bag with some cool water and set aside to rehydrate. Add 1 tablespoon of oil and 1 tablespoon of water to 1 package of the cookie mix. Add the rehydrated raspberries and stir well. Put the additional teaspoon of oil in a frying pan and heat on a medium-low flame. Divide the batter into thirds and drop the balls of dough into the frying pan.

Gently press each cookie down with a spatula. Cook for about 3 minutes until the bottom browns. Flip and cook the other side. Cool for a few minutes before eating as the chocolate and nuts will be very hot.

Follow these same steps for each of the other 3 bags of cookies and raspberries when you're ready to eat them.

Cocoa Mocha Fry Cookies

Makes 12 cookies (3 per package)

This rich cookie goes well with a glass of milk or a cup of coffee.

AT HOME

Combine the flour, cocoa, instant coffee, brown sugar, baking soda, and salt. Add the chocolate chips and hazelnuts. Stir well. Divide into 4 equal parts, and place each of the 4 parts in a ziplock bag. Package the oil with the other vegetable oil you are taking on your trip.

AT CAMP

Combine 1 package of the mix with 1 tablespoon of oil and 1 tablespoon of water. Put an additional teaspoon of oil in a frying pan and heat on a medium-low flame. Divide the batter into thirds and drop the balls of dough into the frying pan.

   Gently press each cookie down with a spatula. Cook for about 3 minutes until the bottom browns. Flip and cook the other side. Cool for a few minutes before eating because the chocolate and nuts will be very hot.

   Follow these same steps for each of the other 3 bags of cookies when you're ready to eat them.

¾ cup all-purpose flour

¼ cup unsweetened cocoa powder

1 teaspoon instant coffee granules

¼ cup dark brown sugar

½ teaspoon baking soda

¼ teaspoon salt

½ cup mini-chocolate chips

¼ cup chopped hazelnuts

5 tablespoons, plus 1 teaspoon vegetable oil

4 tablespoons water

Traditional Anise Biscotti

Makes 14–16 servings

2 ⅓ cups all-purpose flour

2 teaspoons baking powder

¼ cup butter, softened

1 cup granulated sugar

3 eggs

1½ teaspoons anise flavoring or 4–5 drops anise oil

1 egg yolk

Anise is a spice that has the flavor of licorice. The recipe for this hearty Italian cookie came from a family friend named Antoinette. You make these at home before your outing as they travel well in a backpack and freeze well. Use different extracts to change the flavor if you do not like anise. Biscotti are the perfect accompaniment to a hot cup of coffee.

At Home

Preheat the oven to 350°F. Mix the flour and baking powder together in a large bowl. Set aside. Cream the butter and sugar together in a separate large bowl. Stir in the 3 eggs one at a time, and then add the anise. Add the wet ingredients to the dry ingredients. You may have to knead the ingredients together with your hands.

Form the dough into two loaves about 1 ½ inches thick. Beat an egg yolk and brush the top of each loaf with it. Place the loaves on a nonstick baking sheet and bake for 20 to 25 minutes.

Remove from oven and let them cool. While the loaves are still warm, cut each into 1-inch-thick slices. Move your oven rack to the top position and set the oven to broil. Toast the biscotti pieces on both cut sides until they're golden. Allow the cookies to cool. Wrap them tightly in plastic wrap, place them in a ziplock bag, and freeze the cookies until your trip.

Tip

You can replace the anise with almond flavoring and add ¼ cup of sliced almonds to the dry ingredients.

Strawberry Shortcake

Makes 2 servings, plus 2 leftover biscuits

This recipe makes dessert and 2 extra biscuits to wrap up and enjoy with butter and jam the next day. Do not substitute oil or margarine for the butter in this recipe because the dough will not be the right texture.

AT HOME

Put the white sugar in a ziplock freezer bag with the dried strawberries. Sift the remaining dry ingredients once and pour them into a ziplock bag. Package the butter with any other butter that you will take on your trip. Pack a piece of plastic wrap for the leftovers.

AT CAMP

Mix 1 tablespoon of butter and the flour with your fingertips until the mixture the mixture looks like small beans. Add ½ cup of water and mix until you have very soft dough. Do not knead. Divide the dough into fourths. Place the balls of dough in a parchment-lined pan for baking and slightly flatten them. Bake for 20 minutes.

Meanwhile, add ⅓ cup of water to the sugar and strawberries and let sit until strawberries are rehydrated. Add more water if needed. The mixture should be saucy.

When the biscuits are cooked, let them cool slightly. Cut 2 of them in half. Place the bottom half of a biscuit on a plate, and pour some of the strawberry mixture over it. Replace the top of the biscuit and top with more of the strawberry mixture. Repeat for the other biscuit. When the other two biscuits have cooled, wrap them in plastic wrap.

¼ cup white sugar

1 cup freeze-dried strawberries

1 cup all-purpose flour

2 teaspoons baking powder

½ teaspoon salt

¼ cup brown sugar

½ cup water

1 tablespoon butter

Chocolate Fondue

½ cup Toblerone chocolate,
chopped into pieces

A selection of dipping items

Makes 2 servings

It has been said that the way to a person's heart is through their stomach. I made this recipe the first time I went camping with my boyfriend—I guess it worked because he married me.

AT HOME

Cut the Toblerone chocolate into 1-inch chunks with a sharp knife, and place them in a ziplock freezer bag. Package an assortment of items such as pound cake, dried pears, marshmallows, graham crackers, oatmeal cookies, banana chips, dates, fresh orange sections, dried pineapple, dried cherries, or anything else you can think of to dip into the chocolate.

AT CAMP

Use 2 different-size pots; put water in the larger pot along with a couple of rocks and then place the smaller pot inside the first. The rocks keep the pot off of the bottom, which allows space for water underneath and keeps the chocolate from scorching. Heat over a medium flame.

Break up the chocolate in the smaller pot and melt it over the hot water. Turn the stove off when the chocolate is melted. Using a fork, dip your items in the chocolate.

TIP

If you have leftover melted chocolate, pour in some nuts or granola and stir. If the chocolate is still hot, let it cool a little before placing it in a ziplock bag to eat as a snack later in your trip.

Mango Berry Crunch

Dehydration Time: 5–15 hours
Makes 2–3 servings

This warm, comforting dessert also makes a good breakfast.

AT HOME

Place the mango pieces and blackberries on separate lined dehydrator trays. Dry for 5 to 15 hours or until the fruit is leathery and has no moisture. Package the fruit in a ziplock freezer bag. Package the cereal and brown sugar separately in freezer bags, and place them in the bag with the fruit. Add the butter to other butter you are taking on your trip.

AT CAMP

Cover the fruit mixture with ⅔ cup boiling water and allow it to rehydrate for about 30 minutes. Heat 1 tablespoon of butter in a pot or frying pan over medium heat. Add the sugar and stir until combined. Drain the fruit and add it to the sugar mixture. Stir until heated through and then add the cereal. Cook for 1 minute and serve.

½ cup canned or fresh mangoes, chopped

½ cup frozen blackberries

1 cup sturdy flake cereal

⅛ cup brown sugar

1 tablespoon butter

⅓ cup all-purpose flour

¼ cup unsweetened cocoa powder

½ cup vanilla sugar

1½ tablespoons powdered whole egg

½ teaspoon baking powder

¼ teaspoon salt

¼ cup white chocolate chips

¼ cup dark chocolate chips

¼ cup walnuts, finely chopped (optional)

¼ cup dried cherries

⅓ cup butter

Black Forest Brownies

Makes 4 servings

A funny thing happened when I was making these brownies. I accidentally grabbed the dried cherries instead of the raisins—what I call a happy accident. They're like Black Forest cake without whipped cream.

AT HOME
Mix the flour, cocoa, sugar, egg powder, baking powder, and salt together. Add the chocolate chips, nuts, and cherries and stir. Place in a ziplock freezer bag. Add the butter to the other butter that you are taking on your trip.

AT CAMP
Melt ⅓ cup butter in a pot over low heat. Pour the melted butter and 2 tablespoons water into the ziplock freezer bag containing the dried ingredients and mix well. Pour the batter into a pot or pan lined with parchment paper, and bake for 25 to 30 minutes or until the edges are set and dry. Let cool and serve. Wrap any leftovers in plastic wrap for the next day.

Basic Bannock

Makes 4 servings

Many believe that bannock originated with Native cultures, but it was the Scottish who brought this bread to North America. Traditionally, bannock is baked on a stick, but it also cooks well in a frying pan.

At Home

Mix the dry ingredients, and pour them in a ziplock freezer bag. Add the oil to the other vegetable oil that you are taking on your trip.

At Camp

Add enough cold water to the bannock mix to make sticky dough. Cook the dough in a frying pan. When the bottom is golden, flip the bannock to cook the top.

If your pan is smaller than 9 inches in diameter, divide the dough in half and cook half at a time. You want the bannock to be about ½ inch thick before cooking. Allow to cool. Wrap any leftovers in parchment paper, and store them in a ziplock freezer bag.

Tips

Bannock is good to dip in soups or stews and also makes great sandwiches.

Add a tablespoon of sugar and dried fruit to the dry ingredients for a sweet bannock.

Add roasted garlic powder to some butter and use the bannock as a base for garlic bread.

1 cup all-purpose flour

1 tablespoon baking powder

⅛ teaspoon salt

1–2 tablespoons vegetable oil

Chapati

1 cup unbleached all-purpose flour

½ teaspoon salt

2 tablespoons vegetable oil

Makes 4 servings

A traditional unleavened bread common in India, chapati accompanies curry dishes, soups, stews, dal, and hummus well.

At Home

Mix the salt and flour together, and pour it in a ziplock freezer bag. Pack the oil with any other vegetable oil that you are taking on your trip.

At Camp

Add water to the contents of the freezer bag a little at a time to make a thick dough. Add 1 tablespoon of vegetable oil, and knead the dough through the bag, with the zipper open, for a few minutes. Close the bag and let the dough sit for 30 minutes to rest.

Divide the dough into 4 balls. Flatten each ball between your palms until you have ¼-inch-thick circles. Lightly grease a pan with vegetable oil. Fry the circles of dough in the pan over medium-high heat. Turn them once during cooking. When the bread is golden brown and spotty, it's ready to be eaten.

Cornbread

Makes 2–4 servings

Cornbread accompanies chili or stew well; it's even great for breakfast with a drizzle of honey or topped with berries and maple syrup.

AT HOME
Package the powdered egg and milk powder in separate small ziplock bags or pieces of plastic wrap. Mix the remaining dry ingredients, and pour them into a medium-size ziplock freezer bag. Put the packages of powdered egg and milk powder in the bag of dry ingredients. Pack the butter with the other butter you are taking on your trip.

AT CAMP
Add 2 tablespoons water to the powdered egg and mix well. In a separate bowl add ⅓ cup water to the milk powder and mix well. Then pour the egg into the milk and stir to combine. Melt ¼ cup butter over low heat, and stir it into the milk mixture. Stir the dry ingredients; then add the wet ingredients and combine just until moistened.

   Line your pan or pot with parchment paper and grease the paper with 1 tablespoon butter. Pour the batter into the lined pan, and bake for 20 minutes or until a toothpick or knife inserted in the center comes out clean.

TIP
Make the cornbread even more delicious by adding a little cayenne and cheddar before baking it.

1 ½ tablespoons powdered egg

1 ½ tablespoons nonfat powdered milk (enough to make ⅓ cup milk)

½ cup all-purpose flour

1½ teaspoons baking powder

¼ teaspoon salt

¼ cup white sugar

½ cup yellow cornmeal

⅓ cup, plus 2 tablespoons water

¼ cup, plus 1 tablespoon butter

1 cup all-purpose flour

2 teaspoons baking powder

½ teaspoon salt

½ cup water

1 tablespoon butter or shortening

Basic Biscuits

Makes 6 biscuits

This recipe is a great base for all sorts of dishes. To sweeten the dough, add a few teaspoons of sugar and a handful of raisins or currants. If you want to keep it savory, add your favorite herbs and a little garlic.

AT HOME

Sift the dry ingredients once and place them in a ziplock bag. Package the butter (or shortening) separately, and put it in the ziplock bag with the dry ingredients.

AT CAMP

Mix the butter (or shortening) with the flour mixture using your fingertips until the mixture looks like small beans. Mix in ½ cup of water until you have very soft dough. Do not knead. Shape into 6 biscuits.

Place in a pan lined with parchment paper for baking. Bake for 20 minutes. If you are preparing these in a frying pan, cook until they're golden on the bottom; then flip them and cook until they're done.

TIP

Do not use margarine or oil because it will make the biscuits tough and they will not cook properly.

Basic Crepes

Makes 6 crepes

Crepes are so versatile that they're perfect for breakfast, dessert, or even dinner. If you are making a savory stuffed crepe for dinner, use half the sugar that the recipe calls for.

AT HOME
Combine the dry ingredients, except powdered vegetable shortening, and place it in a ziplock bag. If you're using butter, pack it with the other butter you are taking on your trip. If you're using powdered vegetable shortening, put it in a small bag.

AT CAMP
Add water to the flour mixture and beat with a fork until smooth. Put a little butter or powdered vegetable shortening in a frying pan, coating the bottom. Pour about ¼ cup of the batter into the pan and immediately lift the pan away from the heat. Rotate the pan to make a thin circle. Place the pan back on the heat and cook the crepe until the edges are done. Then flip it and cook the other side until it's golden.

TIP
If you are going on a short trip or plan to have crepes within the first few days of a longer trip, you can make the crepes at home. To keep them for your trip, place the cooled crepes between sheets of waxed paper and then place them in a large ziplock freezer bag. You'll need to use them in the first two or three days.

¼ cup nonfat powdered milk

¾ cup all-purpose flour

¼ teaspoon baking powder

¼ teaspoon salt

1 teaspoon white sugar

1 tablespoon whole powdered egg

1 cup, plus 2 tablespoons water

Butter or powdered vegetable shortening

Basic Yeast Dough

Makes 2–3 servings

This easy yeast dough works well for focaccia, cinnamon buns, herb bread, and pizza.

1 heaping teaspoon (½ envelope) rapid-rise yeast

½ teaspoon salt

1 cup all-purpose flour

½ teaspoon sugar

2 teaspoons vegetable or olive oil

½ cup warm water

AT HOME

If the yeast you buy does not come packaged in an envelope, put it in a small ziplock freezer bag. Mix the flour and salt together, and place it in a ziplock freezer bag. Put the yeast envelope or package into the bag with the flour. Add the sugar and the oil to what you are taking on your trip.

AT CAMP

Put ½ cup warm water in your cup and mix in ½ teaspoon of sugar. Sprinkle the rapid-rise yeast into the water, and let it sit for a minute or two. Pour the liquid ingredients into the dry ingredients and add 2 teaspoons of vegetable or olive oil. (Use olive oil to make pizza or herb bread and vegetable oil to make sweet bread like cinnamon buns.)

Knead for 5 minutes or until the ingredients are well combined and the dough is elastic. Shape it into 6 buns, a loaf, or a pizza crust. Bake for 10 to 15 minutes or until golden.

Herb and Olive Focaccia

Dehydration Time: 5–12 hours
Makes 2–4 servings

Leftover focaccia is a great base for sandwiches.

AT HOME

Place a ziplock freezer bag of the yeast dough mix and its
"At Camp" instructions into a large ziplock freezer bag. Dehydrate the olive pieces for 5 to 12 hours or until thoroughly
dried. Put the onions and garlic in a small ziplock bag, and
place it in the bag with the dough mix. Wrap the rosemary in
plastic wrap, and put it in the bag of dough as well. Pack the
olive oil with the other olive oil that you are taking on your
trip. Pack the salt and pepper with the other salt and pepper
you are taking.

AT CAMP

Add boiling water to the olives and onions in a single Nalgene bottle and let them rehydrate. Drain off any excess
liquid. Prepare the dough, and let rise according to the recipe
directions. If the weather is cold, you can place the ziplock
bag inside your jacket to help the dough rise.

Once the dough has risen, press it into a pot or pan lined
with parchment paper. Drizzle with 1 or 2 teaspoons olive
oil. Sprinkle with rosemary and garlic. Top with onions and
olive pieces. Sprinkle with salt and black pepper to taste.

Place in an Outback or reflector oven, and bake for 10
to 12 minutes after the oven is preheated. Once the bread
has cooked through and is golden, remove the loaf from the
heat. Let it cool for a few minutes before eating so that the
olives do not burn your mouth.

1 recipe *Basic Yeast Dough*
(page 212)

5 olives (whatever variety you
prefer), chopped

1 tablespoon dried onion

½ teaspoon dried roasted garlic

¼ teaspoon dried rosemary

2 teaspoons olive oil

Kosher salt to taste

Chapter 10

BEVERAGES

Staying hydrated is extremely important, especially in the backcountry. While on wilderness trips, however, I often meet people who are not drinking enough fluids and are starting to suffer from the effects of dehydration, which include headache, nausea, muscle cramps, fatigue and loss of coordination. A close friend recently learned that dehydration can happen as easily in winter as it can in the summer heat. On a winter hike we took together, he was wearing snowshoes and a very warm down parka; neglecting to layer his clothing was a big mistake and he started to sweat. He replaced fluids with a thermos of coffee, which did not provide adequate hydration. About halfway through the hike he started to stumble and was complaining of nausea. Thankfully he recognized the signs and asked if I had any electrolyte replacement crystals in my first aid kit—luckily, I did. Had he been alone and unaware of the symptoms of dehydration, the situation could've been much more serious.

Take a variety of hot and cold drinks on longer trips. If it is cool or damp, the hot fare adds a bit of comfort, but on a hot summer afternoon, a cooler drink is better. In areas where the water is brackish, adding a flavoring to it makes it more palatable. On a short hiking or paddling trip where you can take a cooler, freeze juice boxes and use them as your ice source. It is nice to have cold juice after all the food from the cooler has been used. The following are some ideas for hot and cold drinks:

- Tang, served hot or cold
- Hot chocolate
- Cocoa
- Powdered milk
- Lemonade, served hot or cold
- Herbal and fruit teas
- Coffee
- Crystal Light or other drink crystals

- Apple cider
- Jolly Rancher (Drop one hard candy in the bottom of your drinking bottle.)
- Ovaltine mixed with powdered milk, served hot or cold
- Jell-o or other flavored gelatin powder, served hot
- Powdered Gatorade

When making beverages such as coffee or tea, you should consider a few things. The first is how you will brew your coffee or loose tea (tea bags are obviously very convenient). Some people use camping percolators, and others use a kettle. Lexan coffee presses also work well for tea. Most people I have met in my travels use a simple camp pot to boil water and then pour the water into a cup containing the ingredients. For some recipes and larger groups the beverage can be brewed directly in the pot. Some teas, such as green varieties, are brewed in cooler water than what is ideal for black or orange pekoe tea.

If you plan to make a camp pot of coffee or tea, put the ingredients in a cone-style coffee filter, roll down the top, and staple it a few times. Disposable tea filters are readily available and are basically just an unbleached tea bag that you fill yourself. They work well for coffee and come in sizes ranging from a single-serving bag to one big enough for an entire pot. Another method is to use cheesecloth spice bags, which have a little drawstring. If you can't find cheesecloth bags, put your loose tea on a square of cheesecloth, bundle it up, and tie the top closed with a little string.

Hot chocolate, or cocoa, is a nice dessert replacement for wilderness trips. It will also warm you and give you the extra fat you need to stay warm in colder weather.

While having an alcoholic beverage is sometimes nice on a winter trip, indulge with caution as it can give you a false sense of warmth. Remember to consume alcohol in moderation and understand that the effects can be more powerful at higher altitudes.

Water Treatment

Just because a water source looks safe doesn't mean that it is; you'll want to take measures to keep from contracting giardia or other parasites. Some of the several methods available are more effective than others. Boiling your water works well, but you have to allow it to cool and then transfer it from one bottle to another repeatedly to aerate it or it will taste flat. Water filters will not remove viruses, which is not a big concern in North America. Filters are faster than chemical treatments but can be weighty. Filters will also remove some of the other harmless particles floating in the water. Another benefit of filtering water is that you can get water faster while on the trail. With chemical treatment you may have to wait for 30 minutes for the water to be safe for consumption. Chlorine dioxide treatments such as AquaMira and Pristine work by combining two chemicals and letting them soak in the water. Chlorine dioxide kills everything in the water, leaves little aftertaste, and is used in many local water treatment facilities. The water treated with chemicals may have harmless particles floating in it but those will settle during the treatment process. Chemicals can also be less cost-effective than a filter and they also have an expiry date. Iodine may not effectively destroy cryptosporidium parasites and has an awful taste—do not use iodine if you are pregnant.

Mayan Hot Chocolate

⅓ cup unsweetened cocoa powder

⅓ cup Nestlé Nido or other powdered whole milk

1 tablespoon powdered coffee creamer

¼ cup vanilla sugar

⅛ teaspoon cinnamon

⅛ teaspoon crushed red chili pepper

Makes 4 servings

The movie Chocolat *was the inspiration for this drink.*

At Home
Mix the dry ingredients together, and place them in a zip-lock freezer bag.

At Camp
Shake the bag of dry ingredients to ensure they are well combined. Place 4 tablespoons of mix in a cup and carefully fill it with 8 ounces of boiling water. Stir until the ingredients dissolve. Repeat for each desired serving.

Raspberry Hot Chocolate

⅓ cup freeze-dried raspberries

¼ cup nonfat powdered milk

⅔ cup hot cocoa mix

Makes 4 servings

Since freeze-dried fruit can easily be made into a powder, you can replace the raspberries with any freeze-dried fruit you prefer. If you like them, bananas are a great choice.

At Home
Grind the freeze-dried raspberries in a blender or food processor until you have a fine powder. Mix the berry powder with the remaining ingredients, and put it in a ziplock freezer bag.

At Camp
Shake the bag of dry ingredients to ensure they are well combined. Place 5 tablespoons of mix in a cup and carefully fill it with 8 ounces of boiling water. Stir until the ingredients dissolve. Repeat for each desired serving.

Toffee Coffee Hot Chocolate

Makes 4 servings

What could be more decadent than a cup of hot chocolate with a hint of coffee and a topping of Skor?

AT HOME

Mix the hot chocolate powder, powdered milk, and instant coffee together, and place the mixture in a ziplock freezer bag. Wrap the marshmallows and toffee bar separately in plastic wrap, and place both packages in the bag with the powder.

AT CAMP

Remove the marshmallows and the toffee from the bag. Break the toffee into pieces. Shake the bag of dry ingredients to ensure they are well combined. Place 4 tablespoons of mix in a cup and carefully fill it with 8 ounces of boiling water. Stir until the ingredients dissolve. Repeat for each desired serving. Top each cup with ¼ of the marshmallows and ¼ of the toffee pieces.

⅔ cup hot cocoa mix

⅓ cup Nestlé Nido or other powdered whole milk

1 tablespoon instant coffee

½ cup miniature marshmallows

1 2-ounce Skor bar or 2 ounces other chocolate-covered crunchy toffee

Chocolate Mint Hot Chocolate

1 cup (4 servings) hot cocoa mix

4 bite-sized peppermint patties

Makes 4 servings

This craveable recipe is very comforting after a cold hike.

At Home
Put the hot cocoa mix in a ziplock freezer bag. If the peppermint patties are not individually wrapped, then wrap each one in a small piece of plastic wrap and place them in the bag with the mix.

At Camp
Place 4 tablespoons, or 1 serving, of hot cocoa mix and an unwrapped peppermint patty in a cup and carefully fill it with 8 ounces of boiling water. Stir until the ingredients dissolve. Repeat for each desired serving.

Kermode Bear Hot Chocolate

Makes 4 servings

The Kermode bear, also known as the Spirit Bear, is a rare, white subspecies of the North American black bear indigenous to the British Columbia rainforest and Princess Royal Island.

AT HOME

Grind the anise seed and white chocolate in a coffee grinder or blender until the chocolate is in fine pieces. Mix in the powdered milk, and place the powder in a ziplock freezer bag.

AT CAMP

Shake the bag of dry ingredients to ensure they are well combined. Place 3 tablespoons of mix in a cup and carefully fill it with 8 ounces of boiling water. Stir until the ingredients dissolve. Repeat for each desired serving.

TIP

Don't use chocolate chips for this recipe. They tend to clump because they are made to hold their shape, to an extent, when heated.

¼ teaspoon anise seed

⅓ cup white chocolate

½ cup Nestlé Nido or other powdered whole milk

Peanut Butter Cup in a Cup

Makes 4 servings

²/₃ cup hot cocoa mix

¹/₃ cup nonfat powdered milk

4 teaspoons peanut butter

You would almost swear that there is a peanut butter cup in this hot chocolate.

At Home

Mix the dry ingredients together, and place them in a zip-lock freezer bag. Package the peanut butter in a leakproof container or add it to any other peanut butter you are taking.

At Camp

Shake the bag of dry ingredients to ensure they are well combined. Place 4 tablespoons of mix and 1 teaspoon of peanut butter in a cup and carefully fill it with 8 ounces of boiling water. Stir until the ingredients dissolve. Repeat for each desired serving.

Hazelnut Mocha

Makes 4 servings

This recipe is one of those happy accidents. My family and I were at the end of a backpacking trip, the weather was miserable, and we didn't have enough coffee for everyone. So I scrounged through our food and came up with this—it was a real hit!

AT HOME
Mix the dry ingredients together, and place them in a ziplock freezer bag.

AT CAMP
Shake the bag of dry ingredients to ensure they are well combined. Place 4 tablespoons of mix in a cup and carefully fill it with 8 ounces of boiling water. Stir until the ingredients dissolve. Repeat for each desired serving.

⅔ cup hot cocoa mix

⅓ cup Nestlé Nido or other powdered whole milk

1 tablespoon hazelnut-flavored instant coffee

Malted Mocha

4 tablespoons hot cocoa mix

4 tablespoons malted milk powder

¾ cup nonfat powdered milk

4 tablespoons powdered coffee
   creamer

1 tablespoon instant coffee

Makes 4 servings

This drink tastes very much like malted milk balls.

At Home
Mix the dry ingredients together, and place them in a zip-lock freezer bag.

At Camp
Shake the bag of dry ingredients to ensure they are well combined. Place 4 tablespoons of mix in a cup and carefully fill it with 8 ounces of boiling water. Stir until the ingredients dissolve. Repeat for each desired serving

Buttered Rum Mocha

⅔ cup hot cocoa mix

⅓ cup Nestlé Nido or other
   powdered whole milk

1 tablespoon instant coffee

½ teaspoon rum extract

2 teaspoons butter

Makes 4 servings

Rich, decadent, and comforting, this drink is perfect for a rainy day.

At Home
Mix the dry ingredients together with the rum extract, and place them in a ziplock freezer bag. Pack the butter with the other butter you are taking.

At Camp
Shake the bag of dry ingredients to ensure they are well combined. Place 4 tablespoons of mix in a cup and carefully fill it with 8 ounces of boiling water. Stir until the ingredients dissolve. Add ½ teaspoon butter to each cup, and stir until the butter has melted. Repeat for each desired serving.

Caramel au Lait

Makes 4 servings

When I was barely out of kindergarten, my brother Bruce used to take me camping in late November. He would make a drink similar to this for his girlfriend and himself.

AT HOME

Mix the dry ingredients together, and place them in a ziplock freezer bag. Leave the caramels in their wrappers, and place them in the bag with the powder.

AT CAMP

Shake the bag of dry ingredients to ensure they are well combined. Place 4 tablespoons of mix and an unwrapped caramel in a cup and carefully fill it with 8 ounces of boiling water. Stir until the ingredients dissolve. Repeat for each desired serving.

⅓ cup nonfat powdered milk

1 tablespoon powdered coffee creamer

2½ teaspoons instant coffee

4 bite-sized, individually wrapped caramels

Hot Butterscotch

Makes 4 servings

This drink tastes like butterscotch pudding in a mug.

AT HOME

Grind the chips into a powder in a blender or food processor. Put the chips and the powdered milk in a ziplock freezer bag together. Divide the marshmallows into fourths, and wrap each fourth in a piece of plastic wrap. Put those bundles in the bag with the dry ingredients.

AT CAMP

Place 4 tablespoons of mix in a cup and carefully fill it with 8 ounces of boiling water. Stir until the ingredients dissolve, and top with the contents of one of the marshmallow bundles. Repeat for each desired serving.

1 cup butterscotch chips

1 cup nonfat powdered milk

½ cup miniature marshmallows

Chocolate Almond Coffee

Makes 4 servings

This drink tastes like almond biscotti dunked in a cup of hot coffee.

4 tablespoons powdered coffee creamer

4 teaspoons sugar

4 teaspoons instant coffee

8 teaspoons unsweetened cocoa powder

1 teaspoon pure almond extract

AT HOME
Mix the dry ingredients and almond extract together, and place them in a ziplock freezer bag.

AT CAMP
Shake the bag of dry ingredients to ensure they are well combined. Place 4 tablespoons of mix in a cup and carefully fill it with 8 ounces of boiling water. Stir until the ingredients dissolve. Repeat for each desired serving.

Harvest Hot Chocolate

Makes 4 servings

Hot chocolate combined with pumpkin pie spices makes for a soothing cup of decadence.

⅔ cup hot cocoa mix

⅓ cup Nestlé Nido or powdered whole milk

¼ teaspoon ginger

¼ teaspoon cinnamon

AT HOME
Mix the dry ingredients together, and place in a ziplock freezer bag.

AT CAMP
Shake the bag of dry ingredients to ensure they are well combined. Place 4 tablespoons of mix in a cup and carefully fill it with 8 ounces of boiling water. Stir until the ingredients dissolve. Repeat for each desired serving.

Caramel Apple Chai

Makes 2 servings

The spiciness of chai tea works well with the apples and sweet caramels.

AT HOME

Put the powdered milk in a ziplock freezer bag. Measure the loose chai tea and dried apple slices into a cheesecloth bag or tea filter and then place them in a ziplock freezer bag with 3 caramels. Put this bag inside the bag with the powdered milk.

AT CAMP

Unwrap the caramels and put them in a pot with 2 ½ cups water, the tea bag, and the powdered milk. Bring to a simmer over medium-low heat, stirring often so that the milk does not stick. Simmer for 3 to 5 minutes or until the tea is the strength you desire and the caramels have melted.

Remove the cheesecloth bag and divide the tea between 2 camp cups. Sweeten to taste.

½ cup nonfat powdered milk

4 dried apple slices, chopped

2 tablespoons loose chai tea

3 bite-size, individually wrapped caramels

Sweetener, such as sugar or honey, to taste

2 tablespoons vanilla-flavored
instant coffee

1 cup nonfat powdered milk

¼ cup chocolate protein powder

4 teaspoons honey

Backpacker's Power Breakfast

Makes 4 servings

A fast, tasty protein boost to get you started.

AT HOME
Mix the dried ingredients together, and put them in a zip-lock freezer bag. Pack the honey in a leakproof container.

AT CAMP
For each serving mix 5 tablespoons breakfast powder, 1 teaspoon honey, and 1 cup of cool or air temperature water in a leakproof bottle. Shake vigorously until the protein powder is dissolved.

4 single-serving pouches hot apple
cider mix

⅓ cup freeze-dried fruit

Infused Cider

Makes 3–4 servings

This fruity cider is a tasty alternative to iced tea. Try using freeze-dried fruits such as mangoes, peaches, raspberries, strawberries, or even bananas in this recipe. You could even combine several fruits to suit your taste.

AT HOME
Place the pouches of cider mix and freeze-dried fruit into a ziplock freezer bag.

AT CAMP
Put the cider mixture and 8 ounces of water for each pouch of cider in a Nalgene bottle. Close the lid and let the bottle sit in the sun for at least 30 minutes. If it isn't sunny the day that you're making it, use hot water and let the mixture infuse until it cools to air temperature.

Strawberry Lemonade

Makes 4 servings

This very summery and pink drink is made with freeze-dried strawberries.

AT HOME
Grind the freeze-dried strawberries in a blender or food processor until you have a fine powder. Put the lemonade powder in a measuring cup with the freeze-dried strawberry powder. Divide the measurement by 4, and record the single-serving amount on a piece of paper. Put the note and both powders in a ziplock freezer bag.

AT CAMP
Shake the package of dry ingredients to ensure they are well combined. Measure 1 serving of powder into a cup or water bottle. Add 8 to 10 ounces of water, depending on how strong you like your lemonade. Stir or shake and let sit for a few minutes.

⅓ cup freeze-dried strawberries

4 servings instant lemonade powder

¼ teaspoon dried citrus zest

2 or 3 fruit tea bags

Sugar or honey (optional)

Wilderness Sun Tea

Dehydration Time: 5–6 hours
Makes 3–4 servings

Sun tea is very easy to make and is refreshing on a hot day.

AT HOME
Zest a piece of citrus, being careful to cut off only the outer part of the skin and avoid the pith. Dry on a lined dehydrator tray for 5 to 6 hours. Place the dried zest on a small piece of cheesecloth and tie it into a pouch with cotton string. Pack the zest pouch and tea bags in a ziplock freezer bag. Pack the honey or sugar with any other amount that you are taking.

AT CAMP
Place the tea bags, zest bag, and 32 ounces of water in a Nalgene bottle. Close the lid and let the bottle sit in the sun for at least 30 minutes. Sweeten as desired.

TIP
If the tea is too strong, simply add a little more water.

Trail Sangria

Makes 3–4 servings

This drink is a delicious treat for adults on a trip. If you do not drink alcohol or want to make a version appropriate for children, replace the wine with nonalcoholic wine or cranberry juice crystals. Wine will not keep long in the backcountry, so it is best to make this in the first 3 or 4 days.

At Home

Package the berries and lemonade powder together in a ziplock freezer bag. Put the wine in a large leakproof container. Pack the orange and a piece of cheesecloth.

At Camp

Early on the day you plan to have the sangria, slice the orange and add it, peel and all, to the wine or juice made from crystals. Add the freeze-dried berries as well, and close the lid tightly. Let the fruit soak in the wine all day. After you have set up camp for the night, use cheesecloth to strain the sangria into camp mugs.

⅓ cup freeze-dried mixed berries (blueberries, raspberries, and strawberries)

1 tablespoon lemonade powder

2 cups red wine, such as Rioja, Shiraz, or Merlot

1 orange

A piece of cheesecloth

Over 21 Blueberry Tea

Makes 2 servings

2 ounces Grand Marnier liqueur

2 ounces Amaretto liqueur

2 orange pekoe single-serving tea bags or equivalent loose tea with a reusable tea bag

Sugar to taste

Contrary to its name, this tea does not contain any blueberries although it has a similar flavor. This adult tea makes a nice after dinner treat in lieu of dessert.

AT HOME
Put the tea bags in a ziplock freezer bag. Mix the liqueurs together and pack them in a leakproof container. Pack the sugar with any other sugar you are taking.

AT CAMP
Put 1 tea bag or equivalent loose tea in each camp cup. Boil enough water for both cups of tea. When the water reaches a rolling boil, fill each cup with water, leaving enough room for 2 ounces of liqueur in each cup. Let the tea steep for a minute or so and remove the tea bag or leaves. Shake the bottle of liqueur and divide it between the 2 cups. Sweeten with sugar to taste.

Chapter 11
Making Camp Food
Fun for Children

Wilderness travel with children can be a very rewarding experience for everyone involved. One of the keys to a successful trip is food—a good meal can brighten a miserable day. Before you head out with your little ones, you need to consider several things, including the age of the children, nutritional needs, likes and dislikes, ease of preparation, and the fun factor. You should also take the time of year and weather into account.

Because young children are constantly on the go, they have high energy needs to begin with. With camping those needs increase, even more so with a wilderness trip. My husband and I found that our little boy at age 5 ate about a fourth to a third more than he did at home. His appetite also varied as much as it did at home. Some days he would be famished, verging on insatiable, and other days he had little appetite. Kids need good food and a balanced diet, even when camping—be sure to include a variety of fruits and vegetables. Make sure that the foods you bring are something that the children will enjoy because even the best foods won't do them any good if they refuse to eat. If you have a picky child, sneak a few vegetables in by grinding the freeze-dried varieties into a powder and then adding them to a soup or sauce. Grind freeze-dried fruit into a fine powder, and mix it into their drinking water to improve the taste and give them a few more nutrients. Avoid commercially available energy bars and protein powders. They often contain far more vitamins and minerals than a young child needs and have ingredients that aren't suitable for children.

Kids can become dehydrated very quickly especially when they are active—make sure they drink enough water.

Some kid-friendly snack foods include:

- Peanut butter and crackers
- A cored apple stuffed with peanut butter, sunflower seeds, and raisins
- Gorp
- Vegetable chips
- Fresh fruit
- Dried fruit
- Fresh vegetables
- Homemade energy bars
- Granola or cereal bars
- Pumpkin or sunflower seeds
- Baked goods left over from the previous night
- Sesame snaps (made of sesame seeds and honey)
- Fruit leather
- Vegetable leather
- Yogurt leather
- Freeze-dried vegetable snacks
- Freeze-dried fruit snacks
- Snack crackers such as Goldfish cheese crackers

Meal Planning for Families

Meal planning for families isn't much different than planning meals for any other small group. The most important thing is to make sure that children's nutritional needs are being met. To make sure they like the food you plan to pack for them, try the foods at home first. Judging how much food they will eat is difficult—every child is different. Before going on a long wilderness journey, try to go on a weekend trip to help gauge how much they will eat. Try to vary the menu as well so they won't get bored with the food.

Involving your child in the planning process can make the trip more exciting for them. Let them look at the maps with you and play a part in planning and making the food at home and at camp. Take them shopping and talk about the ingredients, which teaches them about the different foods. Little tasks can help build a child's self-esteem and build life skills. Examples include dipping the apples in lemon juice and putting the fruit on the trays for drying. Measuring the ingredients for dry mixes can make a great math lesson, and most children like to use measuring spoons and cups. You could even buy them their own set of measuring spoons. Making foods like granola bars and wrapping them up together in waxed paper can be a fun activity. Your child can help you make gorp for the group; it's even more enjoyable to let them go wild and make their own bag of gorp or pick one treat for the group for the trip. Even just helping you pack the dried foods into ziplock bags can make them feel proud.

At camp children can help by shaking the pudding at camp or stirring ingredients that aren't on a camp stove. If you make pizza, let them add the toppings. Children can also help with dishes and camp kitchen cleanup. To make camp food fun, you can do things like drop a Jolly Rancher or a gummy worm into a bottle of water for a sweet treat. Maybe you could make up a gross name for a food that might look a little strange or sing silly songs about camp food with your child while you are cooking dinner. If you are building a cooking fire, have the child help you collect tinder or deadfall. When you're in an area where you have to hang a food bag, let the child help you find the perfect spot.

I've watched our little boy become excited as he helps us prepare for wilderness trips. By getting him to help, it not only teaches him the importance of preparing for a trip but it gives us a chance to create memories with him. The excitement continues at camp, and keeping him involved makes him feel like a big boy.

2 ½ tablespoons Jell-o or other fruit flavored gelatin powder such as strawberry-banana

¼ teaspoon pure vanilla extract

Enough nonfat powdered milk to make 1 cup of milk

1 cup water

½ cup plain yogurt

Yogurt Smoothie

Makes 1–2 servings

You'll need a leakproof bottle with a wide opening such as a Nalgene.

AT HOME

Mix the jelly powder, vanilla extract, and nonfat milk powder together, and place in a ziplock freezer bag. Pack the yogurt in a leakproof container, or take along the ingredients to make *Trail Yogurt* (see page 65).

AT CAMP

Put the dry ingredients in the bottle and add 1 cup of water. Mix until the powder dissolves. Add ½ cup of yogurt and secure the lid. Shake until well combined. Pour into camp cups.

Red-Eyed Spotted Sugar S-s-snakes

Makes 4 servings

Kids get a charge out of these. Children cooking any food over a fire should always be supervised by a responsible adult.

At Home

If the yeast is not in an envelope, package it in a small ziplock freezer bag. Mix the flour, raisins, and salt together, and place in a ziplock freezer bag. Package the cranberries or cherries in a small piece of plastic wrap. Put the yeast envelope or package and the bundle of fruit into the bag with the flour mixture. Add the sugar, butter, and the oil to what you are taking.

At Camp

Put ½ cup of warm water in a cup, and mix in ½ teaspoon of sugar. Sprinkle the rapid-rise yeast into the water and let sit for a minute or two. Pour the liquid ingredients into the dry ingredients in a ziplock bag. Add 2 teaspoons of vegetable oil. Remove the air from the ziplock bag and close the seal. Knead the dough by squeezing the bag with your hands for 5 minutes or until the ingredients are well combined and the dough is elastic.

Divide in half and shape each piece into a snake. Peel the bark off one end of four long, sturdy sticks; you may have to whittle the ends a little. Wrap each snake around a stick, and press two cranberries into the dough for the red eyes. Bake over hot campfire coals for 10 to 15 minutes or until golden. When the dough is cooked and still hot, spread a little butter on each snake and sprinkle them with white sugar.

1 heaping teaspoon or ½ envelope rapid-rise yeast

1 cup all-purpose or unbleached flour

¼ cup raisins

½ teaspoon salt

1 tablespoon dried cranberries or cherries

¼ cup sugar

1 tablespoon butter

2 teaspoons vegetable oil

½ cup warm water

Toasted Banana Wraps

2 large whole-wheat tortillas

½ cup chocolate chips

2 fresh bananas or 1 cup
   rehydrated freeze-dried
   bananas

Makes 2–4 servings

Bananas and chocolate go well together, and kids can help make this fun dessert. If you are backpacking, use freeze-dried bananas.

AT HOME

Put the tortillas in a large ziplock bag, placing a piece of parchment paper between them. Put the chocolate chips in a ziplock freezer bag. Pack 2 fresh bananas if you are car camping or 1 cup of freeze-dried bananas if you are backpacking.

AT CAMP

If you are using freeze-dried bananas, rehydrate them in a little cold water, letting them sit until they are soft and then drain off any excess liquid. Mash 1 banana or half of the rehydrated bananas with a fork on one half of one of the tortillas. Cover the mashed banana with half of the chocolate chips. Fold the other half of the tortilla over the filling and press gently to seal.

Place the tortilla in a preheated frying pan over medium-low heat. Toast one side and then flip and toast the other side. The chocolate should be melted and the tortilla lightly toasted. Repeat with the remaining ingredients to make the second wrap.

Peanut Butter and Banana Chip Wraps

Makes 2 servings

2 large whole-wheat tortillas

¼ cup dried banana chips, broken into small pieces

½ cup chunky peanut butter

This recipe is one of my son's favorites when we go car camping or backpacking. It has a bit more crunch than a traditional peanut butter and banana sandwich.

At Home

Put the tortillas in a large ziplock bag, placing a piece of parchment paper between them. Put the banana chips in a ziplock freezer bag. Package the peanut butter in a leakproof container.

At Camp

Divide the peanut butter between the wraps and spread evenly. Sprinkle the crushed banana chips on each wrap and roll up.

Crunchy Blueberry Banana Leather

Dehydration Time: 6–15 hours
Makes 4–6 servings

¾ cup frozen blueberries, puréed

¼ cup applesauce

¼ cup sliced almonds

¼ cup banana chips, broken

Kids enjoy helping sprinkle the crunch on this fruit leather.

AT HOME

Purée the blueberries and mix with the applesauce. Spread the blueberry applesauce purée about ¼-inch thick on a lined dehydrator tray. Break the banana chips into small pieces. Sprinkle the purée with sliced almonds and banana chips.

Dry until the mixture is pliable like leather. Cut it into pieces and wrap them in plastic wrap.

Octopus Wieners

Makes 1 serving

1 wiener

1 roasting fork

This is more of a technique than a recipe that kids really seem to get a charge out of. Take a small cooler bag if you plan to do this, and make it on the first night of your trip.

AT CAMP

Cut each end of the wiener lengthwise in a cross so that each end has four pieces. Be careful to leave the middle 2 inches of the wiener uncut. Poke a sharpened stick or roasting fork through the center of the wiener, and roast it over hot coals until the ends curl up like the tentacles of an octopus.

Stuffed Pears

Makes 2 servings

The chocolate hazelnut spread in this recipe has some good nutrients, and the flavors complement each other.

AT HOME
Package the chocolate hazelnut spread in a leakproof container. Place the granola in a ziplock freezer bag. Bring along a fresh pear.

AT CAMP
Cut the pear in half lengthwise. Scoop out the seeds with a spoon and remove the stem. You will be left with a depression in the center of each pear half. Mix the chocolate hazelnut spread and granola together and place in the pear cavity. If you have extra filling, spread it on the cut side of the pear.

Press the cut sides of the stuffed halves back together, wrap the pear in foil, and bake it in hot coals for 15 minutes. Allow to cool before unwrapping.

TIP
You can also eat the stuffed pear without baking it.

2 tablespoons chocolate hazelnut spread, such as Nutella

2 tablespoons granola

1 pear

2 tablespoons miniature
    marshmallows

2 tablespoons chocolate chips or
    chocolate bar pieces

2 tablespoons chopped nuts
    (optional)

2 tablespoons dried cherries

2 unpeeled bananas

Aluminum foil

Banana Boats

Makes 2 servings

When I was a youngster, I participated in a 4-H outdoor living course. We made these treats on a five-day camping trip. I had forgotten about them until my mother mentioned them a few years ago. This recipe is more suitable for car camping but could be done on a shorter backpacking trip.

AT HOME
Package each of the ingredients, except for the bananas, in separate snack bags. Take along some aluminum foil.

AT CAMP
Slice 1 banana, with the skin still intact, in half lengthwise, being careful not to slice through the bottom skin. You will have something similar to the shape of a boat. Put your fingers in the cut and gently pry it open. Fill with half of the remaining ingredients and push the two sides back together. Repeat for the other banana.

Wrap both bananas in aluminum foil, and place them directly on the hot coals for about 20 minutes. Remove from the fire, peel back the foil, and enjoy. You can eat the bananas right out of the foil.

TIP
Modify the filling to suit your tastes. I prefer broken chocolate-covered butter toffee, pecans, and marshmallows.

Apple Crisp Sandwich Cookies

Makes 2 servings

This yummy snack tastes like apple crisp but requires much less effort.

AT HOME
Wrap the cookies in plastic wrap. Place the apple butter in a leakproof container and pack an apple. If you are taking cheese, wrap it.

AT CAMP
Cut the apple into very thin slices. Spread ½ tablespoon of apple butter on the flat side of each cookie and set aside. Top two of the cookies with the apple slices. Then place the other cookies, apple butter side down, on top to make a sandwich. Serve with slices of cheddar cheese if desired.

TIP
If you don't have apple butter, use a single-serving container of apple sauce.

4 oatmeal cookies

2 tablespoons apple butter

1 Royal Gala apple

Small block of cheddar cheese (optional)

½ cup maple syrup

1 pan clean snow

Winter Maple Candy

Makes 6 or more servings

When I was 8 years old, I enjoyed reading about making candy with molasses in the cold winter months in Little House in the Big Woods *by Laura Ingalls Wilder. My wonderful elementary school teacher helped my class make it. This recipe can be made as taffy or hard candy and is a real treat when hiking in winter; I make mine with maple syrup.*

AT HOME
Pack the maple syrup in a leakproof container. Put a piece of waxed paper in a ziplock freezer bag.

AT CAMP
Find some untouched clean snow. Pack as much snow as you can into a pan. Heat the maple syrup to a boil over a medium flame, being careful not to scorch it. Let it boil for 3 to 5 minutes; the longer you boil, it the harder your candy will be.

   Allow it to cool for a few moments and then pour it over the pan of snow. Place the candy on a plate and let any moisture evaporate, which should only take a few minutes. Wrap any leftovers in plastic wrap so that the pieces don't stick together.

TIP
Stir some chopped pecans into the syrup before pouring it on the snow.

Chapter 12
MORE ELABORATE DISHES

Sometimes my family and I still car camp or base camp, especially when we want to spend time with friends or family members who do not enjoy true wilderness camping. Often when we car camp it is because the trip to the trailhead or access point is just too far to make in one day. This frontcountry camping offers a lot more flexibility with food and can include fishing trips, car camping, paddling trips that involve base camping, or even staying at a rustic cabin or cottage. Under the right circumstances and with a small soft-sided cooler bag, some of these recipes can even be used for the first night of a weekend backpacking trip. One big difference between frontcountry camping and wilderness camping is the ability to bring a large cooler, which gives you a great deal of flexibility when it comes to your menu. Here are a few storage tips for frontcountry camping trips that will help keep your vehicle organized and your food fresh:

- Use a large Rubbermaid container with a lid for your kitchen equipment and dry goods.

- Store baked goods in a small cardboard box.

- Keep fruits and vegetables out of direct sunlight.

- Tupperware containers are great for storing food inside a cooler.

- Bring a plastic sink and store your camp soap, dish cloth, and drying towels inside.

- Keep cutlery in a plastic container.

- Wrap frozen foods in 2 layers of freezer paper and deep freeze them at home.

- Transfer peanut butter, jelly, and condiments to small leakproof containers.

- Remove excess packaging from store-bought items. (Take individually wrapped granola bars out of the box, for example, and pack in a ziplock storage bag.)

- Freeze juice boxes and water bottles to keep the contents of the cooler cold.

- Only open the cooler if you need to.

Cardboard Box Oven

My family and I celebrate Thanksgiving every year by going camping and cooking a turkey in a cardboard box. Set up on the ground away from your tent, the oven is lined with foil and has a rack suspended inside it. A pie plate, placed on a few rocks inside the oven, holds preheated charcoal briquettes. You are probably thinking the same things we did when we first tried this— will it catch fire? Will it reach and maintain a hot enough temperature to roast a turkey? The first time we tried it, we were really skeptical because it was late fall and cold enough to snow, but our turkey dinner was brilliant and became a yearly tradition. We've since cooked everything from turkey to apple pie. Several years ago, to satisfy our curiosity, we tested the interior temperature with a pyrometer and were surprised to find that the oven was very accurate. This is a fun project for the whole family and works incredibly well. You can even fold down the oven and reuse it several times. To make the oven, you need the following supplies:

- 2 wire coat hangers or 4 feet of sturdy wire

- 1 large cardboard box that closes completely

- 1 wire rack, that fits comfortably inside the box

- 1 aluminum pie plate (large enough to hold 10 charcoal briquettes)

- 1–2 rolls heavy duty aluminum foil

- 8 marble-size stones

- 1 bag presoaked charcoal briquettes (10 briquettes for every hour that you will be baking)

- 1 pair pliers

- 1 pair barbeque tongs

- 1 utility knife

Locate a box that is large enough to fit what you will cook and the wire rack. It should be large enough so that whatever you are cooking has at least 6 inches of clearance above and below the rack with the box on its longest side. Lay the box on its side and cut 2 holes (each approximately 1 inch by 3 inches) into the back, a few inches off the ground, for ventilation.

Line the interior of the box, including the flaps, with heavy duty barbeque foil. Fold some foil over the ends of the flaps to help keep it in place. When the box is completely lined, poke a sharp knife through the foil at the ventilation holes, and fold the foil over the edges.

Cut a 20-inch section out of each of 2 coat hangers or sturdy wire—these will support the cooking rack. Bend each piece of wire into a large U shape. Lay the box on its side again. Note the height at which you would like to position the wire rack to cook your meal. Remember that you need to leave about 6 inches between the bottom of the rack and the bottom of the box.

With one hand holding the foil lining in place and the other hand holding the wire, carefully poke both ends of the wire through one side of the box. The bottom of the U will be on the outside of the box and the ends will be inside. To secure the rack inside, bend the edges of the U-shaped wire upward with a pair of pliers. Repeat on the other side of the box using the second piece of wire. Set the rack on the wires and check that it is secure and level. If it isn't level, adjust the other side as necessary. When the rack is secured properly, it holds the foil in place, and both the box and rack will be quite stable.

Place the stones in a circle (6 inches wide) in the bottom of the box. Preheat 10 charcoal briquettes (see instructions below), and place them in a disposable pie plate. Put the plate on top of the rocks. Carefully fold the box flaps in and place a piece of wood or a rock against the opening to keep it closed. If the box slides when you do this, put a tent stake or two in the ground behind it to secure it.

How to Preheat the Charcoal Briquettes

Build a campfire before you start cooking. Place the briquettes in the fire to preheat them about 10 to 15 minutes before you need them. When you're ready for the charcoal, use barbeque tongs to remove it from the fire and transfer it to the pie tin inside the oven.

The briquettes stay hot for 1 hour; so if you are cooking something like a roast or turkey you will have to replace the briquettes every hour. Be sure to start preheating each batch of charcoal 15 minutes before you need them. Each preheated briquette adds another 35°F to the cooking temperature—so 10 briquettes equals approximately 350°F. If you need to increase the temperature, simply increase the number of preheated briquettes as necessary.

Tips

When using 10 preheated briquettes, cooking times are the same as for a household oven set to 350°F. If you are cooking something like a roast or poultry and want to catch the drippings for gravy, put the meat inside an oven roasting bag and in a roasting pan. If you do not rip the foil, you can reuse the oven several times. If you do not plan to reuse the oven, separate the foil from the cardboard, and recycle the materials or dispose of them properly.

Breakfast Bagels

1 package precooked bacon or "vegetarian bacon"

2 multigrain bagels

2 tablespoons butter

2 tablespoons whipped salad dressing or mayonnaise

Boston lettuce

2 slices Swiss cheese

1 tomato

Salt to taste

Cracked black pepper to taste

Makes 2 servings

This is my family's version of a BLT.

At Home

Put the cheese, lettuce, salad dressing, and butter in a cooler before you leave. Pack the tomato so that it is protected. Pack the rest of the ingredients with the dry goods you are taking.

At Camp

Warm the bacon in a frying pan over medium heat for 2 minutes. Meanwhile slice the bagels in half. Add the butter to the pan and fry the bagels cut side down until they are golden. Place the bottom halves on a plate, and spread a little salad dressing on each one. Add the lettuce followed by the cheese, bacon, tomato, salt, and pepper. Put the tops on the bagels.

Stuffed French Toast

Makes 2 servings

A sauce of blueberries, strawberries, and raspberries makes for a yummy addition to this French toast stuffed with mascarpone cheese and berries.

AT HOME

Wrap the bread slices in plastic wrap. Pack the bread, sugar, and cinnamon with any other dry goods you are taking. Pack the butter with any other butter you are taking. Place the remaining ingredients in a cooler just before you leave.

AT CAMP

Place the lemon zest and ½ cup of the berries in a small pot with 1 tablespoon of maple syrup. Bring to a boil over medium heat, remove from heat, and set aside. Mix the remaining ¼ cup of berries with ¼ cup mascarpone and 1 tablespoon of sugar. Spread half of the berry and cheese mixture on top of a slice of bread, and top with a second slice. Repeat with the other 2 pieces of bread and set aside.

   Beat 2 eggs in a small pot with the milk, cinnamon, and a pinch of salt. Preheat a frying pan over medium heat and add ½ tablespoon of butter. Dip one of the sandwiches briefly in the egg mixture, making sure that both sides are lightly coated with the egg mixture. Fry the sandwich, turning once, until both sides are golden. Dip and fry the second sandwich. Add the remaining maple syrup to the reserved berries, and pour it over the French toast.

¾ cup fresh or frozen mixed berries

1 teaspoon lemon zest

¼ cup maple syrup

1 tablespoon sugar

¼ cup mascarpone or cream cheese

2 eggs or equivalent made from
   dried scrambled egg mix

¼ cup milk or equivalent made from
   powdered milk

¼ teaspoon cinnamon (optional)

Pinch of salt

4 ½-inch-thick slices French bread

1 tablespoon butter

Eggs Benedict with Smoked Salmon

4 eggs

4 slices smoked salmon

2 English muffins

1 0.9-ounce package Knorr (or similar brand) hollandaise sauce mix

Butter as directed on the hollandaise mix instructions

Salt and pepper to taste

Makes 2 servings

Eggs Benedict is one of my family's favorites, but we reserve it as a special brunch treat for camping trips because it is so decadent.

AT HOME

Pack the eggs and salmon in a cooler when you are ready to leave. Pack the English muffins and Hollandaise mix with your dry goods, and take along any ingredients required for the mix as listed on the package. Take some aluminum foil and a pot cozy.

AT CAMP

Make the hollandaise in a small pot according to the package directions, and place it in a pot cozy. Use a fork to split each English muffin in half. Toast the muffins and wrap them in foil to keep them warm.

Put a pot of water on to boil, crack 4 eggs into the pot, and let the water simmer to cook the eggs. The eggs will be cooked when the whites are firm and the yolk is still runny. If you prefer your yolks harder, leave the eggs in the water a little longer.

As the eggs come close to being cooked, place the English muffin bottoms on each plate. Place a piece of smoked salmon on each muffin half. Top with a poached egg and a spoonful of hollandaise and then season to taste.

TIP

If you have any leftover hollandaise, put it in a ziplock freezer bag and store it in your cooler. You can use it in a day or two on vegetables such as asparagus or broccoli. Hollandaise is also delicious on a grilled rib eye steak.

Monte Cristo

Makes 2 servings

Basically a French toast sandwich with a savory twist, a Monte Cristo makes a hearty breakfast or a delicious brunch.

AT HOME
Wrap the bread slices in plastic wrap. Pack the bread and seasonings with the dry goods you are taking. Place the remaining ingredients in a cooler just before you leave.

AT CAMP
Beat 2 eggs in a small pot with ¼ cup milk, and add salt and pepper as desired. Put 3 slices of ham, a slice of Swiss cheese, and a tomato slice between 2 pieces of bread. Repeat with the other 2 pieces of bread, and set the sandwiches aside. Preheat a frying pan over medium heat, and add ½ tablespoon of butter.

Dip one of the sandwiches briefly in the egg mixture, being sure both sides are coated with the egg mixture. Fry the coated sandwich, turning once, until both sides are golden. Dip and fry the other sandwich until golden.

2 eggs

¼ cup milk

Salt and pepper to taste

6 very thin slices Black Forest ham

2 slices Swiss cheese

1 tomato (optional)

4 ½-inch-thick slices French bread

1 tablespoon butter

Chipotle Steak Sandwiches

Sandwich

½ pound sandwich steak (or sirloin steak sliced ¼ inch thick)

2 large crusty buns

2 large slices Havarti cheese (enough to cover the bun)

1 small onion

1 tablespoon vegetable oil

Salt and pepper to taste

Sauce

1½ teaspoons chipotle hot sauce

1 teaspoon mustard powder

1 tablespoon Worcestershire sauce

⅓ cup ketchup

2 cloves garlic, minced

1 teaspoon honey

1 tablespoon vegetable oil

½ teaspoon salt

Makes 2 servings

The sauce for these steak sandwiches is smoky and spicy. Serve these on a plate since they get a little messy, much like a sloppy Joe.

At Home

Mix all the sauce ingredients together, and pour the sauce into a ziplock freezer bag. Slice the thin steak into 1-inch strips about 4 inches long, and put the strips in the bag with the sauce. Compress as much air out of the bag as possible and seal it; freeze the meat mixture until you are ready to leave.

Wrap the buns in plastic wrap, wrap the cheese, and pack an onion. Add the oil to any other vegetable oil you are taking.

At Camp

Make sure that the meat mixture is thawed before you begin. Slice the onion. Pour 1 tablespoon of oil in a frying pan over medium heat. Sauté the onion until it becomes translucent.

Add the thawed steak mixture to the pan and cook until the steak is as done as you prefer. Pile the steak on each bun and top with a slice of Havarti cheese.

Tip

For a slightly different flavor, add sliced mushrooms and green peppers to the pan when you add the onions.

Marinated Grilled Vegetable Sandwiches

Makes 2–3 servings

Meat eaters will enjoy the hearty texture of the portabella mushrooms in this great-tasting vegetarian sandwich. It makes a great side dish, too.

AT HOME

Mix the oil, vinegar, mustard, and garlic, pour the marinade into a leakproof container, and store it in your refrigerator until you are ready to leave. Pack the mushrooms in a paper bag, and store the vegetables as you normally would. Take along a large ziplock freezer bag. Pack the buns with any other dry goods you are taking.

AT CAMP

Cut each pepper lengthwise into 4 pieces. Slice the zucchini and eggplant lengthwise. Cut the mushrooms in half. Place the vegetables in the freezer bag. Add the marinade, and gently stir the vegetables to coat them. Let the mixture sit for a half hour or more.

Preheat the grill, and cook the vegetables directly on the grill until they are tender and heated through. When the vegetables are done, pile them on the buns.

Sandwich

1 sweet green pepper

1 sweet red pepper

2 portabella mushrooms

1 small zucchini

1 baby eggplant

Salt and pepper to taste

2 Italian-style rolls such as panini or ciabatta

Marinade

¼ cup olive oil

¼ cup red wine vinegar

½ teaspoon Dijon mustard

1 clove garlic, minced

Chicken Fajitas

Makes 4–6 servings

⅔ cup onion

⅓ cup sweet red peppers

⅓ cup sweet green peppers

⅓ cup plum tomatoes

2 tablespoons olive or vegetable oil

1 pound fresh boneless chicken

1 teaspoon cumin

2 teaspoons chili powder

½ teaspoon salt

¼ teaspoon black pepper

⅛ teaspoon cayenne pepper

⅔ cup sour cream

⅔ cup guacamole

⅔ cup salsa

⅔ cup Monterey Jack or cheddar cheese, grated

4–8 10-inch tortillas

Fajitas are easy to make and fun to eat. You'll need to take a 1 cup plastic measuring cup with you, or you can use a wide-mouth Nalgene that has measurements marked on the side.

AT HOME

Cut the chicken into 1-inch strips, place it in a ziplock freezer bag, and freeze it until you leave. Pack the bag of chicken and the vegetables, condiments, and cheese in a cooler before you leave. Pack the spices in with your dry goods, and take along some aluminum foil.

AT CAMP

Slice the onion and peppers into ½-inch strips. Chop the tomatoes. Set the vegetables aside. Grate the cheese and set it aside.

Heat the oil in a frying pan over medium-high heat. Add the chicken, and stir fry until it is browned on all sides. Add the spices and turn to coat the meat. Add the onions and cook until they start to become translucent. Then add the peppers and tomatoes. Cook until the peppers are tender crisp.

Spoon some of the filling into the center of each tortilla and top with sour cream, guacamole, salsa, and grated cheese as you desire. Roll up and repeat for the remaining tortillas.

Guacamole

Makes 3–4 servings

Serve this guacamole as a dip or use it in fajitas or tacos.

At Home
Put the cumin and garlic salt together in a small ziplock freezer bag. Package the avocados so that they will not bruise. Package the cilantro in a ziplock freezer bag with a damp paper towel wrapped around the bottom of the stems and keep refrigerated until you are ready to leave. Then store it in a cooler. Pack the lemon, lime, and tomato in a bag or box and store them so that the tomato won't get bruised.

At Camp
Cut both avocados in half and remove their pits. Score the flesh in a crisscross fashion, cutting all the way to the skin. Use a spoon to scoop out the chunks and place them in a bowl. Remove the cilantro leaves from their stems and chop. Discard the stems. Cut the tomato in half and remove the seeds. Put the cilantro and tomatoes in with the avocados and set aside.

   Cut the lemon and lime in half and juice them. Pour the juice in the freezer bag containing the cumin and garlic, and slosh around to mix. Pour the seasoned juice over the avocado mixture, and stir gently to combine. Allow to sit for 10 minutes to let the flavors combine. Serve with tortilla chips or vegetable sticks or use as a topping for other dishes.

½ teaspoon cumin

¼ teaspoon garlic salt

2 ripe avocados

2 tablespoons fresh cilantro

1 lemon

1 lime

1 plum tomato

Steak and Strawberries with Balsamic Reduction

½ cup balsamic vinegar

2 8-ounce strip loin steaks

¼ teaspoon cracked black pepper

½ teaspoon kosher salt

1½ tablespoons butter

⅓ cup fresh strawberries

Makes 2 servings

Strawberries and balsamic vinegar go wonderfully together and are even better on a juicy steak that has been grilled to perfection. This recipe was inspired by my good friend Claude Lauzon and is best served with a crisp spinach salad.

At Home

Freeze the steaks in a ziplock freezer bag until you are ready to pack your cooler. You can make the balsamic reduction a day or two before you leave. Heat ½ cup of balsamic vinegar in a small pot over medium-low, and cook slowly until it reduces by half. Remove from heat. The syrup will thicken as it cools.

Pour the syrup into a plastic container and refrigerate until you leave. Pack the butter with the other butter you will take on your trip. Pack the strawberries so that they will not be bruised, and pack the seasonings.

At Camp

Season the steaks with salt and cracked black pepper, and grill them to the desired level of doneness. Remove the meat from the grill and let rest for 5 minutes.

Meanwhile melt ½ tablespoon of butter in a small pot. Chop the tops off the strawberries and slice them. Add the strawberries and sauté just until the berries are warm and start to soften. Add the balsamic reduction to the straw-berries and heat through. Remove from the heat and add 1 tablespoon of butter. Stir to combine until the butter is melted. Spoon the sauce over the steaks.

Asian Flank Steak

Makes 3–4 servings

This recipe is great served with rice and a salad dressed with Asian-style vinaigrette.

AT HOME
Mix all of the ingredients together, and put in a ziplock freezer bag with the flank steak. Freeze until you are ready to pack your cooler for your trip.

AT CAMP
Let the meat thaw and marinate in the cooler for 24 hours. Remove the steak from the marinade, and place it on a hot barbeque grill or on a grate over hot campfire coals. Discard any leftover marinade.

Cook until the steak reaches your desired level of doneness. Let the meat rest, wrapped in foil, for 15 minutes before cutting. While the steak sits, prepare a salad and some rice. Slice the steak thinly across the grain.

TIP
Leftovers of this dish are a nice addition to a salad or a wrap.

1 ½–2 pounds flank steak

2 green onions, sliced

⅓ cup tamari sauce

¼ cup vegetable oil

1 teaspoon crushed red chili peppers

½ teaspoon black pepper

1 teaspoon fresh ginger, minced

Chicken Diane

Makes 2 servings

2 boneless, skinless chicken breasts

1½ tablespoons olive oil

1½ tablespoons butter

1½ tablespoons Dijon mustard

¼ cup chicken stock

2 teaspoons Worcestershire sauce

2 ounces Cognac or brandy

1½ tablespoons lemon juice

3 tablespoons green onions

1 tablespoon dried parsley

I have no idea who Diane is, but this recipe has been one of my family's camping favorites for decades. This dish pairs wonderfully with baby new potatoes, broccoli, and a salad of baby mixed greens dressed in lemon vinaigrette.

At Home

Place the chicken breasts between 2 pieces of plastic wrap and pound them with the flat side of a meat mallet or the bottom of a small heavy pot until they are about ¾ inch thick. Place the tenderized meat in a ziplock freezer bag, and freeze until you are ready to pack your cooler. Pack the oil with any other olive oil that you are taking. Do the same with the butter.

Mix the Dijon mustard, chicken stock, and Worcestershire sauce, and pack in a leakproof container. Keep the mixture refrigerated until you pack your cooler. Pour the Cognac in a leakproof container. Pack a lemon, some green onions, and some parsley.

At Camp

Chop 3 tablespoons of green onions, cut the lemon in half, and set both aside. Heat 1½ tablespoons of olive oil in a frying pan over medium heat. Add the chicken breasts and brown each side for 5 minutes. Move the chicken to a plate.

Pour the chicken stock mixture, Cognac, parsley, and juice of half the lemon into the pan. Season with salt and pepper and simmer the sauce for about 5 minutes.

Return the chicken to the pan and continue simmering until the chicken is cooked through. Transfer each chicken breast to a plate and turn off the stove. Add 1½ tablespoons of butter to the sauce, stir to combine, and pour it over the chicken breasts.

Greek Souvlaki

Makes 2–3 servings

There is a lot of garlic in this traditional Greek recipe. It's great served with a salad and rice.

AT HOME

Cut the meat into 1-inch cubes. Mix the remaining ingredients together, except the tzatziki. Place everything in a ziplock freezer bag, compressing as much air out as possible. Place the meat mixture in the freezer until you are ready to leave. Just before you leave, pack the tzatziki and bag of meat in your cooler.

AT CAMP

Fill a bag or container with water and soak the bamboo skewers for an hour. Put the meat on the skewers and grill on a rack over hot campfire coals or on a barbeque until the meat is cooked through. Serve with a salad, rice, and tzatziki.

TIP

Tzatziki is a Greek condiment made with sour cream or yogurt that sometimes contains dill.

1 pound fresh pork tenderloin, lamb, or chicken breasts

⅛ cup olive oil

2 tablespoons lemon juice

3 cloves garlic, minced

2 teaspoons fresh oregano or 1 teaspoon dried oregano

6 bamboo or metal skewers

1 8-ounce container tzatziki

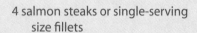

4 salmon steaks or single-serving size fillets

1 peach

1 mango

1 red grapefruit

1 tablespoon lime juice

2 tablespoons fresh ginger, grated

¼ cup cilantro, chopped

¼ cup red onion, minced

1 jalapeño pepper, minced

Citrus Mango Grilled Salmon

Makes 4 servings

The citrus salsa and marinade for this dish enhances the flavor of the salmon. It is best served with a salad of mixed baby greens and a light vinaigrette. If you prefer, substitute tuna for the salmon.

At Home

Place the salmon in a ziplock bag and seal. Dice the peach and mango and place in a bowl. Cut the grapefruit in half and set one half aside. Use a grapefruit knife to remove the segments of fruit from the remaining half. Add the grapefruit chunks to the other fruit in the bowl and then squeeze the juice from the reserved grapefruit half into the bowl.

Add the lime juice, ginger, cilantro, onion, and pepper to the bowl. Pour the marinade into a leakproof container. Refrigerate the marinade and the salmon until you pack your cooler.

At Camp

Early in the day that you are going to eat this meal, put half of the marinade in with the salmon and return the fish to the cooler. Reserve the remaining salsa and store in a cooler. At dinnertime remove the salmon from the marinade. Discard the marinade.

Grill or pan-fry the salmon until cooked through, about 6 minutes on each side. Place each piece of salmon on a plate, and top it with the reserved salsa.

Tip

It is important to oil your grill to keep the salmon from sticking. You can spray it with a nonstick cooking spray or put a little oil in a ziplock bag with a paper towel. Before grilling the fish, remove the paper towel from the bag with tongs and wipe the grill.

Maple Salmon

Makes 2 servings

This is a simple salmon dish with a Canadian twist.

AT HOME

Freeze the salmon in a large ziplock freezer bag. When you are ready to leave, put it in a cooler. Combine the maple syrup and Worcestershire sauce in a leakproof container. Pack a lemon. Pack the oil with the other vegetable oil you are taking.

AT CAMP

Make the marinade in the morning of the day you are going to eat this so that the salmon may absorb the flavors all day. Cut the lemon in half, and squeeze the juice from one half into the bag with the salmon. Add the maple syrup and Worcestershire sauce mixture to the bag. Compress as much air out as you can, seal the bag, and return it to the cooler.

When you're ready to prepare the salmon, preheat your barbeque or prepare hot coals in the campfire, keeping the heat medium-low. Oil the rack. Place the salmon on the grill, and cook for about 5 minutes on each side. Turn the salmon only once—it's fragile. It is cooked when the flesh flakes easily and appears opaque. Be careful not to overcook because it dries out the fish.

2 6-ounce salmon fillets

⅛ cup maple syrup

1 tablespoon Worcestershire sauce

1 lemon

Salt and pepper to taste

¼ cup vegetable oil

¼ cup all-purpose or unbleached flour

¼ teaspoon salt

¼ teaspoon pepper

8 sheets fresh lasagna

½ cup canned artichoke hearts

½ cup asparagus

2 tablespoons butter

2 cloves garlic

3 cups assorted mushrooms (cremini, portabella, porcini, and oyster)

1⅓ cups low-sodium vegetable stock

½ cup fresh or frozen peas

⅓ cup sour cream

1 tablespoon tamari sauce

2 tablespoons fresh parsley

Pasta with Artichoke Cream Sauce

Makes 4–6 servings

This decadent recipe is fairly quick to make. I like to use a variety of mushrooms to add an earthy flavor. You'll need two burners for this recipe and a bamboo or metal steamer.

AT HOME

Mix the flour, salt, and pepper together, and put it in a ziplock bag. Pack the tamari sauce and vegetable stock in leakproof containers and keep them, along with the pasta, asparagus, peas, parsley, butter, and sour cream in the refrigerator until you are ready to pack your cooler. Pack the mushrooms in a paper bag and store in a cool, dry place.

AT CAMP

Bring a pot of salted water to boil. Meanwhile cut the pasta into 1-inch strips crosswise and set it aside. Drain the artichoke hearts, cut each one into fourths, and set them aside. Cut the asparagus into 2-inch pieces. Put the asparagus into the steamer, place it on top of the pot of boiling water, and steam for 5 minutes.

Melt the butter in a large skillet or pot. Mince the garlic. Sauté the mushrooms and garlic until all the liquid has evaporated. Add the flour mixture and cook for 1 minute. Stir in 1⅓ cups vegetable stock and bring to a boil. Add the peas, turn down the heat, and let the sauce simmer for 4 to 5 minutes.

Meanwhile remove the steamer from the other pot. Pour the pasta in, and let it cook according to the package directions. Immediately add the asparagus and artichoke hearts to the sauce. Add the sour cream and tamari sauce and stir to heat through. Chop the fresh parsley and add it to the sauce. Drain the pasta and mix it with the sauce until coated.

Spinach Salad with Red Currant Vinaigrette

Makes 3–4 servings

Even the pickiest eater in our extended family loves this salad. It is a great side for grilled meats.

AT HOME

Hull the strawberries and cut them in half. Remove the stems from the spinach. Chop the onion. Melt the red currant jelly with the mango vinegar in a small pot over medium-low heat. Let cool and then transfer to a leakproof container and store in the refrigerator. When you are ready to leave, pack all the ingredients, including the dressing, and a can of mandarin oranges in a cooler.

AT CAMP

Combine the spinach, strawberries, mandarin oranges, and onions together in a bowl. Shake the dressing and pour it over the salad. Toss gently to coat.

1 cup strawberries

7 cups baby spinach

¼ green onions or chives

¼ cup red currant jelly

3 tablespoons mango, cranberry, or red wine vinegar

½ cup canned mandarin oranges, drained

Salad

1 head romaine lettuce

1 8-ounce strip loin steak (about 1 inch thick)

3 plum tomatoes

1 small red onion

2 large dill pickles

6 large olives, pitted (whatever variety you prefer)

Dressing

2 tablespoons Dijon mustard

½ cup olive oil

2 tablespoons red wine vinegar

1 teaspoon capers

1 ½ tablespoons dried parsley

½ teaspoon kosher salt

½ teaspoon cracked black pepper

Steak Salad

Makes 2 servings

This stacked-up steak salad has many layers of flavor.

AT HOME

Put the steak into a freezer bag and freeze until you are ready to leave. Make the dressing the day before your trip by combing all the ingredients and refrigerating in a leak-proof container. Put the pickles in a small ziplock freezer bag, and store them in the refrigerator until you are ready to leave. Pack the vegetables in a box or container so that they are protected from being crushed.

AT CAMP

Wash and prepare the lettuce as you would for any salad. Season the steak, and grill until medium-rare or your desired level of doneness. While the steak is grilling, chop the tomatoes, slice the pickles lengthwise, slice the onion into rings, and chop the olives. Put half of the lettuce on a large plate, and set the rest aside.

Remove the steak from the grill, and slice it into ¼-inch strips across the grain. Place half of the steak on top of the lettuce on the plate. Top with half of the tomatoes, onions, and pickles, in that order. Shake the dressing, and pour half of it on the layers you have made so far.

Top with the remaining half of the lettuce, steak, tomatoes, onions, and pickles. Drizzle the salad with the rest of the dressing, and garnish with chopped olives.

Avocado, Crab, and Pasta Salad

Makes 2–3 servings

Avocados give this salad a delightful buttery taste. If you didn't mind the weight of the fruit and avocado, you could take this for the first or second night of a wilderness trip.

At Home

Measure the pasta, and pack it in a ziplock freezer bag. Put the pouch of crab in the bag as well. Wrap the tarragon in plastic wrap and put the bundle in the pasta bag. Pack the oil with any other olive oil that you will take on your trip. Pack the fruit and vegetables in a box or container to protect them from bruising. Put the crab in the cooler.

At Camp

Cook the pasta, strain off the water, and let the pasta cool. Finely chop ¼ cup of red onion, and add it to the pasta. Cut the avocado in half, and remove the pit. Score the flesh in a crisscross fashion, cutting all the way to the skin. Use a spoon to scoop the chunks into the pasta mixture.

Cut the skin off both the blood orange and the grapefruit. Remove 6 or 7 sections from each, leaving the membrane behind. Cut the sections in thirds, and add them to the cooled salad.

Squeeze 1 tablespoon of juice from the remaining orange pieces, and do the same with the grapefruit. Mix the juice, tarragon, and oil together, and drizzle it over the salad. Add the crab, season the salad with salt and pepper, and gently stir to combine the ingredients.

Tip

This recipe works great with fresh crab too. If you're using it, store the meat in a freezer ziplock and refrigerate it until you are ready to leave.

---

1 ¼ cups small pasta shells (uncooked measurement)

1 small red onion

1 ripe avocado

1 small red grapefruit

1 blood orange

¼ teaspoon tarragon

1 tablespoon olive oil

3 ½-ounce pouch of premium crabmeat

Salt and pepper to taste

1 cup eggplant, diced

4 tablespoons extra virgin olive oil, divided

4 whole garlic cloves

2 cups cheese tortellini

1 tablespoon walnuts

1 tablespoon balsamic vinegar

1 tablespoon honey

2 tablespoons fresh parsley

4 basil leaves

Parmesan cheese as desired

½ teaspoon black pepper

¼ teaspoon kosher salt

½ cup scallions

⅔ cup cherry or grape tomatoes

Cheese Tortellini Dinner Salad

Makes 4–6 servings

This hearty salad has lots of flavor and can be served warm or cold.

At Home

Toss the diced eggplant and garlic cloves in 2 tablespoons of extra virgin olive oil. Arrange in a single layer in a casserole dish and roast at 400°F for 30 minutes. Remove the eggplant and garlic from the oven and mash with a fork. Allow it to cool and then place it in a ziplock bag.

Cook the tortellini according to the package directions. Drain well. Toss the tortellini with 1 tablespoon of extra virgin olive oil, let it cool, and place it in a ziplock bag.

Toast the walnuts in a dry frying pan for a few minutes. Let cool and package in a piece of plastic wrap. Mix the vinegar, honey, and 1 tablespoon extra virgin olive oil in a leakproof container. Pack the fresh herbs, Parmesan, salt, pepper, and onions separately. Pack the tomatoes. Store all of the ingredients, except the tomatoes, in the refrigerator until you are ready to pack your cooler.

At Camp

Remove the tortellini and eggplant bags from the cooler and allow them to warm to air temperature. Mix the dressing in the leakproof container with the eggplant mixture. Cut the tomatoes in half. Add the tortellini, herbs, toasted walnuts, and onions to the eggplant mixture. Mix well so that the dressing coats the tortellini. Garnish with thinly sliced or grated Parmesan cheese.

Tip

Store tomatoes at room temperature because they lose their flavor when kept in a refrigerator.

Key Lime Pie

Makes 6–8 servings

This pie is so easy to make when you are camping; it works best when you have a cooler to chill it in. My family has been known to make this on backcountry trips in cooler weather.

AT CAMP

Open the package containing the prepared graham cracker crust. Peel enough of the rind from one of the limes for 1 teaspoon of zest, and cut the rind into small slivers, being careful to avoid the white pith. Cut all the limes in half, and squeeze the juice into a pot or bowl until you have about ½ cup of juice.

Add the zest and the sweetened condensed milk to the juice. Stir until the filling has thickened, and pour it into the crust. Garnish with more lime zest if desired. Cover the pie and place it in the top of a cooler to set for about 1 hour.

1 graham cracker crust

6 key limes or 3 regular limes

14 ounces sweetened condensed milk

Campfire Orange Cupcakes

1 single-layer yellow cake mix

6 large oranges (1 for each person)

1 egg (only if required for cake mix)

Vegetable oil (as directed for the cake mix)

Makes 6 servings

This is a fun way to serve a cake and works best with a group. The nice thing is that there are no dessert plates to wash.

At Home

Pack an egg and vegetable oil as required for the cake mix, one orange for each person in your group, and the cake mix itself. Pack some aluminum foil.

At Camp

Cut one end off each orange, about 1 inch from the end. Each orange should have an opening about 2 inches wide. Set the tops aside. Scoop out the fruit and reserve both the fruit and the skins. Squeeze the juice from the pulp. Set the juice aside and discard the pulp.

Prepare the cake mix according to the package directions, substituting orange juice for the water or milk required for the mix. Fill 1 orange ⅔ of the way with cake batter. Replace the top and wrap the orange in foil. Repeat with the rest of the oranges.

Bake the cakes by placing the oranges directly onto hot campfire coals for 15 to 20 minutes or until the cake is fully cooked.

Grilled Fruit Skewers

Makes 6 servings

Grilling fruit enhances its flavor. This dish is so simple yet so tasty.

AT HOME
Put the liqueur in a leakproof bottle. Place the brown sugar in a large ziplock freezer bag. Pack the fruit so that it won't bruise. Pack the bamboo skewers.

AT CAMP
Soak the bamboo skewers in water for about 1 hour. Add the liqueur to the ziplock freezer bag containing the brown sugar, mix well, and set aside. Cut the pineapple, peaches, and bananas into 2-inch by 1-inch chunks. Place the fruit chunks in the bag, and let them marinate for about 15 minutes.

Thread the fruit on the skewers, making sure that you have some of each fruit on every skewer. Reserve the marinade. Grill the fruit for about 10 minutes on a rack over hot coals or a barbeque grill, turning often so that the fruit doesn't burn. Occasionally spoon some of the marinade over the fruit. Be careful to stand back so that you don't get burned if the marinade flares up—a metal spoon with a long handle works well for this. Remove the fruit from the grill or fire, allow it to cool slightly, and serve.

¼ cup Grand Marnier or rum

½ cup brown sugar

1 small pineapple

2 peaches

2 bananas

6 bamboo skewers

Chai Mulled Fruit

1 d'Anjou or Bartlett pear

1 Royal Gala or Fuji apple

1 red or black plum

1 medium peach

2 medium oranges

1 tablespoon brown sugar

2 tablespoons raisins

1 chai tea bag

Makes 3–4 servings

The spices from the tea infuse the fruit and make for a delicious dessert.

AT HOME

Pack the fruit so that it won't bruise. Add the chai tea bag to the dried goods you are taking, and add the sugar to any other brown sugar you are taking.

AT CAMP

Peel and core the pear and apple. Peel the plum and peach and remove the pits. Chop the pear, apple, plum, and peach into bite-size pieces. Peel the rind from one orange, and cut it into small slivers, being careful to avoid the white pith. Juice both oranges into a pot. Add the brown sugar and stir until dissolved. Add the pear, apple, plum, peach, and raisins.

Place the pot over medium heat and bring the fruit mixture to a boil. Add the tea bag, reduce the heat, and allow the fruit to simmer for 5 minutes or until it starts to soften. Remove the pot from the heat, and take out and discard the tea bag. Let the fruit sit covered for 5 minutes.

Grilled Oranges with Chocolate Drizzle

Makes 2 servings

These oranges are sweet and yummy. The cinnamon and chili powder in the chocolate sauce gives them a Mexican twist.

At Home

Pack the oranges. Pack the oil with any other vegetable oil you are taking. Package the chocolate, cinnamon, and chili powder together in a ziplock freezer bag. Put the cream in a leakproof container, store it in the refrigerator, and pack it in your cooler when you are ready to leave.

At Camp

Cut the oranges into ¾-inch thick slices, leaving the peel on the fruit, and brush lightly with vegetable oil. Grill on a rack over hot campfire coals or on a barbeque grill until the fruit softens and is hot through.

While the fruit is cooking, melt the chocolate. Use two different-size pots; put water in the larger pot along with a couple of rocks and then place the smaller pot inside the larger one. Place the chocolate mixture in the smaller pot, add the cream, and gently stir until the chocolate has melted and formed a sauce. Transfer the fruit from the grill to plates and drizzle with the chocolate sauce.

2 oranges

2 tablespoons vegetable oil

¼ cup broken chocolate bar pieces or chocolate chips

¼ teaspoon cinnamon

⅛ teaspoon chili powder

⅛ cup heavy cream

2 teaspoons raspberry jam

4 graham crackers

1 2½-ounce milk chocolate bar

2 large marshmallows

Raspberry S'mores

Makes 2 servings

S'mores are even more decadent with a dollop of raspberry jam inside.

AT HOME

Package the jam in a leakproof container. Wrap the graham crackers in plastic wrap. Pack the marshmallows and the chocolate bar.

AT CAMP

Spread raspberry jam on 2 graham crackers. Top with enough of the milk chocolate to cover each cracker. Toast the marshmallows. Place one toasted marshmallow on top of the chocolate on each cracker. Top with another graham cracker and serve.

Pumpkin Pecan Bake

Makes 4 servings

Not quite pumpkin pie and not quite fruit crisp, this dessert is a great finish to a turkey dinner on a fall camping trip.

AT HOME

Mix the cinnamon and ginger for the pie with the brown sugar, and place in a ziplock freezer bag. Pack the can of pumpkin. Put the whipping cream or milk in a leakproof container, and pack it in the cooler when you are ready to leave. Pack the eggs carefully. Add both amounts of butter to what you are taking. Mix all of the topping ingredients, except the butter, and place them in a ziplock freezer bag.

AT CAMP

Mix the brown sugar mixture with ⅛ cup of softened butter. Beat 2 eggs in a separate bowl and then mix them with the butter and sugar. Stir in the can of pumpkin. Add ⅓ cup of cream and ¼ teaspoon of salt, and mix until well blended. Pour into a pan or Dutch oven, and bake for 45 minutes to 1 hour or until firm.

Meanwhile, add ¼ cup softened butter to the bag with the topping ingredients and mix well. When the main layer has finished baking, cover it with the topping mixture and bake for another 8 minutes or so. Keep a close eye on the topping as it overcooks easily. It is done when the topping is golden brown.

TIP

This recipe can be baked in a box, reflector, Dutch, or Outback oven.

Pie

½ teaspoon cinnamon

¼ teaspoon ground ginger

½ cup brown sugar

⅛ cup butter, softened

2 eggs

14 ounces canned, puréed pumpkin

⅓ cup whipping cream or whole milk

¼ teaspoon salt

Topping

¼ cup flour

¼ cup brown sugar

¼ teaspoon ground ginger

¼ teaspoon cinnamon

⅓ cup pecans

¼ cup butter, softened

Chapter 13

FOR THE CANINE COMPANION

You need to consider a few things when planning food for your dog for a camping or paddling trip. Pack the food so that moisture does not get into it and it stays fresh. Be sure to double bag the dog food to keep the smells and flavors from infiltrating your food. You'll also have to hang the dog food with your food pack, or put it in with your other food in a bearproof container. Don't forget to take some cookies or training treats for your canine companion.

Remember to keep your pet well hydrated—with treated water, if possible. That said, since it is almost impossible to keep dogs from drinking out of lakes, ponds, and streams, talk to your vet about additional vaccines to protect your pet.

Depending on the length of your trip and the size of your dog, you might want to consider letting him carry some of his own food and treats. Specially designed dog packs are available for dogs of all sizes. The packs are usually similar in design to a saddle bag for a horse. Collapsible dog bowls made from nylon are a great idea for both food and water. They dry quickly and are lightweight and compact. Both these products are available in larger pet stores and in some outdoor stores. You can also buy outdoor gear for your pet from Ruff Wear (www.ruffwear.com), Granite Gear (www.granitegear.com), and Wolf Packs (www.wolfpacks.com).

Carrot Dog Cookies

Makes 60 cookies

½ cup instant nonfat powdered milk

1¼ cups unbleached flour

½ cup whole wheat flour

¼ cup wheat germ

1 teaspoon dried parsley

1 egg

½ cup carrot baby food

¼ cup canola or vegetable oil

1 teaspoon honey

¼ cup water

My family's dog goes crazy for these cookies. We don't even have a chance to ask him to do a trick for the cookie—he does them all before we even get a treat out of the bag.

At Home

Preheat the oven to 350°F. Mix the dry ingredients together in a medium-size bowl. Beat the egg in a separate medium-size bowl. Mix the baby food, oil, honey, and water with the egg. Add the wet mixture to the dry ingredients, stirring to combine. Knead the mixture for 5 minutes.

Flour your hands. Roll the dough into ½-inch balls. Flatten the balls between your palms until they are about a ¼ inch thick. Place them ¼ inch apart on a nonstick baking sheet, and bake for 55 minutes to 1 hour.

Allow the treats to cool completely and then package them in ziplock freezer bags, compressing as much air out as possible. Store the treats in the freezer until you are ready to leave.

Tip

Be sure that the baby food doesn't contain onion or garlic as those ingredients can sometimes make your furry friend ill.

Peanut Butter Dog Cookies

Makes 60 cookies

What dog doesn't like peanut butter? These treats go over really well.

AT HOME

Preheat oven to 350°F. Mix the dry ingredients together in a medium-size bowl. Beat the egg in a separate medium-size bowl. Mix the peanut butter, oil, honey, and water with the egg. Add the wet mixture to the dry ingredients, stirring to combine. Knead the mixture for 5 minutes.

Flour your hands. Roll the dough into ½-inch balls. Flatten the balls between your palms until they are about a ¼ inch thick. Place them ¼ inch apart on a nonstick baking sheet, and bake for 55 minutes to 1 hour.

Allow the treats to cool completely and then package them in ziplock freezer bags, compressing as much air out as possible. Store the treats in the freezer until you are ready to leave.

½ cup instant powdered soy milk

1¼ cups unbleached flour

½ cup whole wheat flour

¼ cup wheat germ

1 teaspoon dried parsley

1 egg

½ cup all-natural peanut butter

⅛ cup canola or vegetable oil

1 teaspoon honey

¼ cup water

½ cup instant nonfat powdered
milk

1 ¼ cups unbleached flour

½ cup whole wheat flour

¼ cup wheat germ

1 teaspoon dried parsley

1 egg

½ cup chicken baby food

¼ cup canola or vegetable oil

1 teaspoon honey

¼ cup chicken stock

Chicken Dog Cookies

Makes 60 cookies

*Since these cookies should be kept cool, they are suitable
for cold-weather trips, dayhikes, and car camping. They
are full of flavor—my family's dog can't get enough of
them.*

At Home

Preheat oven to 350°F. Mix the dry ingredients together in
a medium-size bowl. Beat the egg in a separate medium-
size bowl. Add the baby food, oil, honey, and chicken stock
to the egg and stir well. Add the wet mixture to the dry
ingredients, stirring to combine. Knead the mixture for 5
minutes.

   Flour your hands. Roll the dough into ½-inch balls.
Flatten the balls between your palms until they are about a
¼ inch thick. Place them a ¼ inch apart on a nonstick baking sheet, and bake for 55 minutes to 1 hour.

   Allow the treats to cool completely and then package
them in ziplock freezer bags, compressing as much air out
as possible. Store in the freezer until you are ready to leave.
If you're taking them on a warm-weather trip, store them
in a cooler in a zippered freezer bag.

Tip

Be sure that the baby food doesn't contain onion or garlic
as those ingredients can sometimes make your furry friend
ill.

Glossary of Special Ingredients

adobo sauce A mixture of ingredients such as peppers, garlic, onions, and tomatoes. Canned chipotle peppers are often found packed in it.

anise flavoring (anise extract) A liquid extract with a flavor similar to that of licorice. Anise oil can be used as a substitute but only use ¼ of the amount of flavoring a recipe calls for because it is highly concentrated.

anise seed A seed used in cooking and baking that has a mild licorice flavor. If you cannot find anise seed, substitute fennel seed, which is slightly sweeter.

artichokes The flower of a plant from the thistle family. The heart of the artichoke is the best tasting part.

balsamic vinegar A fruity and dark vinegar made from unfermented white grape juice. It has a slightly sweet flavor. It lasts 3 to 6 months after being opened.

basmati rice A long grain rice popular in India that is available in white and brown varieties.

blood orange A citrus fruit with a deep red flesh that is less acidic than a navel orange.

candied ginger (crystallized ginger) Pieces of peeled gingerroot or stem ginger that have been simmered in a mixture of sugar and water. Candied ginger can be found in the baking section of most grocery stores.

capers The buds of a plant related to the cabbage and popular in Mediterranean cuisine as a garnish. They are usually sold pickled, which imparts a slightly sour and salty flavor.

celery leaves The leaves of the celery plant. They have a milder flavor than the stalks and are a great addition to salads and wraps.

chipotle hot sauce A spicy condiment made from red jalapeño peppers that have been smoked. This smoking process gives the peppers a sultry flavor.

chipotle peppers Smoked jalapeño peppers that have a medium heat level. They are well suited to sauces and meat dishes as they add a smoky flavor and a little heat.

chipotle purée   A purée of mashed chipotle peppers and adobo sauce.

chocolate protein powder   Made from whey protein, it can be found at health food stores and places that specialize in nutritional supplements.

clarified butter (drawn butter or ghee)   Butter that has been heated and from which the milk solids have been removed. This process gives the butter a higher smoke point and reduces its risk of spoilage if it's being stored without refrigeration.

coconut powder   Made from dried coconut that has been ground fine, this powder can be purchased in stores that specialize in Indian or Thai cuisine.

couscous   Usually made from durham semolina in Moroccan and Israeli varieties. Moroccan couscous is a small grain couscous and is not as large or round as the Israeli, or pearl, couscous. Couscous also comes in instant varieties, which are more suitable for the recipes in this book.

creamed coconut   A concentrated coconut product sold in blocks. It still contains moisture and is somewhat pastelike. You can add water to it to make coconut milk. Look for it in the Asian section of larger grocery stores. It's different from coconut cream, which is a liquid similar to coconut milk and is usually found in cans.

cumin seeds   Flavorful seeds often found in Indian and Mexican cuisine. They impart a strong flavor, so a little goes a long way.

demerara sugar   A raw cane sugar with a brownish color that can be interchanged with other raw sugars such as turbinado or muscovado sugar. It is especially nice in coffee and cocoa drinks.

dried mushrooms   These fungi come in many varieties and can be easily reconstituted. Reserve the rehydrating liquid to add extra flavor to your dish.

ghee   *See* clarified butter.

guacamole   A condiment made primarily of avocado and cilantro. It often has a creamy texture and is commonly served with Mexican foods.

habanero peppers   Similar to Scotch Bonnet peppers, these are excruciatingly hot, but they impart a fruity flavor.

hickory smoke (liquid smoke) A liquid often used in smoking meats and making jerky and that can be used to add smokiness to other recipes as well.

hollandaise sauce mix A powdered mix made of eggs to which milk or butter is usually added to create a sauce. Hollandaise is traditionally served over vegetables and eggs Benedict.

Hungarian paprika Most often used in goulash, this spice is made from dried peppers and available in sweet, or mild, and hot forms. Hungarian paprika is much more flavorful than Spanish paprika.

instant custard powder A corn flour–based instant mix used to make English-style custard with a pudding-like consistency. Instant custard powder is unlike traditional English custard in that it does not contain eggs.

instant wild rice A variety of natural wild rice that has been processed to shorten its cooking time.

jasmine rice A variety of long grain rice commonly used in Thailand. It has the subtle aroma of jasmine and is slightly shorter grained than basmati rice.

kosher salt Coarse and flaky in comparison to table salt, it is also noniodized. Because of its coarse texture, kosher salt adheres to food much better than table salt does.

lemon zest The exterior yellow part of the lemon rind without the white pith. The zest contains lemon fragrance and flavor along with oils and adds another layer of flavor to salads and other foods.

lime zest Similar to lemon zest, it comes from the exterior green part of the lime rind, without the white pith. The zest contains lime fragrance and flavor along with oils and can be used in a variety of ways.

Maggi seasoning A preservative-free, bottled condiment made from natural vegetable proteins created in the 1800s by the Maggi family in Switzerland. It is a great addition to rice and pasta dishes that contain chicken or mushrooms. It is often used in Asian cuisine and can be found in the Asian section of most grocery stores.

mango chutney A jamlike condiment often used in curry dishes and made from mangoes, sugar, ginger, and other spices. It can be found in the Indian section of larger grocery stores and in specialty markets.

maple sugar Maple syrup that has been boiled down until granulation occurs. It has an intense maple flavor, is a nice addition to hot drinks, and can be reconstituted into syrup.

mascarpone cheese An unripened Italian cream cheese that is very smooth. Since it is perishable, you can only use it when you are taking a cooler.

malted milk powder *See* powdered milk.

milk powder *See* powdered milk.

mustard powder (English mustard) A hot mustard that should be used in smaller quantities than the prepared mustard commonplace in North America.

Nestlé Nido A whole milk powder found in the Mexican section of many grocery stores. Its high milk-fat content, 26 percent, makes it ideal for increasing the fat content in hot drinks and cereals on winter trips.

orange zest Similar to lemon zest, it comes from the exterior of the orange rind, without the white pith. The zest contains a strong orange scent and flavor along with oils and can be used in a variety of ways.

pepitas A hulled pumpkin seed that makes a nice addition to trail mix and salads.

plum tomato (Roma tomato or Italian tomato) An oval-shaped tomato with a firmer texture and more concentrated flavor than regular tomatoes due to the reduced amount of juice and seeds.

powdered egg Made from whole eggs, it can be used to replace the eggs in most recipes.

powdered milk (milk powder) Made from dehydrated milk solids and available in both instant and regular varieties. Instant dissolves very quickly in water, making it preferable for the backcountry. Skim or nonfat powdered milk has a longer shelf life but a less rich taste than powdered whole milk like Nestlé Nido and Milkman; the higher fat content of the latter make them good for trips in cooler weather. Powdered soy milk, nondairy and made from soybeans, has a rich texture and creaminess and can be substituted for skim or whole powdered milk. Malted milk powder, such as Ovaltine, has a chocolate malt flavor, can be used hot or cold, and is meant to be mixed with milk.

powdered scrambled egg mix A combination of whole egg powder, powdered milk, and powdered vegetable oil to which one just adds water. It is excellent for making scrambled eggs, omelets, and French toast.

quinoa The seed from the goosefoot plant, which is native to South America. It is an excellent and complete protein, containing essential amino acids and also magnesium, riboflavin, and iron. Quinoa should be rinsed before cooking to remove any bitterness caused by the natural coating of saponin. It has a fluffy consistency with a slight nuttiness and a bite similar to pasta.

Roma tomato *See* plum tomato.

rubbed sage Dried and crumbled sage leaves that are aromatic and a great accompaniment to poultry. It can also be used to make sage butter, which is delicious on ravioli or other pasta.

saffron threads The handpicked stamens from the Saffron crocus (*Crocus* sativus L.). Because saffron is handpicked, it is quite expensive compared to other spices and herbs. It imparts a gentle flavor and wonderful yellow color.

seafood seasoning A combination of celery seed, mustard seed, red pepper, bay, cloves, cardamom, salt, paprika, and allspice. One example is the brand Old Bay Seasoning.

smoked gouda A cheese with a firm but creamy bite and a smoky flavor. It is most often smoked with hickory chips.

smoked salmon A fillet of salmon that has been smoked and cured.

sour cream powder Freeze-dried sour cream that can be used in a variety of ways but is not suitable for making standard sour cream. It adds a tangy flavor to soups and pasta dishes such as stroganoff.

Sriracha chili sauce A Thai hot chili sauce made with sun-ripened peppers, garlic, and sometimes fish extract. It is very hot and is sometimes used as a dip.

stem ginger *See* candied ginger.

stone ground mustard (Creole mustard) Similar to whole-grain mustard except that the seeds are slightly crushed or ground, giving the mustard an interesting texture. It has a spicier flavor than other prepared mustards.

sun-dried tomatoes Made from Roma tomatoes that have been dried in the sun, they have a concentrated flavor and can be bought dry or in jars with oil. The dry kind can be used in trail mix, salads, soups, pasta, and bannock. The kinds that are packed in oil aren't suitable for backcountry trips.

Swiss chard (spinach beet) A leafy vegetable with properties similar to spinach. It tastes a little like beets and is sturdier than spinach. Chard is great on its own or in soups.

tahini (sesame paste) Ground white sesame seeds with a texture similar to that of peanut butter. It's most often used to make hummus.

tamari sauce Very similar in taste to soy sauce, but it does not contain wheat. It has a lighter flavor than regular soy sauce.

teriyaki sauce A Japanese sauce typically made from mirin, soy, and sake. Mirin, a type of rice wine, gives teriyaki its sweetness.

textured vegetable protein (TVP) A dehydrated product made from soy flour. TVP provides fiber and protein and has a texture similar to ground beef.

Thai green chilies A small, very hot chili that is also known as a bird chili.

turmeric A very yellow and pungent spice often used in Indian cooking and in prepared mustard.

tzatziki sauce A condiment used in Greek cuisine that contains cucumbers, dills, and sometimes garlic. It is usually made from yogurt but is sometimes made with sour cream.

vanilla protein powder *See* chocolate protein powder.

vanilla sugar Made by placing a vanilla bean in white granulated sugar so that the sugar absorbs the vanilla flavor. You can sometimes find vanilla sugar in the baking section or in specialty shops, but it is just as easy to make your own.

wasabi paste A Japanese condiment that comes from Japanese horseradish. If you can't find the paste, you can buy wasabi powder and follow the package directions to make the paste.

wasabi peas Peas that have been dried with a coating that contains wasabi. They are crunchy and hot—a great addition to a savory trail mix.

white pepper Less pungent than black pepper with a milder heat, it is often used for aesthetic reasons.

yogurt culture A freeze-dried powder with bacterial cultures that is used to make yogurt. It comes in different varieties, one for making regular yogurt and another for making yogurt with *Casei, Bifidus,* and *Acidophilus* cultures, which have added health benefits. The regular culture is recommended for the trail yogurt recipe in this book.

Glossary of Cooking Terms

beat Mix ingredients until they are smooth.

blanch Cook fruits or vegetables briefly in boiling water and then dunk them in ice water.

blend Mix ingredients together well by hand or in a blender.

chop Cut into small pieces.

combine Stir ingredients just until they come together.

dice Cut into ⅓-inch cubes.

grind Create very fine pieces or a powder using a blender, food processor, or spice grinder.

mince Chop into fine pieces.

mix Stir ingredients together until they are well combined.

purée Mash or blend food until it becomes a paste.

simmer Cook a liquid on a stove at a temperature at which small bubbles just break the surface.

Measurement Conversions

These tips will help you measure ingredients more precisely at home or at camp and help prevent cooking disasters.

• Always use level measurements unless indicated otherwise in a recipe.

• When dividing commercial ingredients like muffin or cake mix, be sure to shake or mix the dry ingredients well before splitting the portions.

• Never measure spices or seasonings over your food—a mistake can easily ruin your meal.

• The measurements marked on some water bottles and other gear are inaccurate; verify the markings at home before your trip.

• Measure liquid ingredients at eye level.

• A large folding measuring spoon that doubles as a scoop is a great addition to a backcountry kitchen.

Conversions Within the English System	
A pinch	⅛ teaspoon
3 teaspoons	1 tablespoon
1 tablespoon	1/16 cup
2 tablespoons + 2 teaspoons	⅙ cup
2 tablespoons	⅛ cup
4 tablespoons	¼ cup
5 tablespoons + 1 teaspoon	⅓ cup
6 tablespoons	⅜ cup
8 tablespoons	½ cup
10 tablespoons + 2 teaspoons	⅔ cup
12 tablespoons	¾ cup
16 tablespoons	1 cup
48 teaspoons	1 cup

Metric Conversions

Volume	
⅛ teaspoon	0.5 milliliter
¼ teaspoon	1 milliliter
½ teaspoon	2 milliliters
¾ teaspoon	4 milliliters
1 teaspoon	5 milliliters
1 tablespoon	15 milliliters
¼ cup	60 milliliters
⅓ cup	80 milliliters
½ cup	120 milliliters
⅔ cup	160 milliliters
¾ cup	180 milliliters
1 cup	225 milliliters
2 cups or 1 pint	450 milliliters
3 cups	675 milliliters
4 cups or 1 quart	1 liter
½ gallon	2 liters

Temperature	
250°F	130°C
300°F	150°C
350°F	180°C
400°F	200°C
450°F	230°C

Mass	
½ ounce	15 grams
1 ounce	30 grams
3 ounces	85 grams
3 ¾ ounces	100 grams
4 ounces	115 grams
8 ounces	225 grams
12 ounces	340 grams
16 ounces or 1 pound	450 grams

Index

Laurie Ann March is an avid backpacker, hiker, and wilderness canoeist. Her first nature experiences were shared with her big brother, Bruce, who backpacked and hiked all over Canada throughout his life. Laurie's relationship and wilderness experiences with her brother instilled a deep respect for nature and love of the outdoors in her.

The outdoors isn't merely a hobby for Laurie—it is her passion. She is an instructor of a wilderness cooking course in which she teaches and supports students who are learning the special skills needed to prepare food for wilderness excursions. Laurie enjoys her work as owner and editor of the popular outdoors e-zine www.OutdoorAdventureCanada.com. Laurie is not just an author and outdoorswoman; she is also a mother, wife, artist, and photographer.

Laurie lives in Ontario, Canada, where she backpacks, hikes, and paddles with her husband, Bryan, and her son, Tobias. Seeing nature through her son's eyes is one of her greatest rewards.

For more information about wilderness cooking and printable trail instructions and to read Laurie's blog, which covers food finds and other tidbits, please visit www.AForkintheTrail.com.